GRAMMAR AND COMPOSITION

Generating Sentences and Paragraphs SECOND EDITION

Hulon Willis

Bakersfield College

Holt, Rinehart and Winston

New York   Chicago   San Francisco   Atlanta   Dallas

for Stevie and Susan

Library of Congress Cataloging in Publication Data

Willis, Hulon.
Grammar and composition.
Published in 1967 under title: Structural grammar
and composition.
Includes index.
1. English language—Rhetoric. 2. English
language—Grammar—1950–   I. Title.
PE1408.W614 1976   808'.042   75-26646
ISBN: 0-03-089846-3

Preface

Though this book covers important aspects of composition that, when taught, do not call for any grammatical analysis or terminology, its title includes the word *grammar* because the parts that deal with sentence composition and conventional usage do involve some grammatical analysis. However, I avoid a multitude of complexities of English grammar because they have no bearing on the teaching of composition. The grammatical analysis used in this book is elementary and is intended to be a *tool* useful in the teaching of composition.

I believe that instruction in basic grammatical analysis and in the nature of large sentence constituents is certainly *one* way of teaching many students to write better. Part 1 provides a minimal foundation in grammatical analysis. Part 2 is designed to improve the students' syntactic maturity by increasing their ability to use large sentence constituents—such as appositive phrases, which few students use—in composing mature, well-formed sentences rather than childish ones. I use the term *sentence expansion* as a name for the large sentence constituents (apart from central predications) that carry full ideas that students too often express in a series of simple sentences. I do not, however, mean that I think students should try to make the composition of long sentences their chief goal. I mean only that we should try to teach our students to compose sentences that sound like good writing rather than like recorded casual conversation or like the writing of an average eighth grader.

The grammatical system I use is an updated, scholarly-traditional system. I am quite willing to admit that Noam Chomsky is the Einstein of modern linguistics and that some of the new grammars are closer than scholarly-traditional to the ultimate truth of the structure of English. However, these new grammars, for me at least, are very nearly unusable as tools to employ in talking to students about weaknesses in their sentence composition. So far as I can tell, scholarly-traditional grammar is the only such tool. The various generative grammars and others are, in my opinion, subject matter for advanced linguistic study, not usable tools in composition and literature classrooms.

Perhaps an analogy will make my point clearer. When, in the 1920s, the new physics of Einstein, Planck, Heisenberg, and others destroyed classical physics and Newton's laws of motion as ultimate truth, classical physics remained an indispensable tool in the training of such professionals as engineers and architects. Though not the ultimate truth, classical physics is *a* truth and is essential. If textbooks of classical physics had been junked in the twenties and thirties (as happened to texts of traditional grammar in the sixties) and engineers and architects had been taught only relativity and quantum mechanics, our new bridges and buildings would probably have collapsed. With Newton's laws of motion, even a bright high school student can predict an eclipse to the second. To predict one using only the physics of relativity would require a huge bank of computers and a considerable amount of time. In short, advancement toward ultimate truth does not, in many fields, diminish the usefulness of traditional non-ultimate truths. It may be that the marked decline in the writing ability of college freshmen, a decline that has recently received widespread publicity, is partly due to the disappearance from the public schools of scholarly-traditional grammar as a tool in the teaching of composition.

Thus, though the scholarly-traditional grammatical system that I use does not tell the ultimate truth about the structure of English, it most certainly tells a serviceable truth, for it provides a good tool for teaching certain aspects of composition (and for unraveling knotty problems of syntax in poetry, too). It also provides a simple means for moderately well-educated people to talk about their language. As the noted linguist Francis P. Dinneen said, scholarly-traditional grammar "provides the most widespread, influential, and best understood method of discussing Indo-European languages in the Western World."

Though the subject matter of this text clearly falls into four parts, instructors can easily vary their assignments to suit their own preferences. For example, assignments can be made in Part 3 before instruction in Part 1 is undertaken. Or, for another example, the exercises in Chapter 23 may be used in a number of ways: at the beginning of the course for diagnostic purposes, at the beginning and end of the course to test overall progress, as a kind of final exam for Parts 1 and 2, or for class discussion of sentence composition.

A traditional correction chart, with chapter references, is printed on the inside front cover. An index to grammatical terms, with page references, is printed on the inside back cover.

An instructor's manual consisting of a key to the exercises in this text is free to teachers. To secure one, write to the English Editor, College Department, Holt, Rinehart and Winston, 383 Madison Avenue, New York, N.Y. 10017.

Bakersfield, California   H.W.
January 1976

Contents

PART 1

THE BASIC SYSTEM
OF ENGLISH GRAMMAR

1
Introduction to
the Study of Writing
in College

THE COLLEGE COMPOSITION REQUIREMENT

Almost every American college requires its entering students to enroll in an English course designed to teach them to write better. College educators have three general reasons for imposing this near-universal requirement. First, they understand that college work itself demands writing competence. Throughout college, students must write definitions, tests, exams, various kinds of reports, and term papers. Thus the freshman composition course has an immediate usefulness. The more a student improves his writing effectiveness, the more likely he is to make high grades in all his courses. Furthermore, because of a general upgrading of academic standards in our time, American colleges are increasingly demanding of their students higher levels of competence in writing. Poor writers are finding it more and more difficult, if not impossible, to graduate from college. For this reason, the college composition requirement is a highly practical one. No other college course so much affects all other courses.

Second, college educators also understand the importance of effective writing in most of the professions that college students prepare for. Thus they maintain the composition requirement because of its long-range usefulness. As our society becomes more and more complex, fewer and fewer occupations are open to people who cannot write clearly and precisely. It is not enough for the college graduate to bring knowledge to his new job; he must also bring the ability to express himself effectively. It is literally true that even in a time of shortages many companies reject technically well-trained applicants because of deficiencies in their language usage. In maintaining a composition requirement, college educators recognize that effective use of language is perhaps the most important single factor in the success of the majority of college graduates.

Finally, college educators recognize that graduating from college is not just an end in itself and that one's occupation is not his whole life. Reading, of course, plays a much larger part in our lives than writing, but for most Americans of even moderate education writing competence is a valuable personal and social asset. As

3

our increasingly complex society provides us with more leisure, we engage in more organizational and social activities that test our literacy. And too often adult Americans are embarrassed by their inability to write clearly and correctly. As much as any other college course, then, the composition requirement benefits the student apart from its value for future occupational demands.

Most students willingly give lip service to the belief that effective use of language is necessary for a successful college career, for desirable employment thereafter, and for social accomplishment; but privately most of them regard their composition courses with a notable lack of enthusiasm. In fact, many dread their English courses and feel frustrated as they try to write acceptable papers. It would be convenient now to tell you that with this composition text you can easily and painlessly learn to write better. But no such claim can ever be truthfully made. Good writing is far too complex a skill to be acquired quickly with a magical formula. There is no such thing as "skillful writing in ten easy lessons." But this text can give you some concepts and insights that will help you better to understand the process of composition, and perhaps that understanding will lead not only to your learning to write better but also to your getting more personal satisfaction from the creative act of composing. The remainder of this introductory chapter, then, will explain some concepts that you should understand and some attitudes that you should develop in order to study composition successfully. Read the following sections carefully. They may clear your mind of some misconceptions about language and writing that are widespread and that have severely retarded the progress of countless composition students.

THE FRUSTRATION AND THE SATISFACTION OF WRITING

College students are not the only ones who experience frustration in trying to write well. Almost every writer agonizes over some of his sentences when he knows they will be read by a critical audience, for writing well is a painful process. Sometimes the writing process goes smoothly for any writer, but the difficult passages inevitably come. And usually even the smooth passages that seemed almost to compose themselves need revision after all. You will have a healthier attitude toward your composition course if you understand that even professional writers share with you and your classmates a feeling of agony as they try to develop an extensive piece of writing for critical readers. Few writers can escape the pain of writing.

But the very aspect of writing that is a source of frustration is also a source of satisfaction. Simply put, the frustration a writer often feels in trying to express an idea just right turns into a feeling of accomplishment and genuine pride when he does achieve his goal. So do not be easily discouraged when you have a difficult time getting a paper started, or when a particular sentence seems especially hard to compose, or when you find you must revise or amend a passage you thought already good. Almost all writers experience the same difficulties. For example, a writer for *Time* magazine said he once spent 70 hours at the typewriter to write a five-page article. Stick to your task until you accomplish it, and the feeling of pride, even elation, will come. Remember that the more a passage of writing appears to be simple, clear, and just naturally good, the more likely its author worried about it and took pains to get it just right. No one who is writing even close to his best can escape the hard labor and pain of writing.

The satisfaction to be derived from writing is special, for its source is the act of creating. Nothing gives the human mind and soul more pleasure than creativity. You should understand that the sense of satisfaction with which a writer is rewarded does not derive only from the writing of poetry or other so-called creative writing, such as short stories and personal essays. All writing is creative, and all worthwhile writing—even English themes and essay tests—can be a source of personal pleasure. Such pleasure can be yours if you approach your writing in a spirit of creativity, knowing that you will often agonize as you compose but that your finished product, even when just a single well-written sentence, will be a source of pride. Of course, people like to be praised for what they have done well, and so if as a student you are to experience the joy as well as the frustration of writing, you must be praised when you write well and not just criticized when you write poorly.

THE IMPORTANCE OF FORM AS WELL AS CONTENT IN WRITING

Student writers frequently complain that they just do not have anything to write about. But the source of their frustration is not often a lack of information, ideas, opinions, insights, convictions, skills, memories, experiences, knowledge. In spite of their feelings of deficiency in subject matter, most writers agonize most not over what to say but how to say it. More often than "I just don't have anything to write about," teachers hear "I know what I want to say, but I don't know how to say it." When the idea is there but the words will not come right, the writer is frustrated. But when at last the words do come right, he experiences the high pleasure of creativity.[1] The source of both the frustration and the satisfaction of writing, then, is the fact that one idea can be expressed in many ways. Finding the best way (or even an acceptable way) is often difficult but always rewarding.

You should understand, then, that a sentence is not like an equation. It does not have one fixed form. In composing a sentence, you don't just get *the* answer and that is that. Even the simplest fact or idea can be expressed in several different sentences, and a moderately complex idea can be expressed in innumerable ways. Of the many ways of expressing an idea, no one way is necessarily best, but most of the ways are ineffective—that is, awkward, unclear, wordy, dull, inexact, or bumbling. Most writers ponder and reponder, revise and re-revise, to find clear, exact, and pleasing ways of expressing their ideas. *A chief purpose of your composition course is to develop your ability to search for effective form in expressing your ideas.*

The following is the opening paragraph of an impromptu theme written by a high school junior:

[1] The use of *he, him,* and *his* to refer to indefinite sex or to groups composed of both sexes is firmly rooted in tradition and should not be thought of as a sign of sexism. See Chapter 37 for a discussion of this controversial point.

Every individual has a set of values which motivates him, and frequently he assumes that his values are the only "good" ones. He knows that other individuals have different beliefs and desires, but he is positive that, if made aware of the soundness of his, everyone else would adopt them, forgetting their own. One often finds it difficult to see how important other things can be to other people.

You might think this high school junior was copying from, or at least remembering, a passage written by a more mature writer. But here is the process she went through to achieve her good finished passage:

> ~~There are many motives for the actions of men.~~
> ~~Each individual has~~
> ~~Mankind~~
> ~~M~~ Every individual has a set of values which motivates him, and frequently he assumes that his ~~set~~ values are ~~the only ones that count are important~~ the only ~~really~~ "good" ones. He knows that other individuals have ~~their own belie~~ different beliefs and desires, but he ~~assumes that~~ is ~~sure~~ positive that, if made aware of the ~~real im~~ soundness of his ~~valu set values,~~ everyone else would ~~forget their own and adopt his~~ adopt them, forgetting their own. ~~An individ~~ One ~~can~~ often finds it difficult to see how important ~~something can~~ other things can be to other people.

The writer of this passage did not go through such a painful process of composing a clear and pleasing paragraph *because* she was just a high school junior, but *in spite of* her youth. The more mature a writer is, the more likely he is to ponder his composition and to revise it for exactness and smoothness.

Form and content are both important in writing. One cannot write without structure; neither can one write without ideas. In fact, an idea is at best vague until it is given clear form. An important concept for you to understand is that the human mind must go through a *composing process* to give clear, exact, and pleasing form to ideas. The very word *compose* means "to put together." Thus the composing process demands that you *manipulate* language and that you *choose* the effective form and avoid the ineffective. The manipulation and the choice are the source of both the frustration and the satisfaction of writing, for they are the result of creativity.

THE DIFFERENCES BETWEEN SPEECH AND WRITING

All normal human beings over three or four years old speak a native language fluently. This apparently simple fact is in reality astonishing, for all languages are so complex that it is truly remarkable that very young and even retarded children learn one (or more) easily. In literate countries most normal seven- or eight-year-olds have also learned to write, in the sense that they can copy printed material and can put into written form simple phrases and sentences that they might speak. Yet in a highly educated country such as ours, only a small percentage of adults can write well in the sense that what they write is clear, exact, logically constructed, pleasingly phrased, and mature enough to appeal to an educated mind— in short, as college-educated people should write and, because of occupational demands, are more and more being required to write. Since a high percentage of Americans now receive more than twelve years of schooling, their general failure to learn to write well might seem as astonishing as the very young child's success in learning to speak a complicated language. But there are reasons why there is often a marked difference between an educated adult's ability to use oral language and his ability to write, and these reasons lie in the differences between speech and writing. An understanding of some of these differences is most important to your study of composition.

Few misconceptions about the nature of writing have hindered composition students more than the general belief that writing is just reproduction of speech. It is not true, as is widely believed, that anyone who can speak well can write well, or vice versa. Though writing obviously is in some ways like oral language, it is also different in many significant ways. *Good writing must be learned apart from oral language.* Many people who speak clearly, fluently, and effectively in their casual talk write quite poorly, and a few who ramble and stumble in their ordinary speech write clearly, precisely, and elegantly. In fact, learning to write well is more likely to improve one's ordinary conversation than learning to talk well is likely to improve one's writing. We probably transfer more techniques from our writing habits to our speech than from our speech habits to our writing.

The differences between writing and talking are so great that one noted scholar of language says that "a composition style foreign to beginning students— whether foreign because of its elegance, or its technical nature, or its contrast with oral style—must be learned *as a foreign language* is learned. . . ."[2] He means that one's normal speech habits, even though admirable, cannot just be transferred to his writing habits. Instead, the student of writing must carefully read the kind of writing that he wants to imitate, must understand its vocabulary and sentence structure, and then must imitate its characteristics in his own writing. *You cannot learn to write educated prose unless you imitate other writing rather than spontaneous speech.* You will have a more affirmative attitude toward your composition course if you realize that it is not tampering with your speech habits[3] but is helping you improve a skill you have only begun to master: how to use words and sentences the way good writers use them.

Speech uses many modes of expressing meaning that writing cannot use. For example, we use meaningful facial and bodily gestures constantly in our talk that we cannot transfer to our writing. We also alter the tone of our voices to give additional meaning to our words, and we have many ways of showing in speech that single words, short phrases, and other fragments are meaningful. In short, the structure of oral language differs considerably from that of written language. Native speakers learn very early the structure of their oral language by imitating speech. If they are to write well as adults, they must also learn the structure of their written language by imitating writing.

Unprepared speech tends to be much looser and more rambling—even jumbled—than writing. And it also tends to omit connective words and ideas

---

[2] Kenneth Pike, "A Linguistic Contribution to Composition," *College Composition and Communication,* XV (May 1964), page 82. (The italics are the author's.)

[3] It is true that students who successfully study composition also improve the clarity and precision of their oral language, but that is a by-product of their study. The purpose of a composition course is not to teach a student to speak "correctly" so that he can write well. Writing is not different from speech because it is more "correct" in its grammar, but for the reasons given above.

necessary in writing. We are simply used to hearing speech that is at times repetitious and at other times full of gaps that we have to fill in ourselves. We accept such structure in oral language, but when we read writing that is rambling or full of gaps in logic, we reject it because we are not used to that kind of structure in writing.

To illustrate the rambling nature of unprepared speech, here is a passage from the oral language of one of our presidents:

> What I do think is here is something that has to be constantly studied, explored, and to keep up with the changing proposals, free cities, and that sort of thing, I mean, in the free city in the sense of an international sense, not the way we are talking about it, that kind of thing. So we have to keep up, abreast of the situation.

And here is a passage from the casual talk of a highly learned scholar of language:

> As far as I know, no one has yet done the in a way obvious now and interesting problem of doing a in a sense structural frequency study of the alternative syntactical in a given language, say, like English, the alternative possible structures, and how what their hierarchical probability of occurrence structure is.

The fact that these men were highly educated and knew their subject matter thoroughly did not keep their spontaneous talk from being jumbled and rambling. If they had been writing, they would have used a different kind of language structure.

Good writing is much tighter, less wordy, and more logical in structure than casual speech. Readers expect this tighter structure with its greater clarity, exactness, and smoothness, and thus a writer must learn to handle the written language differently from the way he handles oral language. Since he has more time for thought and revision, he can give more attention to the structure of his writing. Consider arithmetic. In your head you can do simple problems, but with more time and pencil and paper you can do much more complex problems. The same is true in writing. If you have time and pen and paper *and proper training,* you can write more clearly, precisely, and elegantly than you can talk spontaneously.

Casual speech is likely to use more sentence units, or simpler parts within a long sentence, than good writing. The written language uses more *expansions* of the simpler spoken sentence, because the writer has more time to think about what he is doing. For example, a writer composed the following two sentences for an article in the *Atlantic:*

> My education proceeded under John Carlyle, classicist, who in a presidential year taught Cicero's *Letters,* not out of the book, but out of the Charlotte *Observer,* a morning newspaper. Comparing, day by day, the text with the news stories, he drew parallels, obvious once they were pointed out, between Cicero's advice to his son-in-law, running for some office in Rome, and the maneuvers of the campaigners then raging across the country.

If this writer had been saying the same thing casually to a friend, he would likely have used several more (and more wordy) sentence units to express the ideas that he put into such *sentence expansions* as "classicist," "obvious once they were pointed out," "running for some office in Rome," and so on. He would very likely have had extra sentence units such as "he was a classicist," "they were obvious once they were pointed out," and "he was running for some office in Rome." *The sentence expansions, which reduce the number of sentence units in writing and make for more precise structure, can be learned only through reading and training in writing, for they are not very common in ordinary speech.* Writing can employ such sentence expansions more easily than ordinary speech because the eye is more capable than the ear of following complex structures.

Good writing also uses many kinds of constructions (not just expansions) that are rare or absent in ordinary talk. For example, the following sentence from an article in the *Atlantic* sounds perfectly natural to the reader's ear:

> There is nothing vainglorious about this belief, nor does it represent the zenith of Hoffa's ambitions.

But the use of the "nor does it" construction, as natural as it sounds, is quite rare in everyday talk. Learning to use common written constructions of this sort and sentence expansions, as illustrated in the preceding paragraph, makes learning a composition style different from merely transferring speech to paper.

Finally, workaday speech uses a simpler and more colloquial vocabulary than good writing. Everyday words and even slang terms (such as *snitching, kickback,* and *crackdown*) are certainly not out of place in good writing, and pretentious words and phrases (such as *ego-integrative action orientation* or *processual ethnicity*) are scornfully avoided by most good writers. But in general even highly educated people use a more limited and more informal vocabulary for speech than for writing. There is nothing wrong with such phrases as *put up with, left up to us,* and *a great deal of help to us,* but a good writer would be more likely to choose *tolerate, our concern,* and *valuable to us.* When one is writing, he has more time to select the kind of economical and polished wording that readers expect, whereas listeners are quite satisfied with more wordy and colloquial speech.

As you write, then, imitate other good writing, not your speech patterns. Good writing will sound natural like high-level conversation, but it will differ from casual talk in its use of a greater variety of complicated sentence expansions, fewer rambling and wordy constructions, a more varied and polished vocabulary, and many constructions not often heard in speech. Your progress in composition will accelerate if you understand some of these differences between written and oral language.

THE PLACE OF GRAMMAR IN THE STUDY OF COMPOSITION

Like most words, *grammar* has several meanings. It is most commonly used to mean correctness in speaking and writing. Thus people who say *ain't, he don't, I done it,* and the like are said to use bad grammar or to speak ungrammatically, and people who make no "errors" in their use of English are said to use good grammar. This meaning of *grammar* must be recognized, because many people use the word in that sense. But in the study of writing in college, *usage* is the term normally applied to the problems of conventional[4] correctness in language, and *grammar* is generally used to mean the structure of a language. We will make this distinction between the two terms and will briefly discuss grammar first. The aspect of grammar that we will be most concerned with is **syntax,** which means **word arrangement** to produce clear meaning. For example, *I drank the beer* is syntactical, for the words are arranged properly; but *I the drank beer* is not syntactical because this arrangement of words is not natural or meaningful in English.

First, we should say that constructions such as *it ain't, she come late, I taken the money,* and so on are *not* ungrammatical. They simply belong to nonstandard dialects, and any dialect, no matter how much it varies from the standard (educated) dialect is grammatical and is as good linguistically and as good for basic communication as any other dialect. Of course, now we are talking about conventional usage, but we needed to make the above point in order to explain clearly a point about grammar.

He ain't got no whiskey is a grammatical sentence because it is one that is completely natural to speakers of some English dialects, and any sentence or construction that occurs naturally in the native speech of any dialect and does not seem odd to those who hear it is grammatical. However, the above sentence represents substandard usage. But consider these two phrases taken from a student paper:

> this pertaining to their possible in getting job
> I stand in correction to say

These constructions are ungrammatical because their kind of syntax does not occur naturally in any English dialect and would puzzle or amuse anyone whose native language is any variety of English. When in haste or panic a writer (or speaker) uses a construction whose syntax is unlike any he has heard before and that is unclear or sounds odd to his readers, he is being ungrammatical.

College students do sometimes write in haste or panic and make *errors in sentence structure.* Such errors are errors in grammar, and one purpose of this text is to help you make fewer of them. For example, we will try to show you why such a sentence as

> By arranging regular study hours helps me make better grades

is ungrammatical.

Also, we should say that an error in **idiom** is (except for some nonstandard but often-used idioms) an error in grammar rather than conventional usage. An idiom is a construction "peculiar" to a language and not literally translatable into another language. In a more general sense, idiomatic English is natural English as

---

[4]A **convention** is just an arbitrary custom or manner of doing something that some group (large or small) openly or subconsciously agree is proper for them. For example, in polite society it used to be a convention for a gentleman to tip his hat to a lady he passed on a sidewalk.

In language, conventional usage does involve **morphology,** which is the aspect of grammar that deals with the formation of words and their meaningful parts, including changes in the form of a word according to its use in a sentence. Thus in *I seen it,* not only conventional usage but also the morphological aspect of grammar is involved. We will touch only lightly on the morphological aspect of grammar.

actually used by native speakers of English. For example, *your views contradict mine* is idiomatic, but *your views contradict with mine* is unidiomatic or un-English. Idioms are so important that a whole chapter in Part 1 will be devoted to them.

However, an even more important purpose of this text is to emphasize the positive rather than just the negative aspects of sentence composition. By learning some aspects of grammar, you can probably learn to write sentences that are more mature and well-formed than those you now write. Visualize a graph with a curve that begins in the lower left-hand corner and swings in nearly a straight line to the upper right-hand corner. Horizontal lines through the graph are labeled in degrees of **syntactic maturity**. This term means the maturity of sentence structure that any individual normally uses in his writing. The lower end of the graph represents the syntactic maturity of an average child just entering the second grade; he uses only simple sentence structure. The upper end represents that of a learned college professor and author; he uses much more complex sentence structure than the child. Where is your point on the line? Wherever it is, one of our intents in this text is to send your point of syntactic maturity up a few notches. For example, we hope that you will develop the ability to write such a sentence as

> After winning the student body election, I was faced with the task of preparing an acceptance speech—no easy matter for one so unused to writing and speech-giving as I,

rather than a passage like this from a student paper:

> I won the student body election, and so I had to prepare an acceptance speech. I had not had much practice in writing or speech-giving, and so this was not going to be easy for me.

Your reaction may be, "What difference does it make? They both say the same thing." One difference is, to paraphrase the famous author James Michener, that in the adult world of college-educated workers the ones who can write mature, well-formed sentences will be sought for the finest jobs and will receive promotions more quickly. And there are other differences, too, that have nothing to do with employment. (Incidentally, to complete our analogy of the graph, we should say that its vertical lines represent extent of vocabulary, for high syntactic maturity and extensive vocabulary usually accompany each other.)

The grammatical system (there are various and diverse systems that describe the structure of English) we are using in this text is basically the **scholarly-traditional system**. We chose it because it is by far the best system for teaching certain aspects of composition and usage and also the best for educated people who occasionally want to have fun by talking about their language. For example, a composition teacher needs a simple way to talk to a student about particular sentences if the student writes one or more such as this, as one student did:

> If you have a good foundation of what is right and wrong makes you a good Christian.

Or, because people of some education are curious about language and get fun out of discussing it, someone might turn his curiosity to this old joke:

He: Call me a taxi.
She: O.K. You're a taxi.

Of the various grammatical systems now available, only the scholarly-traditional one will let people indulge in a little *simple* grammatical analysis as to why the above is a joke. (The point is that the *He* sentence has an indirect object (*me*) and a direct object (*taxi*), but *She* interpreted the sentence as though it had a direct object (*me*) and an object complement (*taxi*), as in such a sentence as *We elected Sam president,* in which *Sam* is the direct object and *president* the object complement.)

We need to make two more points in this section. First, the scholarly-traditional grammatical system we use is modern and updated; it is not the old eight-parts-of-speech grammar with sentence diagramming. And second, *we will deal only with those aspects of grammar that are useful as a tool to help students learn to write better.* We will avoid all other aspects of grammar, for your instructor will not have time to teach subtleties of grammar that are not useful in teaching composition.

Material for studying sentence structure from both positive and negative points of view will be given in Part 1 of this text.

THE PLACE OF USAGE IN THE STUDY OF COMPOSITION

"Errors" in conventional usage are not errors in grammar, but simply represent words and constructions normally used in nonstandard dialects but not in the standard dialect. (Actually, there is not just one standard dialect in American English, but several, which differ from each other only slightly, especially in writing. And most people have at least a few aspects of their language usage that do not fit what many other people consider the standard dialect.) Thus really we should not use the term *correct conventional usage,* but rather *standard usage* or *preferred usage,* for no dialect is inherently bad and no one needs to be ashamed of his dialect. Nevertheless, it is a hard fact of life that people are often judged unworthy of holding a particular job or of circulating in certain elements of society because their writing and speech depart too far from what is considered standard.

Here are some examples of "errors" in conventional usage, with the incorrect words italicized:

Professor Turley has hardly *no* sense of humor.
Then it *begun* to rain hard.
Each of these candidates *are* well qualified.
Both *him* and his boss were jailed for embezzlement.
There *is* at least four different versions of this poem.

As you no doubt know, for standard usage the italized words should be *any, began, is, he,* and *are.* Though sound logical arguments can be given for simply accepting these dialectal variations in our language, people who want to rise on the economic and social ladders must bow to social pressure and avoid nonstandard usage.

Students who make errors in conventional usage are often helped by an elementary study of grammar. Part 4 of this text will deal with conventional usage; your teacher may want to assign some chapters in that part early in the course.

There is one further point we must make. Though good writing requires reasonably standard usage, standard usage by itself will not make writing good. For example, here is a paragraph from a weak, though moving, freshman paper:

> Teen-agers rush into marriage unable to stem the tide financially, resulting the failure of improving themselves for a better foundation for the future. Failure to prepare for the future in marriage results in an unhappy home, broken homes, children to suffer, etc. Some older people are not exempt. All ages become unhappy, discouraged, nothing to cling to. Their only hope, is to do the best they can, not give up but keep on trying.

As badly written as this paragraph is, it contains no errors in conventional usage. It has no incorrect verb, pronoun, or modifier forms. None of its constructions are the kind commonly used in nonstandard dialects but not in the standard dialect. Instead, the paragraph is weak because of its unidiomatic expressions, its faulty sentence structure, and its weak development. Thus, though conventional usage cannot be ignored, Parts 2 and 3 of this text are perhaps more important than Part 4.

THE IMPORTANCE OF THE SENTENCE IN THE STUDY OF COMPOSITION

When you have a long paper to write, you are likely to feel that any individual sentence in it will be almost insignificant. You feel the magnitude of your whole task. But the individual sentence is one of the principal keys to good writing. No matter how extensive a piece of writing is, its quality finally rests in the quality of its individual sentences. If a person can write well-formed sentences—clear, precise, mature sentences—he can quickly learn (or, more likely, already knows) how to develop larger units of writing. A person who is inadequate to the task of composing good sentences is already defeated in his effort to produce a whole paper of quality. Of all the main principles of composition—organization of the whole paper, paragraph development, sentence composition, word choice, and correct usage—students can most fruitfully study the art of sentence composition. Learn to compose good sentences, and these other skills will naturally follow.

As paradoxical as it may sound, the sentence (unless it is quite simple) is the most complex unit of composition, more complicated in structure than either a paragraph or a whole paper. Anything is complex in proportion to the number of its basic parts and the intricacy of their arrangement. Most mature sentences in written language have more parts (clauses and phrases) than paragraphs have parts (sentences), and the relationships between phrases and clauses in a sentence are more complicated than the relationships between sentences in a paragraph. *Thus the sentence is in a true sense a composition in miniature.* When you study the art of sentence composition, you in effect study all the principles of composition; and when you have mastered the English sentence, you can write well. One university professor, who teaches English at the University of California, Berkeley, summarized his philosophy of the teaching of writing in this way:[5]

> All the basic principles of composition operate in the composition of the sentence. A good sentence, like a good essay or a good book (and far more than "a good theme"), requires a reasoned organization, a point of view, a consistent and appropriate tone, form, and diction. The principles of composition can be far more easily [taught] in the sentence than in longer compositions.

No college student is too good or too poor a writer not to profit from this approach.

Parts 1 and 2 of this text are designed to give you training in the art of sentence composition as it is practiced in good writing. Remember that this instruction is not intended to "purify" your language by interfering with your natural speech habits, but to add to your language skills by teaching you to compose the kind of carefully thought out sentences found in good writing but not often in casual speech. Think of a person already expert in adapting his walking to the normal situations of everyday life—taking a child for a walk, strolling with a date, hurrying to catch a train, carrying bags of groceries. When he first tries to dance, he is awkward, even though he uses the same legs that he walks with. A fluent speaker, too, is always awkward when he first tries to write, even though he uses the same basic vocabulary and grammar that he talks with. There are many subtle differences between walking and dancing and between speaking and writing. When learning to dance or write, one must learn something new, not unlearn something already acquired.

---

[5] Jackson Burgess, "Sentence by Sentence," *College Composition and Communication*, XIV (December 1963), page 259.

EXERCISE 1
Review

Directions: Without referring to the previous chapter, write out a short answer to as many of the following questions as your instructor requires.

1. Why does almost every American college require all its students to enroll in a composition course?
2. Why is writing so often a source of frustration?
3. Why is writing well a source of satisfaction?
4. What is meant by "a composing process"?
5. Why is good writing not just a reproduction of speech? What are some of the differences between casual speech and writing?
6. What is the meaning of *grammar* as the word is generally used by the public?
7. What is the meaning of *grammar* as the word is used in this text?
8. What aspect of grammar is most useful in the study of writing?
9. What is the meaning of *conventional usage?* Why is *preferred usage* or *standard usage* a more exact term than *correct usage?*
10. How can writing be incorrect other than in usage?
11. Why is the individual sentence so important in writing?
12. Why is the individual sentence "a composition in miniature"?

2
The Parts of Speech: Content Words

Because this text in part bases its instruction in composition on grammar, it is necessary for its users to have an elementary understanding of the basic system of English grammar. Chapters 2 through 10 will define and illustrate the basic grammatical terms and concepts you need to know in studying composition. We will avoid, however, discussion of the many complicated aspects of grammar that are not useful in learning to write better. Our aim is to use grammar as a *tool*, and the aspects of grammar that serve as a tool in the teaching of composition are elementary and not difficult to learn.

Our language is made up of words, and words function as **parts of speech.** The parts of speech fall into two categories: (1) **content words,** which are nouns, verbs, adjectives, and adverbs and which make up the vast majority of our vocabulary; and (2) **structure words,** most of which do carry some meaning but which also serve to form a structural framework so that the content words can be fitted into sentences. This chapter will be devoted to the content words and Chapters 3, 5, 6, and 7 to the structure words that you will need to understand in studying composition. Chapter 4 shows how content words and two classes of structure words (discussed in Chapter 3) can be arranged to form basic sentence patterns.

The four kinds of content words—nouns, verbs, adjectives, and adverbs—are also called the **form classes,** because technically they are best identified by form, rather than by meaning or function. We will show how they are identified by form but will also mention other ways of identifying them. But in studying parts of speech, remember that in English a word may be classified as more than one part of speech. For example, the word *present* (if we ignore its stress pattern, or pronunciation) may be classified as a noun, a verb, and an adjective.

NOUNS

A simple and serviceable definition of *noun* is that it is the name of anything that exists or that can be conceived. For advanced grammatical study that definition is not wholly satisfactory, but it is useful for our purposes. Understanding that definition will help to give you a natural feel for identifying nouns.

A noun is identified by form on the basis of whether it can be made plural or possessive or both. A paradigm, which is a set of related forms, is used to determine whether a word is a noun by form. If a word will fit into any two of the four slots in the following paradigm, it is a noun.

	singular		*plural*
stem	*possessive*	*plural*	*possessive*
book	(a) book's (cover)	books	(these) books' (covers)
goose	goose's	geese	geese's
chaos	chaos's	—	—
—	—	pants	pants'

The last two examples in the paradigm may seem a little strange, but such constructions as *chaos's effect on the political convention* and *his pants' stylishness* are certainly grammatical English expressions. Almost all nouns in English will fit into the noun paradigm. An understanding of the noun paradigm will give you a natural feel for identifying nouns. For example, just an elementary understanding of the paradigm will tell you at once that such a word as *courageous* is not a noun.

Another useful method of identifying nouns is to understand that almost all of them can be (or at times must be) preceded by the definite article, *the,* or by one of the indefinite articles, *a* and *an,* or by a possessive pronoun or noun, such as *my* or *Jack's.* These structure words, as well as some others, are called **determiners** because they determine something about the nouns that follow them. Of course, other words can come between the determiner and its noun, as in *the expensive, Renaissance-style house.*

Finally, there are a number of **noun-forming suffixes** that, when you become aware of them, will help you develop a natural feel for recognizing nouns. These suffixes are added to other parts of speech, and occasionally to other nouns themselves, to form nouns. Here are the most common of them:

act + **or** (sometimes spelled *er* or *ar*) = actor
lovely + **ness** = loveliness
appear + **ance** = appearance
place + **ment** = placement
devote + **ion** (sometimes spelled *tion, ation,* or *sion*) = devotion
drain + **age** = drainage
science + **ist** = scientist
social + **ism** = socialism
note + **ice** = notice
king + **dom** = kingdom
girl + **hood** = girlhood
friend + **ship** = friendship
fail + **ure** = failure
active + **ity** = activity

There are other, less common, noun-forming suffixes, but an understanding of these will give you a concept helpful in identifying nouns, as will the other concepts discussed in this section.

English also has many **compound nouns,** which are nouns made up of two or more words but which function just as simple nouns do. Some compound nouns are spelled as one word; some, as two words; and some, as hyphenated words. Examples of compound nouns:

blackboard	high school	mother-in-law
handyman	rocking chair	bull's-eye

In compound nouns spelled as two words, the primary stress is on the first syllable, as in *SPINning wheel,* which means the machine. The pronunciation *spinning WHEEL* would mean a wheel that is spinning. The same is true of spoken compound nouns spelled as one word. For example, *BLUEbird* would mean the species, whereas *blue BIRD* would just mean a bird that is blue (species perhaps not known). The latter construction is known as a grammatical construction rather than a compound noun.

VERBS

A verb is often defined as a word that expresses an action or a state of being. That definition has some usefulness, but is not wholly satisfactory even for elementary grammatical study. For example, in *a fracus occurred, a fracus* expresses an action but is a noun, not a verb.

However, verbs are very easily identifiable by form. Virtually every English verb fits into the verb paradigm, which has five slots. Examples:

stem	third person, singular, present tense	present participle	past tense	past participle
(to) talk	talks	talking	talked	(have) talked
(to) freeze	freezes	freezing	froze	(have) frozen
(to) bring	brings	bringing	brought	(have) brought

Verbs that end in *ed* in both the past tense and past participle are **regular,** and those that do not are **irregular.** Some irregular verbs have identical past-tense and past-participle forms, and some have differing forms, as illustrated in the above paradigm. Except for the *is* form of *to be* and the *has* form of *to have,* every English verb is regular in its third-person-singular, present-tense and present-participle forms. That is, the former is always formed by adding *s* or *es* to the stem (as in *hears* and *guesses*) and the latter by adding *ing* (as in *hearing* and *guessing*). Thus if you can meaningfully add *ing* to a word, you can be sure it is a verb. Also placing *to* in front of the stem (as in *to hear* and *to guess*) makes the infinitive form of all English verbs.

There are three broad groupings of verbs that you need to know.

1. Intransitive verbs. An intransitive verb expresses an action but in a sentence does not have a direct object that receives the action. The sentence subject simply performs an action but not to, for, or against anything or anybody. Examples:

Harry **laughed.**
Joe **had gone.**
The preacher **will be shouting.**

The boldface verbs are intransitive because they do not have direct objects. (Of course, in real sentences such verbs often are modified by adverbs and adverbials, as in *laughed loudly*.)

2. Transitive verbs. A transitive verb expresses an action that has a direct object—that is, something or someone that receives the action. Examples:

Joey **stole** a car.
Marty **is beating** his wife.
Mavis **will save** some money.

The boldface verbs are transitive because they have the direct objects *car*, *wife* and *money*, which receive the actions expressed in the verbs.

3. Linking verbs. A linking verb expresses a state of being, not an action, and is followed either by a predicate noun, which tells what the sentence subject is or renames the subject in different terms, or by a predicate adjective, which describes (modifies) the sentence subject. There are not many linking verbs, the chief ones being *to be, to become, to continue, to stay, to turn, to get, to appear, to remain, to look, to act, to grow, to smell, to taste, to sound, to feel,* and *to prove.* Examples:

Mr. Ford **became** President.
Dr. Chadbourne **remained** dean.
Chris **looks** tired.
Mr. Perez **feels** bad.

The first two boldface verbs are linking because they have predicate nouns (*President* and *dean*) renaming the sentence subjects in different terms or telling what the subjects are. The second two are linking because they have predicate adjectives (*tired* and *bad*) that describe (modify) the sentence subjects. Usually, a linking verb carries in it the meaning of *to be;* for example, in the first three sentences above the verb *is* could replace the linking verbs, and it could in the fourth too except that we might misinterpret the meaning of *bad.*

Most linking verbs can also function as intransitive or transitive verbs, or both, according to the sentence pattern. Example:

Melinda **grew** weary. (linking, with *weary* as a predicate adjective)
My pine tree **is growing.** (intransitive)
Farmer Jones **will grow** corn. (transitive, with *corn* as the direct object)

Also we should say that some normally intransitive and transitive verbs can in special cases function as linking verbs. For example, in

The well **ran** dry

the boldface verb *ran*, which normally is intransitive (*Tiny Alice can run*) or transitive (*José ran the office*), is linking because *dry* is a predicate adjective describing the subject *well*—that is, *dry well.*

Tense

Tense is the feature of a verb that specifies the time of occurrence of the action or state of being. The English tense system is enormously complex, but all you need to know in studying this text is whether the tense of a verb is one of the past, present, or future tenses. Examples:

one of the past tenses: Estella **had been gone** for two hours.
one of the present tenses: Kathie **is coming** to the party.
one of the future tenses: I **will have finished** by noon.

When a verb has one or more auxiliaries, the first auxiliary carries the tense: *had* in the first example, *is* in the second, and *will* in the third. Thus the verb *has been gone* is one of the present tenses because *has* is a present-tense auxiliary.

ADJECTIVES

An adjective has traditionally been defined as a word that modifies a noun or pronoun, but that definition is inaccurate because nouns, verbs, and sometimes adverbs may also modify nouns. The adjective has also been defined as a describing word, but that definition is faulty too because such a noun as *a quarrel* and such a verb as *staggers* contain description. But there are characteristics of adjectives that can help you develop a natural feel for identifying them. First, most adjectives can be identified by form on the basis of their fitting into a paradigm. We start with the so-called **comparable paradigm,** which is as follows:

stem	comparative degree	superlative degree
kind	kinder	kindest
intelligent	more intelligent	most intelligent

The *more* and *most* in this usage have the same meaning as the *er* and *est* suffixes. They are used to produce smooth sound, for *intelligenter* would sound awkward.

But the comparable paradigm alone will not identify an adjective, for adverbs use the same comparative forms. Thus the adjective paradigm must be expanded. If a word can be compared and can also either be made into an adverb by the addition of *ly* or into a noun by the addition of *ness*, it is an adjective. Examples:

stem	comparative degree	superlative degree	ly	ness
rapid	more rapid	most rapid	rapidly	—
early	earlier	earliest	—	earliness
happy	happier	happiest	happily	happiness

Most adjectives will fit this paradigm.

Another simple test for identifying adjectives is this: if a word will meaningfully fit into both of the blank slots in the following kind of sentence, it is an adjective:

21

This _____ teacher is very _____.

Any common noun can replace *teacher* and any determiner can replace *this*. Examples:

My **gentle** horse is very **gentle**.
Your **raunchy** dog is very **raunchy**.
That **sexy** secretary is very **sexy**.

The boldface words are adjectives, as is almost any word that will fit this pattern. Most adjectives will, though a few will not.

Another simple test for identifying adjectives is this: if a word *other than* a noun will fit the blank slot in the following kind of sentence, it is an adjective:

Marcia seems _____.

Any proper or common noun can replace *Marcia*. Examples:

My cat seems **arrogant**.
Professor Lowry seems **kooky**.
History seems **boring**.

The boldface words, since they are not nouns, are adjectives. Some other linking verbs, such as *feels* and *appears,* can replace *seems* in this test for identifying an adjective.

Finally, a number of **adjective-forming suffixes** help in the identification of adjectives. Added to other parts of speech (and occasionally to other adjectives themselves), they form adjectives. Here are the most common ones:

outrage + **ous** = outrageous
peace + **able** = peaceable
girl + **ish** = girlish
mercy + **less** = merciless
assert + **ive** = assertive
athlete + **ic** = athletic
mange + **y** = mangy
fortune + **ate** = fortunate
quarrel + **some** = quarrelsome

This is by no means a complete list of adjective-forming suffixes, but knowledge of such suffixes will increase your adeptness at identifying adjectives, as will all the concepts mentioned in this section.

ADVERBS

The usual definition of an adverb is that it is a word that modifies a verb, an adjective, or another adverb. This definition is somewhat useful but not wholly satisfactory, because sometimes nouns and verbs modify verbs and because adjectives and adverbs are often modified by words that are not adverbs. But though adverbs are a difficult group to identify, there are ways to be over ninety-five percent accurate in making such identification.

The so-called pure adverb, which ends in *ly*, is very easily identified by form in a simple paradigm. The large majority of adverbs in English fit into this paradigm:

adjective stem	adverb	comparative degree	superlative degree
sweet	sweetly	more sweetly	most sweetly
soft	softly	more softly	most softly
crazy	crazily	more crazily	most crazily

With a few exceptions, to be noted below, any word that fits into the second slot of this paradigm (the first slot being occupied by an adjective) is an adverb. We do, however, have a few adjectives that end in *ly*, and they should not be confused with adverbs. The chief of these are *kindly, friendly, lovely, comely, lively, queenly, manly,* and *portly.* To make an adverb out of one of these adjectives, we would have to form a word such as *friendlily.* Since such a word is awkward, we resort to such a prepositional phrase as *in a friendly way.*

The necessity of the adverb form, though it has no meaning not included in the adjective form, can be illustrated by these sentences:

*Raul is **courageously**.[1]
*Yam Shang drove the car **courageous** off the cliff.

In the first sentence the adjective form is demanded; and in the second, the adverb form. But only the grammar, not the meaning, of the word changes.

Words ending with the suffixes *ward, wise,* and *ways* are also usually adverbs. Examples:

up + **ward** = upward
money + **wise** = moneywise
side + **ways** = sideways

There are few of these words, and many people object vigorously to the *wise* suffix as producing poor style.

English also has a group of commonly used so-called flat adverbs, which are not formed by adding *ly* to an adjective. The large majority of these express time, place, or manner (a concept we will discuss later). The chief of these are the following:

above	everywhere	hereafter
ahead	everytime	inside
already	far	meantime
always	farther	meanwhile
anytime	fast	never
anywhere	further	now
back	forth	nowhere
before	headlong	often
behind	henceforth	outside
below	here	overhead

---

[1] Any construction in this book preceded by an asterisk is ungrammatical.

seldom	soon	thereafter
since	still	thus
sometime	then	well
somewhere	there	yet

Almost all flat adverbs like these express time (*then*), place (*where*), or manner (*thus*).

3
The Parts of Speech:
Two Structure Classes

Words that do not fit into the form classes discussed in Chapter 2 are called **structure words** because, though most of them carry some meaning, they are necessary to provide the structural framework of sentences. Think of how often you have misunderstood newspaper headlines (such as *Union Demands Increase*) because the absence of structure words has deprived the headline of a clear structural framework. The content words are **open classes** because new ones come into the language frequently. The structure words are **closed classes** because very rarely does a new one enter the language.

In classification, structure words troublesomely overlap. For example, consider the word *that* in these sentences:

> **That** student is a three-letter athlete.
> I know a store **that** sells liquor to minors.
> I know **that** my chances of making an *A* are slim.

Though these *that's* are spelled and pronounced alike, they are three entirely different words with entirely different meanings. They fit into three different categories of structure words. They are no more alike than the word *bear* meaning the animal and the word *bear* meaning to carry. However, we will avoid most of the complexity of structure words because we are using grammar only as a tool in studying composition. (Incidentally, in order to understand better the difference between content and structure words, try defining any one of the three *that's* in the above sentences.)

In this brief chapter we will discuss just two of the structure classes, because with them and the content words we can illustrate the basic sentence patterns in English. It is desirable for you to learn the basic sentence patterns early; and thus, after discussing **determiners** and **verb auxiliaries** here, we will discuss the

29

basic patterns in Chapter 4. After that we will discuss some more structure words and some other elementary grammatical matters.

DETERMINERS

A **determiner** is a **noun marker**—a word that precedes a noun (with perhaps other words between it and the noun) and determines something about the meaning or function of the noun. Here are some examples in boldface:

a pig	**such** a mess	**no** money
an ape	**many** athletes	**my** wife
the soup	**some** beer	**Dick's** Mercedes
that hussy	**those** bikes	**any** method

Sometimes two determiners precede a noun. Examples:

all the cash	**half the** liquor
double his score	**both your** sisters

Any words like these, which announce that a noun is coming, are determiners (but remember that some of these words fit into other structure classes too, with different functions and meanings).

VERB AUXILIARIES

Many verb forms are composed of two or more words, such as *should have been going* and *was being repeated.* The last word is the main verb and all the others are **auxiliaries.** Because several auxiliaries may accompany a main verb form, the number of complete verb forms for any one verb is almost endless. The auxiliaries carry various subtle meanings, including tense. Though the grammar of auxiliaries is very complex, you need to understand little about them in studying composition.

To be, to have, and *to do* are common verbs in English with specific meanings. Some forms of these verbs are also used as auxiliaries, but when they are auxiliaries, they bear no relationship in meaning to the verbs themselves. For example the *have's* in *I have a pony* and *they have gone* are entirely different words. Here are the forms of the above-mentioned verbs that serve as auxiliaries:

to be: am, is, are, was, were, being, been
to have: has, have, had, having[1]
to do: do, does, did

Another group of auxiliaries is called **modal auxiliaries.** They are the following:

shall	can	must
should	could	ought to
will	may	
would	might	

[1] Verb forms that can function as sentence verbs, such as *will be seen,* are called **finite.** Verb forms that cannot function as sentence verbs, such as *having eaten,* are called **nonfinite.** *Having* functions as an auxiliary only in nonfinite verb forms.

These modal auxiliaries carry many subtle meanings. For example, in the sentence *John may leave,* the modal *may* can mean that John has permission to leave, or it may mean that there is a possibility he will leave. (There are some other complex auxiliaries, but they need not concern us in our study of composition.)

Auxiliaries may serve as **verb** or **verb-phrase substitutes.** For example, in such sentences as *yes, he can, I'm sure he did,* and *she probably will,* the auxiliaries *can, did,* and *will* must take their meanings from previous sentences, such as *can he help you,* in reply to which *can* would substitute for *can help you.*

Now you have learned enough about the parts of speech to understand the structure of our chief basic sentence patterns, which are covered in the next chapter.

EXERCISE 3
Determiners and Verb Auxiliaries

1. Explain the difference in meaning between these two boldface determiners:

   a. **The** steak _____

   b. **A** steak _____

2. Explain why the following two boldface determiners cannot be switched while the nouns remain where they are:

   a. **Much** sugar _____

   _____

   b. **Many** apples _____

   _____

3. Not using any of the determiners listed under **Determiners** in this chapter and not using two or more that are essentially the same (such as *your* dog and *his* dog), list five words that can function as determiners.

   _____

4. Try to think of a phrase with three determiners preceding a noun. Do not have any other words in the phrase and especially be sure not to use a preposition, such as in *all of the ale*.

   _____

5. Using a sentence beginning with *I have money,* try to think of the one determiner that can follow as well as precede its noun.

   _____

6. Explain the difference between the *did*'s in the following sentences:

   a. I **did** my daily chores. _____

   _____

   b. Mary **did** pay back the money she borrowed. _____

   _____

7. **See** how many auxiliaries you can use with a main verb form and still have a grammatical verb form.

_____

_____

8. Explain the meanings of the boldface auxiliaries in the following sentences:

a. Alan **should** marry. _____

_____

b. Curtis **should have** arrived by now. _____

_____

c. **Do** you know Alberto? _____

_____

d. **Do** come to see me tonight. _____

_____

e. Jerry **must have** got lost. _____

_____

f. Richard **must** obey the court order. _____

_____

9. You no doubt often hear such a sentence as

   If I **would have** studied, I would have passed.

   What auxiliary would an older person be more likely to use than the boldface **would have?** Is one preferable to the other?

_____

_____

4

The Basic
Sentence Patterns
and Related Matters

INDEPENDENT CLAUSE DEFINED

We combine words, of course, to make sentences. In our casual speech we use many fragments, or nonsentences, because in our flow of conversation the hearers understand many things that the speakers need not say. But most writing is composed of complete sentences, each of which must contain at least one **independent clause**. A **clause** is a unit of words that contains a **subject** and a **predicate**. An independent clause is one that can grammatically stand by itself, beginning with a capital letter and ending with a mark of end punctuation. It may, of course, have reference through pronouns or verb auxiliaries to a previous sentence and thus not be meaningful unless that reference is understood. For example,

> Billy ate the mustard

is an independent clause that carries its own full meaning. But

> He wasn't sure

and

> Of course they could

are also independent clauses even though they must derive most of their meaning by reference to one or more immediatly preceding sentences.

SENTENCE SUBJECT DEFINED

The grammatical term *subject* is very difficult to define, but for our limited purpose of using grammar as a tool to study composition, we can get along very well by identifying the sentence subject as the answer to the question *who?* or *what?* about the sentence verb. Examples:

> My horse ate some locoweed.

What ate? *My horse,* which is thus the subject.

Jerome was promoted to manager.

Who was promoted? *Jerome,* which word is therefore the subject.
Sometimes, of course, the subject is not just a single noun. Examples:

All the students in Calculus 6A are planning to be engineers.

Who are planning? *All the students in Calculus 6A;* that phrase (a **phrase** is a unit of words that does *not* have a subject and predicate) is the subject.

Brock's store in Valley Plaza was robbed last night.

What was robbed? *Brock's store in Valley Plaza;* thus that phrase is the subject.
    A noun-phrase subject like those of the example sentences above is called the **full subject.** The **headword** of the phrase (*students* and *store* in the example sentences) is called the **simple subject.** The headword of a noun phrase is the word to which all the other words in the phrase are attached. Be sure to understand that the simple subject is never the object of a preposition but is the headword of a noun phrase. Example:

Many of the spectators were hurt.

Ask "Who were hurt?" and you might answer *spectators.* But *spectators* is the object of the preposition *of,* and not all the spectators were hurt. Thus the headword *many* is the simple subject (*many were hurt*). Change the sentence to

One of the spectators was hurt

and ask "Who was hurt?" Then you will see why *spectators,* as the object of the preposition *of,* is not the simple subject, because it would require the verb *were* rather than *was.*
    Sometimes **word groups** (defined in Chapter 9) function as sentence subjects. Example:

Winning at poker gives me great pleasure.

The boldface verb phrase is the subject of this sentence, for it is the answer to "What gives?" In the study of composition, however, word-group subjects will be of little concern to us.

SENTENCE PREDICATE DEFINED

The **predicate** of a sentence is what is asserted about the subject. It always contains a verb and may contain one or more **complements.** A complement is a word or word group that completes a meaning initiated in the verb. The chief complements will be illustrated below. Here are examples of predicates:

José **is a genius.**
The farmer **drowned a litter of newborn kittens.**
The union organizers **were unjustly fired.**

The boldface predicates make assertions about the subjects *José, the farmer,* and *the union organizers.* That is, the predicate tells what the subject is or what the subject did or what was done to the subject.

BASIC SENTENCE PATTERNS

There are not many basic sentence patterns in English, though with the use of modifiers (discussed in Chapter 9) an infinity of different sentences can be created. We will illustrate the main basic sentence patterns and, for convenience, will number them. Our illustrations are just basic sentences without modifiers except determiners and verb auxiliaries. A double slash (//) separates the subject from the predicate, and a single slash (/) separates the verb from its complement(s) and complements from each other.

Pattern 1

   subject + intransitive verb ⟶ State of being
   Some guests // have arrived.   no D.O.
   The sun // is shining.

This pattern has no complement of the verb (though of course many modifiers might flesh out the meaning in a real-life sentence of this pattern).

Pattern 2

   subject + transitive verb + direct object
   The President // addressed / Congress.
   Mary // is avoiding / Marshall.

The **direct object** is one of the most common complements. Note that it completes a meaning initiated in the verb. A direct object receives the action expressed in the verb. Most direct objects are nouns or pronouns, but they can be other constructions.

Pattern 3

   subject + transitive verb + indirect object + direct object
   Professor Gooly // gave / Marci / an A.
   My bank // loaned / me / a thousand dollars.

This pattern has two complements. The **indirect object,** usually a noun or pronoun, is the person or thing to or for whom the action in the verb is performed. The indirect object in this pattern can always be transformed into a prepositional phrase beginning with *to* or *for*. Example:

   Professor Gooly // gave / an A to Marci.

Now we have a Pattern 2 sentence with a modifier. Except in a very few cases in which a direct object is understood (such as *Henry wrote me,* with *a letter* being the understood direct object), a sentence with an indirect object must also have a direct object.

Pattern 4

> subject + transitive verb + direct object + object complement
> George // called / Ruth / a liar.
> Maria // made / Sir Toby / happy.

An **object complement** is (with few exceptions) either a noun that tells what the direct object is (*Ruth is a liar*) or an adjective that describes the direct object (*happy Sir Toby*). Patterns 3 and 4 are very common, but only a few verbs will function in either of these patterns.

Pattern 5

> subject + linking verb + predicate noun
> My sister // became / a nurse.
> Bobby // may be / a genius.

A **predicate noun** (which can be a pronoun) is a complement that renames the subject or tells what it is. Of the small number of linking verbs, forms of *to be* are by far the most common and are used with high frequency in our language. Sometimes the infinitive *to be* is used in conjunction with a linking verb. Example:

> Bobby // seems to be / a genius.

Such a sentence is still a Pattern 5 sentence, for *to be* is just used as a filler and does not really add any meaning. That is, *Bobby seems a genius* has the same meaning; the *to be* just makes the sentence sound more natural.

Pattern 6

> subject + linking verb + predicate adjective
> Don // remained / unconscious.
> The patrolman // appeared / drunk.

As a complement, a **predicate adjective** describes (or modifies) the subject. A form of *to be* is the verb most often used in this pattern too, and also *to be* sometimes accompanies another linking verb as a filler. Example:

> The patrolman // appeared to be / drunk.

Often the use of such a meaningless *to be* makes the sentence sound more natural. The basic pattern, however, is the same whether the *to be* is used or not.

The foregoing are the main basic sentence patterns in English and are all that you need to know for your study of composition. To engage in discussion of some complex variations of these patterns and of some rarer patterns would not help in the study of composition and might cause unnecessary confusion.

VOICE

We must, however, explain one very common variation of Patterns 1, 2, 3, and 4, for this kind of sentence will be discussed from time to time in later chapters. **Voice** is a grammatical term having to do with whether a subject performs the action expressed in a verb or receives that action. When the subject performs the action, both the sentence verb and the whole sentence are said to be in the **active**

voice. When the subject receives the action, the verb and the sentence are said to be in the **passive voice.**

Every passive-voice sentence is a transformation of an active-voice sentence. A Pattern 2 sentence can be transformed into the passive voice by making the direct object the subject of the new sentence, putting the subject of the active-voice sentence into a *by* phrase, and altering the verb as necessary (but always having a form of *to be* as an auxiliary). Examples:

> *active voice:* Cranford bit the bullet.
> *passive voice:* The bullet was bitten by Cranford.
>
> *active voice:* Someone stole my car.
> *passive voice:* My car was stolen (by someone).

In the passive-voice sentence, the doer of the action is the object of the preposition *by.* When the doer of the action is unknown or considered unimportant, the *by* phrase is usually omitted.

An active-voice Pattern 3 sentence can be transformed into the passive voice with either the direct object or the indirect object becoming the subject of the passive-voice sentence. Example:

> *active voice:* Georgine gave me the gin.
> *passive voice:* The gin was given me by Georgine.
> *passive voice:* I was given the gin by Georgine.

The *by* phrase could be omitted.

An active-voice Pattern 4 sentence can be transformed into the passive voice only with the direct object becoming the subject; the object complement can never be made the subject of a passive-voice sentence. Example:

> *active voice:* We appointed Roy captain.
> *passive voice:* Roy was appointed captain (by us).
> *ungrammatical:* *Captain was appointed Roy by us.

More often than not, the *by* phrase in a passive-voice sentence is suppressed.

A Pattern 1 sentence can be transformed into the passive voice only when its intransitive verb is modified by a prepositional phrase whose object receives the action of the verb. Example:

> *active voice:* Monique laughed at Jim.
> *passive voice:* Jim was laughed at (by Monique).

In effect, in such an active-voice sentence, *Jim* is the object of *laughed at* rather than being just the object of the preposition *at.* (Incidentally, it is *not* wrong for a sentence to end with a preposition.) A Pattern 1 sentence such as

> Juanita speaks clearly

cannot be transformed into the passive voice. Sentence Patterns 5 and 6 cannot be transformed into the passive voice either.

FAULTY PREDICATION

Though we still have several basic grammatical concepts and terms to define and illustrate before we begin work on the art of composing mature, well-formed sentences, this is the proper place to introduce the sentence error known as **faulty predication,** for it is closely related to the structure of the basic sentence patterns discussed in this chapter.

The grammatical function called predication is simply the fitting of a subject to a predicate to make a statement. The resulting predication is a sentence. But when a sentence is composed so that its subject does not fit properly with its predicate, the error known as faulty predication occurs. The error may be due to carelessness or to faulty thought processes. Here is an example from student writing, with a slash separating the subject from the predicate:

> *faulty predication:* The casting of a ballot for a candidate / sometimes tends to be a popularity contest.

The subject and predicate do not fit together properly because the casting of a single ballot cannot be a popularity contest. What did the student mean? That an election is sometimes a popularity contest? Or that an individual may vote for the most popular rather than the most competent candidate? The predication of the sentence is so faulty that we cannot be sure just what the writer did mean. But even if the writer's meaning were understandable, any experienced reader would be annoyed by the faulty writing and would form an unfavorable opinion of the writer.

Faulty predication is usually not due to faulty grammar as such, but to illogical meaning. That is, a very common sentence pattern (Pattern 5) says that one thing is (or may be, or was, and so on) another thing. Example:

> A television commercial / may be a work of art.

Here the predication is proper, and clear meaning is delivered. From a technical point of view, any sentence that says one thing is another is grammatical. This fact can be demonstrated through the use of made-up words. Example:

> The bliable ponuts / are mugeous phlumpers.

Though these made-up words have no meaning, anyone with a basic understanding of English grammar would know that the sentence is grammatical (even though ponuts may not be phlumpers). The *able* and *ous* suffixes clearly identify *bliable* and *mugeous* as adjectives and the *s* suffix shows that *ponuts* and *phlumpers* are nouns. Grammatically, a noun is being called a noun, and that is sound grammar. But when one thing is called something that it cannot be, the predication is faulty because the meaning, not the technical grammar, is faulty. However, we still call the error one in sentence structure.

Here are other typical examples, from student papers, of faulty predication:

> The next type of advertising / is the radio. (*The radio is a medium of advertising, not a type.*)
> An excellent way to enrich the soil / would be man himself. (*Can man be a way to enrich the soil?*)
> My first impression of my physics teacher / was overbearing and conceited. (*Can an impression be overbearing and conceited?*)
> The hair oil that states "try the 60-second workout" / is a misleading advertisement. (*The hair oil itself is not an advertisement.*)

40

In closing the Brooklyn Navy Yard, dozens of decisions and thousands of details / must be made. (*Decisions are made but details are not.*)

Faulty predications like these are not uncommon in student compositions, but they are infrequent in the writing of students who *think* very carefully about what they want to say as they *compose* sentences.

Faulty predications like the above are nonrecurring, though students can learn not to write them the first time. One commonly recurring kind of faulty predication, however, is the *is when* sentence. Such a sentence is not as serious an error as those illustrated above, but it does represent poor writing. Here is a typical example from a student paper:

Prejudice / is when you make a judgment about a person before you know anything about him.

This predication is faulty because *when* specifies a time, but the subject *prejudice* makes no indication of time. The student should have written such a sentence as

Prejudice / manifests itself when one prejudges a person.

In this revision the subject logically fits the predicate. So beware of the *is when* construction; use it only when the sentence subject specifies time.

5

Six More Classes
of Structure Words

In this chapter we will briefly discuss six more classes of structure words that from time to time you may need to make reference to. The various classes of structure words known as **connectives** are much more important in the study of composition than the six classes discussed in this chapter; thus the two chapters following this one will be devoted to them.

PRONOUNS

Though the personal pronouns can be classified as a subset under nouns, most other kinds of pronouns cannot. Therefore, all pronouns are usually classified as structure words, and it is necessary to separate them into subgroups.

The group of pronouns called the **personal pronouns** refer to people, animals, or things, with the person or thing referred to called the pronoun's **antecedent.** These pronouns show **person, case, number,** and **gender.** Here they are in the form of a paradigm:

First Person

	singular	*plural*
subjective	I	we
objective	me	us
possessive	my, mine	our, ours

Second Person

	singular	*plural*
subjective	you	you
objective	you	you
possessive	your, yours	your, yours

Third Person

	singular	*plural*
subjective	he, she, it	they
possessive	him, her, it	them
objective	his, her, hers, its	their, theirs

The paradigm itself defines the grammatical terms person and number. The genders are, of course, masculine and feminine. **Case** has to do with whether the pronoun functions as a subject (or as a predicate nominative after a form of the verb *to be*), or as the object of a verb or preposition, or as an indicator of possession.

The **reflexive pronouns** are those that end in *self* or *selves* and reflect back to their antecedents. They are the following:

myself	herself	ourselves
yourself	itself	yourselves
himself		themselves

They are used as intensifiers, as in *Mary herself could not calm Tom down*, and as direct objects whose antecedents are the sentence subjects, as in *Rosa cut herself*.

The **relative pronouns** are *who, whom, whose, which, that, who(m)ever*, and *whichever*. They are used to introduce adjective clauses. Example, with the relative pronoun and its antecedent in boldface:

I met a **man** in Orval's Tavern **who** tried to sell me a gold brick.

The **demonstrative pronouns** are *this, that, these*, and *those*. They are the "pointing" pronouns (or determiners), as in *I want **those** books*. When these pronouns are used to refer to whole ideas, as in

Some politicians are corrupt. **This** makes many people distrust the government in general,

they are not demonstrative and are best called **broad-reference pronouns.** (*It* and *which* also function as broad-reference pronouns.)

The **indefinite pronouns** are those that do not refer to definite or specific persons or things. These are the chief ones:

one	anybody	anything
anyone	everybody	nothing
everyone	nobody	everything
someone	somebody	something
no one		

NOUN SUBSTITUTES

The indefinite pronouns really function as **noun substitutes,** as do some other words. Here are the chief ones:

enough	one another	none	all	his
plenty	each other	more	both	its
other	many	most	each one	mine
another	much	much	each	yours
any other	several	either	few	hers
no other	some	neither	less	ours
				theirs

52

These words often fill in for nouns that the hearer or reader understands, as in *I've had enough* (*beer*). Of course, many of the various pronouns also function as noun substitutes; the ones listed in the last column above (except for some uses of *his* and *its*) function only as noun substitutes.

PREPOSITIONS

Prepositions, whose meanings are often hard to express, are the most numerous of the structure classes. They form prepositional phrases in order to express relationships of various sorts between two words. For example, in the phrase *the girl in the string bikini,* *in* expresses a relationship between *girl* and *string bikini.* For reference, here is a list of the most common simple prepositions:

above	besides	into	since
across	between	like	through
after	beyond	near	till
along	but	of	to
among	by	off	toward(s)
around	down	on	under
at	during	outside	until
before	for	over	with
behind	from	past	within
below	in	save	without
beside	inside		

Many prepositions consist of two (or even three) words and thus are called **compound prepositions.** Here are the main ones:

ahead of	because of	out of
apart from	belonging to	owing to
as for	contrary to	rather than
as well as	due to	together with
aside from	inside of	up at
away from	instead of	up on
		up to

Such phrases as *in reference to* (*that*) and *in addition to* (*this*) can be classified as compound prepositions or as one prepositional phrase followed by another.

PARTICLES

So many prepositions function as a part of a verb that they can be separately classified as **particles.** Together with a verb, a particle forms a **verb-particle composite,** and the two words together are one verb. The grammar of verb-particle composites is very complex, but one simple concept about them will be sufficient for our study. This concept is that usually neither of the two words in the composite has its regular meaning and always at least one will not have its regular meaning.

Some verb-particle composites are intransitive. Examples, with the composites in boldface:

1. The lost little boy **turned up.**
2. I think I'll **turn in.**
3. The drunk **passed out.**
4. With a dozen eggs the cook can **make out.**
5. After an hour the prizefighter **came to.**

In the first example there is no literal turning and no direction of up. In Example 4, the *make* does not refer to the cook's work but to her ability to succeed in preparing her dishes with no more ingredients. And so with the other examples. The particles are definitely a part of the verbs.

Some verb-particle composites are transitive. Consider these two sentences:

The tractor ran across a furrow.
I ran across a rare book.

In the first sentence, *ran* is a verb with its usual meaning, and *across a furrow* is a prepositional phrase. In the second, *ran* does not have its usual meaning, and *across a rare book* is definitely not a prepositional phrase. Instead, in the second sentence *ran across* is a verb-particle composite, and *a rare book* is its direct object.

More examples, with the composites in boldface:

1. Mary couldn't **make up** her mind.
2. That **wrapped up** the deal.
3. Lucille could only **stir up** trouble.
4. Can you **look over** my proposal now?

In Example 1, *make* does not have its regular meaning, and *up* does not express direction. *Up her mind* is definitely not a prepositional phrase. In these sentences, *mind, deal, trouble* and *proposal* are direct objects of the verb-particle composites.

With almost all transitive verb-particle composites (*run across* is an exception), the particle must come after the direct object if the direct object is a pronoun. Examples, with the composites in boldface:

1. **Make** it [your mind] **up** quickly.
2. You can really **stir** it [trouble] **up,** can't you?
3. That **wrapped** it **up.**
4. Can you **look** it **over** now?

Note that *make up it quickly, that wrapped up it,* and so on sound ungrammatical.

EXPLETIVES

An **expletive** in grammar is a word without meaning used only as a filler so that a sentence will sound natural. Only two expletives are of concern to us: *there* and *it*. An example:

There is no way to solve this problem.

The *there* in this kind of sentence is an expletive, or filler, without meaning. We use it because such a sentence as

No way to solve this problem is

would sound unnatural. The use of *there* to introduce a sentence is in no way wrong. (The example with *there* is a variation of a Pattern 1 sentence.)
Another example:

It is true that power corrupts many politicians in high office.

The *it* in this sentence is an expletive, or filler, without meaning. We use it in such sentences in order to emphasize the noun-clause subject, which comes last. That is, the sentence

That power corrupts many politicians in high office is true

does not have the same emphatic impact. (The example with *it* is a variation of a Pattern 6 sentence.)

QUALIFIERS

Just as a determiner is a noun marker, so a **qualifier** is an **adjective** or **adverb marker**. It qualifies or intensifies or limits the meaning of the adjective or adverb it modifies. The most common qualifiers are the following (in boldface):

very tired	**somewhat** embittered
quite courageously	**a little** confused
rather courageous	**a lot** better

But any word or phrase that functions as an adjective or adverb marker is a qualifier.
Some form-class words have been converted into qualifiers in set phrases. Examples:

dead right	**fighting** mad
stark naked	**dirt** cheap

Here the adjectives *dead* and *stark*, the verb *fighting*, and the noun *dirt* have been made qualifiers.
Some qualifiers are considered too informal (or colloquial) for use in semi-formal writing. Examples:

mighty pretty	**kind of** bored
plenty mad	**sort of** hungry
awful smart	**real** nasty
awfully good	**a heap** richer

In your college writing you should avoid such low-level qualifiers.
Remember, many words in English fit into more than one form or structure class.

EXERCISE 5
Some Structure-Class Words

1. Write one sentence that has a pronoun in the subjective case (such as *I*), one in the objective case (such as *me*), and one in the possessive case (such as *my*). Do not use *I, me,* or *my*.

＿＿＿＿＿＿＿＿＿＿＿＿＿＿＿＿＿＿＿＿＿＿＿＿＿＿＿＿＿

＿＿＿＿＿＿＿＿＿＿＿＿＿＿＿＿＿＿＿＿＿＿＿＿＿＿＿＿＿

＿＿＿＿＿＿＿＿＿＿＿＿＿＿＿＿＿＿＿＿＿＿＿＿＿＿＿＿＿

2. Write two sentences using *this* as a different kind of pronoun in each one. (Remember that *this* as a determiner is also called a demonstrative pronoun.)

a. ＿＿＿＿＿＿＿＿＿＿＿＿＿＿＿＿＿＿＿＿＿＿＿＿＿＿

＿＿＿＿＿＿＿＿＿＿＿＿＿＿＿＿＿＿＿＿＿＿＿＿＿＿＿＿＿

b. ＿＿＿＿＿＿＿＿＿＿＿＿＿＿＿＿＿＿＿＿＿＿＿＿＿＿

＿＿＿＿＿＿＿＿＿＿＿＿＿＿＿＿＿＿＿＿＿＿＿＿＿＿＿＿＿

3. Write a sentence with at least two nouns in it. Then rewrite the sentence using a noun substitute in the place of each noun.

a. (nouns) ＿＿＿＿＿＿＿＿＿＿＿＿＿＿＿＿＿＿＿＿＿＿

＿＿＿＿＿＿＿＿＿＿＿＿＿＿＿＿＿＿＿＿＿＿＿＿＿＿＿＿＿

b. (noun substitutes) ＿＿＿＿＿＿＿＿＿＿＿＿＿＿＿＿＿

＿＿＿＿＿＿＿＿＿＿＿＿＿＿＿＿＿＿＿＿＿＿＿＿＿＿＿＿＿

4. What relationship does the boldface preposition in each of the following constructions express between the italicized words?

a. *everybody* **but** *the Davises*

＿＿＿＿＿＿＿＿＿＿＿＿＿＿＿＿＿＿＿＿＿＿＿＿＿＿＿＿＿

b. *happiness* **as well as** *money*

＿＿＿＿＿＿＿＿＿＿＿＿＿＿＿＿＿＿＿＿＿＿＿＿＿＿＿＿＿

c. *a painting* **like** *mine*

_____

d. *nobody* **besides** *the very rich*

_____

e. *shouting* **with** *glee*

_____

5. Write a meaningful sentence that has three consecutive propositional phrases.

_____

_____

_____

6. In the blanks in front of the following sentences, put a **PP** if the boldface words are a verb followed by a preposition that has an object and a **V-PC** if the boldface words are a verb-particle composite and the following noun a direct object.

   a. _____ Grace **turned down** my offer.
   b. _____ The car **turned down** the driveway.
   c. _____ Mrs. Poore **walked into** the store.
   d. _____ Mrs. Cashe **bought out** the store.
   e. _____ Mr. Avery **traded in** the Bon Marché.
   f. _____ Mr. Wallett **traded in** his old car.
   g. _____ The student **looked up** the strange word.
   h. _____ The student **looked up** a sooty chimney.
   i. _____ Little Tony **made up** an excuse.
   j. _____ Billy **hid in** an ash can.

7. In the blanks provided, write the (or a) name of the structure class that each of the following words belongs to. Words from the two structure classes discussed in Chapter 3 may be represented.

   a. in _____   b. an _____

   c. terribly _____   d. should _____

   e. some_____   f. it _____

   g. hers_____   h. up _____

   i. this_____   j. do_____

6

Coordinating
Connectives

The structure words known as **connectives** are used, quite obviously, to connect either parts of sentences or sentences themselves. They are extremely important words in our language because they express relationships between ideas, thus contributing to clarity and smoothness in writing. For example, note the jarring effect that you feel as you read these two simple sentences:

> I consider it a privilege to be an American. If I were an Asian, I would not feel inferior.

The omission of the connective *but* between the two sentences jolts the reader as he passes from the first to the second and therefore produces poor writing. Connectives, indeed, are so important that the great English writer Samuel Taylor Coleridge went so far as to say that "a good writer may be known by his pertinent use of connectives." And another great English writer, Thomas de Quincy, said, "All fluent and effective composition depends on the connectives."

In this chapter we will first define and list the three main kinds of coordinating connectives and then will merge all three groups and classify them according to the relationships they express between sentences or parts of sentences. A connective is **coordinating** when it connects two (or more) parts of a sentence that are equal in rank—that is, parts that have the same grammatical structure or that function so identically that they can be thought of as having the same grammatical structure. Naturally, two independent clauses or sentences are equal in rank, and thus any connective between them is coordinating, whether the independent clauses form one compound sentence or two separately punctuated sentences.

COORDINATING CONJUNCTIONS

The **coordinating conjunctions** are important all out of proportion to the small number of them. They are the following:

and	or	for
but	nor	so
yet		

LEARN

Except for *for* and *so*,[1] the coordinating conjunctions can connect virtually any kind of sentence parts, from single content words to independent clauses. This is one of the characteristics that make coordinating conjunctions and conjunctive adverbs separate groups. Examples:

apples **and** bananas
in the house **and** on the roof
waiting patiently **but** not enjoying the delay
curious **yet** afraid
I may go to the dance **or** I may stay at home.

Nor is seldom used unless accompanied by *neither* (see correlatives below). *For* and *so* can connect only independent clauses or sentences, never just parts of a sentence. (But, of course, *for* is a preposition too, and, as that (entirely different) kind of structure word, it can join parts of one sentence.)

CORRELATIVES

The **correlatives** are two-part coordinating connectives, as follows:

both . . . and	not . . . but
not only . . . but (also)	not . . . nor
either . . . or (else)	never . . . nor
neither . . . nor	whether . . . or

These two-part connectives may join independent clauses or parts of sentences. Examples:

Either you will apologize **or** I will bust your nose.
both mustard **and** catsup
not only at the beach **but also** in the mountains
not if he leaves **but** when he leaves
never complains **nor** expects favors
whether drunk **or** sober

The correlatives pose problems in subject-verb agreement (see Chapter 35).

CONJUNCTIVE ADVERBS

The **conjunctive adverbs** are a group of connectives that can connect independent clauses or sentences only. Here is a list of them:

[1] Many grammarians call *so* a conjunctive adverb, which, in fact, it is. But we include it as a coordinating conjunction because when it connects two independent clauses or sentences, a comma preceding it is sufficient punctuation. All the other conjunctive adverbs require semicolons or periods. *For* is included as a coordinating conjunction because no one knows how else to classify it.

accordingly	furthermore	otherwise
afterward(s)	hence	(so)
also	however	still
besides	later	then
consequently	moreover	therefore
earlier	nevertheless	thus

these are not coordinating conjunctions (handwritten annotation)

These words may connect independent clauses with a semicolon between them, thus forming a compound sentence. Examples:

> The nurse failed to administer the prescribed medicine; **therefore** the patient was left in critical condition.
> I wanted to believe the mechanic; **still,** I was not sure of his dependability.

Or a period rather than a semicolon can separate the sentences connected by a conjunctive adverb. Example:

> The nurse failed to administer the prescribed medicine. **Therefore** the patient was left in critical condition.

A writer's stylistic preference must determine whether he uses a semicolon or a period.

Most of the conjunctive adverbs can be shifted to the interior of the second independent clause or sentence. This function is one of the characteristics that distinguish them from the coordinating conjunctions. Examples:

> In June, Maria and Toby seemed ready to be married at last; their engagement, **however,** was postponed still another time.
> Two of our star players were injured. Our chances of winning the championship, **consequently,** were greatly diminished.

Commas are used after, or on both sides of, conjunctive adverbs if a distinct voice pause calls for them. For examples, reread the illustrative sentences in this section.

THE RELATIONSHIPS EXPRESSED BY COORDINATING CONNECTIVES

The coordinating connectives express different kinds of relationships between the sentence parts or whole sentences that they join in equal rank. Though there are subtle variations within each group, these relationships can be classified into six categories.

1. Addition or accumulation. The relationship of addition or accumulation is expressed by *and, both . . . and, not only . . . but also, also, besides, furthermore,* and *moreover.* When one of these connectives is used, one word or word group or whole statement is simply added to another. There is an accumulation of whatever is being discussed. Example:

> The leader of the wildcat strike refused to confer with a neutral arbitration committee; **furthermore,** he announced that he would not negotiate with certain company officials.

Note that any of the other connectives listed above will function logically in the place of *furthermore*. In the case of the correlatives, slight adjustments are necessary:

> **Not only** did the leader of the wildcat strike refuse to confer with a neutral arbitration committee, **but** he **also** announced that he would not negotiate with certain company officials.

When several connectives are available that function alike and express the same relationship, a writer must simply choose the one that sounds best to him.

2. Alternatives. The conjunction *or (either . . . or)* establishes simple alternatives. Examples:

> We may subscribe to *Harper's* magazine, **or** we may use the library's copies.
> I don't know whether he said seven o'clock **or** eleven o'clock.

Since *nor (neither . . . nor)* is the negative form of *or*, it is used when neither alternative is available. Example:

> The prisoners received **neither** mercy **nor** justice.

3. Cause and result. The relationship of cause and result is expressed by *accordingly, consequently, for, hence, so, therefore, thus,* and sometimes *and*. When one of these connectives is used, one of the statements is a cause and the other is the result of that cause. Example:

> Round-the-clock negotiations were scheduled; **thus** the chances of an early settlement increased.

Note that any of the above conjunctive adverbs can replace *thus*, since all express the same relationship. The writer simply chooses the one that sounds best to him. The connective *for* requires that the cause-result sequence be reversed:

> The chances of an early settlement increased, **for** round-the-clock negotiations were scheduled.

Often the conjunction *and* expresses a cause-and-result relationship as well as a relationship of addition. Example:

> The bus stopped suddenly, **and** all the passengers were thrown forward.

The relationship of cause and result is clearly expressed by *and* in sentences of this sort.

4. Contrast. The relationship of contrast is expressed by *but, yet, however, nevertheless, still,* and sometimes *otherwise*. The relationship of contrast is broad and includes such concepts as **contradiction, opposition, paradox, qualification,** and **concession.** It means that between the two statements joined by one of the above connectives there is some degree of contrast. Examples:

> In June, the negotiators appeared on the verge of a settlement; **however,** the strike continued through July.
> Mbono assured the United Nations that his troops had been disarmed; **still,** there was widespread apprehension that fighting would erupt again.

62

Note that any of the above connectives except *otherwise* can replace *however* or *still* with the same relationship. Again, the writer should choose the connective that sounds best to him. The connective *otherwise* can show the relationship of contrast, as in this sentence:

> Light rains still fell along the coast; **otherwise,** the hurricane seemed to have run its course.

Even though they sound too strong for this sentence, the other connectives of contrast can all logically replace *otherwise* in this sentence.

5. Condition. The relationship of condition is expressed by *otherwise* and *or*. The relationship of condition means that the truth of one statement is dependent on the truth of the other. (Usually this relationship is expressed by *if* or *unless,* which are subordinating connectives.) Example:

> We must resist Russian aggression; **otherwise** we may lose our position of world leadership.

Note that *or, either . . . or,* or *or else* will also express the relationship of condition in this sentence.

6. Time. A time relationship is shown by *afterward, earlier, later,* and *then.* These words are used in other ways and function as conjunctive adverbs only when they coordinate two statements. Example:

> On August 10, Chrysler signed a new three-year contract with the UAW; **then,** Ford and GMC accepted the same terms.

Note that *then* can be replaced by any of the other connectives of time, though minor modifications would have to be made in the second statement to accommodate the connective *earlier.*

FAULTY PARALLELISM

When two or more sentence parts are joined by a coordinating connective, they are said to be in **parallel structure,** which means that they are equal in rank. Also we say that such structures are **compounded,** which also means that they are arranged in equal rank. All of the example sentences in the preceding section show sentence parts (or whole sentences) in proper parallel structure. That means that the parts are similar grammatical structures or function so identically that they may be considered to be similar grammatical structures. However, careless or poorly trained writers sometimes use coordinating connectives to connect sentence parts that are not parallel, or equal in rank, or that do not function identically even if they are similar grammatical structures. In such cases, the error in sentence structure known as **faulty parallelism** occurs.

Here is an example with three sentence parts incorrectly placed in parallel structure:

> *faulty parallelism:* Royal Jelly will leave her **beautiful, refreshed,** and remove **the wrinkles from her face.**

The coordinating conjunction *and* signals that the three sentence parts in boldface are in parallel structure, but the first two parts (*beautiful* and *refreshed*) are ad-

63

jectives and the third a verb phrase. Thus the parallelism is faulty, producing poor writing. It is not enough for the writer to say, "Well, you know what I meant." Experienced readers reject bad writing, and personnel officers who hire people for important jobs are experienced readers. The faulty sentence above can be corrected by the use of two sets of parallel structures:

> *correct:* Royal Jelly will leave her beautiful and refreshed and will remove the wrinkles from her face.

Now the adjectives *beautiful* and *refreshed* are properly parallel, as are the two verb phrases *will leave* . . . and *will remove* . . . .

Sometimes two grammatically similar parts can be faulty in their parallelism because one of them does not fit with a word outside the compound structure. Example:

> *faulty parallelism:* I let off my tension by saying **what I want to say** and **how I want to say it.**

The two boldface parts are noun clauses and thus are grammatically similar. Both are functioning as direct objects of the verb *saying*, but the second one (*how I* . . .) cannot grammatically function in that way. That is,

> by saying **what I want to say**

is grammatical, but

> *by saying **how I want to say it**

is ungrammatical. The student writer should have written such a sentence as

> *correct:* I let off my tension by saying what I want to say and by speaking in the way I want to speak.

Now two *by* phrases (*by saying* . . . and *by speaking* . . .) are properly parallel.

Here are other examples of faulty parallelism, with revisions. The sentence parts in faulty and in proper parallelism are in boldface.

> *faulty parallelism:* When we turn on **our TV sets, radios,** or **read magazines,** we are usually seeking entertainment.
> *correct:* **When we turn on our TV sets or radios** or **when we read magazines,** we are usually seeking entertainment.

> *faulty parallelism:* A citizen of this country **is** assured many freedoms, and one of the most important of these **being** freedom of speech.
> *correct:* A citizen of this country **is** assured many freedoms, and one of the most important of these **is** freedom of speech.

> *faulty parallelism:* The poem starts out with an ant **running** into a moth and **is** so busy that he doesn't notice.
> *correct:* The poem starts out with an ant **running** into a moth and **being** so busy that he doesn't notice.

The more conscious knowledge of sentence structure you have, the less likely you are to write sentences with faulty parallelism.

64

EXERCISE 6B
Revising Faulty Parallelism

Directions: Each of the following sentences has two or more parts joined in faulty parallelism. Underline the parts that are in faulty parallelism, encircle the connective that joins them, and be prepared to explain why the parallelism is faulty and to suggest a revision for each sentence. An example sentence is provided to illustrate the procedure.

A person may be brilliant in a specific field (but) he does not have general knowledge.

The parallelism is faulty because the verb auxiliaries *may* and *does* are not similar in meaning.

> *Corrected version:* A person may be brilliant in a specific field but may lack general knowledge.

1. After debating the amendment for a week, yet they did not come to an agreement, the committee members gave up in disgust.

_____

_____

_____

2. Our instructions were to purchase supplies, extra blankets, to leave a forwarding address, and we were to keep in radio contact with the other group.

_____

_____

_____

3. At one time or another Professor Billings was a surveyor, a gandy dancer, washed dishes, and he also played pro baseball.

_____

_____

_____

4. B* Professor Billings had neither a knowledge of human nature and he did no 'ike people.

_____

_____

_____

5. Professor Billings knew that we had cheated and we were pretending that we studied hard.

_____

_____

_____

6. Six players were knocked out on the play but not being seriously injured.

_____

_____

_____

7. To read recommended books and watching educational TV are helpful in gaining a real education.

_____

_____

_____

8. The coach suggested two hours extra practice and that we should go to bed at nine o'clock.

_____

_____

_____

9. The coach thought the play was strategic, effective, and could be used several times.

_____

_____

_____

10. The registrar notified me that I was on probation and I should repeat two courses.

_____

_____

_____

11. When we hunt pheasants, guinea hens, or fish for steelheads, we are helping destroy wild species.

_____

_____

_____

12. A college student has his own rights and one of these being to question his grades.

_____

_____

_____

13. Student demonstrators want participation in policymaking, to have political freedom, and giving minorities a chance at education.

_____

_____

_____

14. Agriculture uses water not only for irrigation, but industry needs great amounts, too.

_____

_____

_____

15. The story opens with a student missing class and is so in love he doesn't notice.

_____

_____

_____

16. Disinfect diapers with boiling, sunshine, or use special antiseptic granules.

_____

_____

_____

17. The books in my library are all paperbacks, many costing only $1.00 and some cost only $.50.

_____

_____

_____

18. The armed forces offer financial security, opportunity for travel, and to learn of people from different cultures.

_____

_____

_____

19. There are two ways to avoid a divorce: One is to never argue about money and second do your share of the work.

_____

_____

_____

20. The flowers are smaller, many having holes in the petals and some petals are discolored.

_____

_____

_____

7

Subordinating Connectives

Just as coordinating connectives join sentence parts equal in rank, **subordinating connectives** join parts that are unequal in rank. The Latin prefix *sub* means "under," and the Latin verb *ordinare* means "to set or place." Thus when a sentence part is subordinate, it is "placed under" another part. There are three categories of subordinating connectives.[1]

RELATIVE PRONOUNS

The **relative pronouns** are these:

who	whose	that
whom	who(m)ever	which
		whichever

A relative pronoun is a connective that joins, or relates, an adjective clause (defined further in Chapter 9) to a noun or pronoun in another part of the sentence. The relative pronoun serves not only as a subordinating connective but also plays a grammatical role (such as being the subject or direct object) in its own clause. Example:

> Senator Phogbound, **who had earlier supported the President,** now turned against him.

As a subordinating connective, the *who* keeps the boldface clause from standing by itself an an independent clause. That is, if no question is intended, then

> who had earlier supported the President

[1] In its entirety, the grammar of subordinate structures is extremely complex, and we will not discuss the aspects of it not useful in studying composition. However, we should note that in some sentences—such as "Bridge is one game **that I could never master**"—a subordinate construction (such as the boldface adjective clause in the example sentence) may contain the most important element of meaning in the sentence. But for the purpose of using grammar as a tool in studying composition, we need not consider that technical fact.

cannot stand alone as a sentence because *who* is a subordinating connective. Also the *who* is the subject of the predicate *had earlier supported the President.*

Another example:

The worker **that the foreman fired** returned that night to commit arson.

Being a subordinating connective, the relative pronoun *that* in the boldface adjective clause prevents the clause from standing alone as a sentence. The *that* also is the direct object of the verb *fired.* In effect, the clause is

the foreman fired that,

with *that* meaning *the worker,* which is the antecedent of the relative pronoun.

A relative pronoun does not express a relationship between ideas, as we have seen that the coordinating connectives do, but instead has a noun or pronoun as its antecedent and simply substitutes for that noun. That is, a relative pronoun means whatever its antecedent means. For example, the above example sentences could be written this way:

Senator Phogbound had earlier supported the President. Senator Phogbound now turned against him.

The foreman fired the worker. The worker returned that night to commit arson.

In considering the art of composing effective sentences, we will study relative pronouns in much more detail in Chapter 20.

SUBORDINATING CONJUNCTIONS

Subordinating conjunctions are connectives that introduce adverb clauses, which are subordinate or dependent just as adjective clauses are. Unlike the relative pronouns, but like the coordinating connectives, subordinating conjunctions express a relationship between two ideas. Thus they are extremely important words in our language, and a close study of them is well worthwhile.

For reference, here is a list of the chief subordinating conjunctions. Of course, you need not try to memorize the list.

after	inasmuch as	provided (that)
although	in case	since
as	in order that	so (that)
as . . . as	in that	so . . . that
as if	less than	than
as soon as	less . . . than	though
as though	like	till
because	more than	until
before	more . . . than	when
fewer than	no matter how	where
fewer . . . than	now that	whereas
however[2]	once	wherever
if		while

[2] *However* as a subordinating conjunction means *no matter how* and is a different word from the conjunctive adverb *however.* So with *that* just understood after it is also a different word from the coordinating conjunction (or conjunctive adverb) *so.*

In Chapter 21 we will study the use of subordinating conjunctions in composing mature, well-formed sentences.

The subordinating conjunctions express seven broad kinds of relationships, which we will now categorize and illustrate.

1. Cause and result. The relationship of cause and result is expressed by *because, inasmuch as, in case, in that, now that, once, since,* and *so . . . that.* Examples:

> We can now forget our differences for another four years, **because the election is over.**
>
> **Inasmuch as the election is over,** we can now forget our differences for another four years.
>
> **Now that the election is over,** we can forget our differences for another four years.
>
> The election is **so** far in the past now **that we can forget our differences for another four years.**

In these sentences the subordinating conjunctions all express the same basic relationship of cause and result: the election being over is the cause, and our being able to forget our differences is the result. With minor changes in wording, the other subordinating conjunctions listed under cause and result can function in the example sentence. There are subtle differences among these connectives so that in any particular sentence one of them usually sounds best. The experienced writer becomes adept at choosing the connective that best suits his particular sentence.

2. Contrast. The relationship of contrast is expressed by *although, however, no matter how, though, whereas,* and sometimes *while.* Examples:

> **Although [or though] he expected to lose the election,** Casey won by a margin of one percent.
>
> Casey won the election by a margin on one percent, **whereas he had expected to lose.**
>
> **While he expected to lose,** Casey won the election by one percent.
>
> **However [or no matter how] hard I study,** I always make a low grade.

There is virtually no difference between *although* and *though* or between *however* and *no matter how.* The latter two do express a relationship of contrast but cannot function in the sentence about Casey. *While* should be used in this meaning in informal speech or writing only.

3. Condition. The relationship of condition is expressed by *if, unless,* and *provided (that).* Examples:

> **If we get a 90 percent voter turnout,** we can win the election.
>
> We can't win the election **unless we get a 90 percent voter turnout.**
>
> We can win the election **provided (that) we get a 90 percent voter turnout.**

4. Manner, method, or comparison. The relationship of manner, method, or comparison is expressed by *as, as . . . as, as if, as though, less than, less . . . than, like, more than, more . . . than,* and *than.* Examples:

> Casey conducted his campaign **as a gentleman should.**
>
> Williamson was **as** thorough in his campaigning **as his finances permitted.**
>
> Gonzales was **more** effective as a campaigner **than Brunner was.**
>
> Brunner campaigned **as though he expected to lose.**
>
> Grunnion acted **like he was angry.**

Many experts think that *like* as a subordinating conjunction should be used only in informal speech or writing.

5. **Purpose.** The relationship of purpose is expressed by *so that* and *in order that*. Examples:

> Casey conducted his campaign on a high plane **so that his image as a political infighter would be modified.**
>
> **In order that he might be known as a friend of the veterans,** Casey advocated Christmas bonuses for them each year.

These examples sound a little stilted. Most writers use phrases beginning with *to . . .* or *in order to . . .* to express the relationship of purpose. Informally, the *that* of *so that* may be omitted when it expresses the relationship of purpose. For example, the *that* in the first example could be omitted.

6. **Time.** A time relationship is expressed by *after, as, as soon as, before, since, till, until, when,* and *while.* (Remember: there is much overlapping in the structure classes; for example, *since* is an entirely different word when it expresses cause and result.) Often a relationship of cause and result is also implied in some of these connectives that express a relationship of time. Examples:

> **When he was confronted with incontrovertible evidence,** Cluckford confessed his part in the crime.
>
> **After the attorney for the defense completed his summation,** the jury were in tears.

The cause-and-result, as well as the time, relationship between the two clauses in each sentence is obvious. But sometimes, of course, a connective of time expresses only a time relationship. Example:

> Grobel had not voted Democratic **since he voted for Roosevelt in 1932.**

The *since* in this sentence is a wholly different word from the cause-and-result *since*.

7. **Place.** The subordinating conjunctions *where* and *wherever* express a relationship of place. Examples:

> **Where the bees are thickest,** Julius seems to be in the least danger of being stung.
> **Wherever you go,** I will pursue you.

NOUN-CLAUSE CONNECTIVES

In Part 2 of this text, which is devoted to the art of composing effective sentences, we will not be much concerned with noun clauses, because they chiefly function as subjects or objects just as nouns do. We will, however, consider their use as appositives (defined in Chapter 9), for in that function they are sentence expansions. Some of the subordinating conjunctions may be used to introduce noun clauses. There is also another category of six connectives that introduce noun clauses. They are the following:

how	what	whether
that	whatever	why

The *that* in this category is an entirely different word from the relative pronoun *that*. As a connective introducing a noun clause, *that* has no meaning; as a relative pronoun, *that* means whatever its antecedent means.

Examples of some of the above connectives in sentences, with the noun clauses in boldface, follow:

> *noun clauses:* **That liars and crooks can be elected to high political offices** seems to reveal a weakness in our political system.
> **Whether you stay or go** is no concern of mine.
> We can't know **what the future will bring.**
> We don't understand **why the stock market keeps declining.**
> *adjective clause:* I want the drink **that Julie turned down.**

In the first example, *that* is a connective without meaning, and the whole noun clause functions as the sentence subject, as does the noun clause in the second example. In the third and fourth examples, the noun clauses are direct objects of the verbs *know* and *understand.* In the adjective clause, *that* means the same as (refers to) *drink.* (Adjective clauses are discussed in Chapter 20.)

EXERCISE 7B
Interchanging Coordination and Subordination

Directions: Each of the first five of the following sentences contains two coordinated statements, and each of the second five has one statement subordinated to the other. Change the coordination to subordination in the first five and the subordination to coordination in the second five. Encircle the connective in each sentence. An example illustrates the procedure.

It was hot when I arrived in Ohrid, (but) the peasant women wore coarse wool skirts and blouses. (coordination)
(Although) it was hot when I arrived in Ohrid, the peasant women wore coarse wool skirts and blouses. (subordination)

1. One's rate of reading speed can affect his academic performance, but still many slow readers do well in college.

_____

_____

2. A large vocabulary is the surest indication of academic success, for a large vocabulary usually indicates that one has superior thinking ability.

_____

_____

3. A college student must be able to conceptualize; otherwise, he cannot handle such courses as anthropology, math, political science, and so forth.

_____

_____

4. Surveys show that married students do better in college than single students; therefore, it does not seem unwise for a college student to marry.

_____

_____

_____

5. Girls make better grades in humanities courses than do boys; boys, however, do far better than girls in science and math.

_____

_____

_____

6. Although there is a high correlation between the size of one's vocabulary and his earning potential, many teachers with large vocabularies do not make much money.

_____

_____

_____

7. Because I distinguished myself in my college career, I can testify to the great value of mental discipline in pursuing academic studies.

_____

_____

_____

8. After the recessional was over, half the graduates went to the Nite Lite to celebrate.

_____

_____

9. Since they are older and more experienced than most entering college students, veterans tend to be more studious in their pursuit of a college degree.

_____

_____

_____

10. Though I was reduced to penury, I managed to complete my college education.

_____

_____

8

Idioms

Though **idioms** are not parts of speech, a brief discussion of them belongs in Part 1 on the Basic System of English Grammar. The word *idiom* comes from the Greek word *idioma*, meaning "peculiarity." Thus in its strict meaning, an idiom is an expression "peculiar" to its language—that is, not readily understandable from its grammatical structure and not literally translatable into another language. For example, the first time a foreigner learning English hears the expression "it looks like rain," he might think that there is a substance that looks like rain but is really something else. Or if the foreigner heard that someone "came into a fortune," he might think that a fortune is a structure that one can walk into. Such expressions are idioms.

We also use the word *idiom* in a broader meaning to apply to constructions that are not "peculiar" and that can be literally translated into other languages. For example, we say that *conflict with, differ from, turn against,* and so on are the proper idioms (rather than *conflict to, *differ against, and so on). Most idiomatic expressions contain one or more prepositions or particles. Here are a couple of typical examples, with the idiomatic expressions in boldface:

> Reinhart **came up against** an insurmountable personal problem.
> Ludwig **came across with** his overdue payment.

Why *came up against* instead of, say, *came out across?* Or why *came across with* instead of, say, *came out with?* The only answer is that idioms in English just are what they are and that's that. Except for its idioms, English is a very easy language for foreigners to learn. But English is so full of idioms that not only do they cause trouble for foreigners learning English but also account for many errors in student writing.

We could list innumerable English idioms, such as *concerned about* and *interested in; be in the movies* and *be on television; contrary to something* and *in conflict with something; a stand on an issue* and *an opinion about an issue;* and on and on. But errors in idiom are usually nonrecurring, and thus a student cannot learn to avoid such errors by memorizing a list of English expressions. Most errors in idiom are due to carelessness, panic, or lack of sufficient acquaintance with the written language.

Here, from student writing, are some examples of errors in idioms, with the *faulty* idiom in boldface and the correct idiom in parentheses after each sentence:

There are many odd dances **popular to** the youth of today. (popular with)
Cars play an important **part of** a teen-ager's life. (part in)
Parents do not **acquaint** their children **to** the facts of life. (acquaint with)
Our educational system is **improving** civilization **to** many ways. (improving in)
A good teacher will have a wide **variety to** her teaching. (variety in)
My moods are **established** primarily **with** the music my generation likes. (established by)
I have a lack of **appreciation towards** the opera. (appreciation of)
My generation is **anxious of** the near future. (anxious about)

Such errors occur less often in casual conversation; in writing, they are due mostly to the writer's fear of, or small acquaintance with, the written language. Much practice in writing and much reading are the student's best guard against making such errors.

Sometimes a faulty idiom is due to misuse of content words rather than of prepositions and particles. Examples, with the faulty idioms in boldface, follow:

Parents too quickly **cast judgments** on their children.
There were tedious **hours of technique** behind his performance.

In English, we do not cast judgments or spend hours of technique. In the first sentence, the student probably meant *cast aspersions on;* and in the second, *hours of practice.* The student's lack of sufficient familiarity with the written language no doubt was the cause of these faulty idioms.

A common error in idiom is due to the omission of the first preposition in a compound structure that requires two different prepositions. Examples:

omitted preposition: George showed great love and devotion to his mother.
omitted preposition: Professor Gobly shows great concern and interest in his students.

Since *love to his mother* and *concern in his students* are not proper idioms, these sentences need *for* after *love* and after *concern,* for *love for* and *concern for* are the proper idioms. Such omission of prepositions is usually due to carelessness.

9
Modifiers and Appositives

MODIFICATION DEFINED

Now that you have an understanding of parts of speech and basic sentences patterns adequate for your study in Part 2 of the art of composing effective sentences, we must introduce and discuss the grammatical function of **modification** and briefly consider **appositives** (defined later in this chapter). A **modifier** is a word or word group that limits, restricts, describes, or adds to another word or word group. For example, consider the phrase *an exciting experience*. The word *exciting* is modifying the word *experience*. Technically, the modifier limits or restricts the word it modifies, for, in this example, without the modifier *exciting* the phrase *an experience* can include not only an exciting experience but also an unexciting one or any other kind. That is, without the modifier the word *experience* has a broader meaning; the modifier limits its meaning. Actually, however, we think of the modifier in terms of its adding to the meaning of *experience,* for now we know something specific about the experience—that it was exciting. Though in grammar the entirety of modification is extremely complex, the definition of it in this paragraph is sufficient for our purposes.

THE THREE KINDS OF MODIFIERS

Modifiers may be classified into three categories.

    1. Adjectivals. Any word or word group that modifies a noun or pronoun is an adjectival by function. Be sure to understand the difference in meaning between *adjective,* which is a form-class part of speech as explained in Chapter 2, and *adjectival,* which is any part of speech or word group that performs the normal function of an adjective, which is to modify a noun or pronoun. We will be concerned chiefly with word-group adjectivals, but briefly we can illustrate for you the fact that parts of speech other than adjectives can modify nouns. Examples of adjectivals that are not adjectives:

a **cotton** dress (the noun *cotton* modifying the noun *dress*)
a **smiling** chimpanzee (the verb *smiling* modifying the noun *chimpanzee*)
the apartment **below** (the flat adverb *below* modifying the noun *apartment*)

2. Adverbials. An adverbial is any word or word group that modifies a verb, adjective, or other adverb (most frequently a verb). As with adjectivals, not all adverbials are adverbs. Examples of adverbials that are not adverbs:

I walked **home.** (the noun *home* modifying the verb *walked*)
Hemingway wrote **standing.** (the verb *standing* modifying the verb *wrote*)

3. Sentence modifiers. The third kind of modifier is a sentence modifier. In this pattern of modification, a word or word group modifies a whole idea (usually that in an independent clause) rather than a single word. Example:

adverbial: Joy Ann behaved **naturally** at the party.
sentence modifier: **Naturally,** Joy Ann behaved at the party.

You can easily see that in the first example, *naturally* modifies the verb *behaved* and is thus an adverbial (and an adverb). But in the second, *naturally* modifies the whole sentence, not a particular word, and is thus a sentence modifier (and an adverb by form).

As preparation for the study of Part 2, you need to understand the nature of certain **word groups,** which you will study as modifiers and appositives that act as **sentence expansions.** You have already seen in Chapter 4 how noun phrases (with noun headwords) can be subjects (and they can be objects and appositives too). Also you will in Chapter 15 be introduced to simple adjective phrases. Our technical term *word group* will not apply to these phrases. Instead, it will apply only to phrases and clauses that do not have noun or adjective headwords. The word groups we will now discuss will play an important role in Part 2 on the art of composing effective sentences.

PREPOSITIONAL PHRASES

You were briefly introduced to simple **prepositional phrases** in Chapter 5 under the heading **Prepositions.** To refresh your memory, such a simple phrase consists of a preposition with an object and perhaps one or more modifiers of the object. Examples:

George, **as well as his older brother,** is a member **of the Masons.**

The compound preposition *as well as* has the object *brother,* which has the modifier *his older;* the preposition *of* has the object *Masons.* Except for the study of subject-verb agreement in Chapter 35, we need not be further interested in simple prepositional phrases.

But some prepositional phrases are grammatically complex and contain whole ideas that might be stated in simple sentences. Some examples, with the whole prepositional phrase in italics, the preposition in boldface, and an indication of how the sentence might continue, follow:

88

Without caring at all about his sister, Rory. . . .
Inside the room filled not only with smoke but also with conniving politicians, an
 argument. . . .
With all the beer consumed, we. . . .

Of course, these constructions are not simple prepositional phrases, but because
they begin with prepositions, we will call them prepositional phrases and will
study them in Chapter 19 as sentence expansions. We will not be concerned with
analyzing their complex structures.

VERB PHRASES

There are various kinds of **verb phrases** that perform various functions in sentences. A verb phrase is composed of a verb form (such as *being, having been,
having been eaten, to have understood,* and so on)[1] plus its complement(s) and/
or modifiers. For example, *known* is just a verb, but *known for his skill at chess*
is a verb phrase.

For the sake of simplicity, we will classify the many kinds of verb phrases
into just three categories, and in Chapters 16, 17, and 18 we will consider them
only as modifiers. As modifiers they act as sentence expansions, carrying full ideas
that could be expressed in simple sentences.

1. **Infinitive phrases.** Any verb phrase that has *to* as a part of the verb we
will call an infinitive phrase. Examples, with the verb phrase in italics, the verb
form in boldface, and an indication of how a full sentence might be constructed
with the verb phrase as a modifier, follow:

*To **find** the quickest method of analyzing this soil,* we . . .
. . . finally arrived, *only to **be met** by a gang of thieves.*
*To **have understood** Professor Gooly's lecture,* one would . . .

We need not be concerned with the names of the subcategories of infinitive
phrases.

2. **Present-participial phrases.** All verb phrases that have an *ing* form as
the verb or a part of it we will call present-participial phrases. These are the
most numerous kinds of verb phrases. Examples, with the verb phrase in italics,
the verb in boldface, and an indication of how the phrase might be a modifier
in a full sentence, follow:

***Drinking** more heavily than usual,* Sam Jones . . .
. . . just sat there, *rapidly **becoming** a nervous wreck.*
*Never **having been understood** by his parents,* Ed . . .
The youngster, ***having been** lost for several days,* was . . .

The more you develop a natural feel for the unity of such phrases, the better
your writing will be.

3. **Past-participial phrases.** Any verb phrase whose verb form is just a past

[1] In this chapter and in Chapters 16, 17, and 18, we will be dealing only with nonfinite verb
forms, that is, those that cannot serve as sentence verbs. Finite verb forms serve as sentence
predicates; for a study of composition we need not discuss them here nor in Chapters 16, 17,
and 18.

participle we will call a past-participial phrase. Here are some examples, with the verb phrase in italics, the past participle in boldface, and an indication of how the phrase might be a modifier in a sentence:

The lake, *probably* **frozen** *at this time of year,* will be . . .
Seen *by the entire audience,* Philip . . .
Clyde, *never* **understood** *by his wife,* began to . . .

Past-participial phrases occur less frequently than the other two types, but learning to use them effectively will improve your writing.

DEPENDENT CLAUSES

In Chapter 4 under the heading **Independent Clause Defined,** we defined a clause as a unified group of words containing a subject and a predicate. An independent clause is one that can stand alone as a sentence, as illustrated in Chapter 4. A **dependent clause** is one that cannot stand as a sentence because it is introduced by a subordinating connective that prevents it from standing alone. There are three kinds of dependent clauses, and each, of course, contains a full idea that could be expressed in a simple sentence. We will study them as sentence expansions in Part 2.

    1. Adjective clauses. An adjective clause is one that is introduced by a relative pronoun—*who, whom, whose, which, that, who(m)ever,* and *whichever*—and that (with one exception, noted below) modifies a noun or pronoun. The modified noun is the antecedent of the relative pronoun. Here are examples, with the adjective clauses in boldface:

Patrolman Rufus Goode, **who has a reputation for treating suspects courteously,** lost his temper when a suspect spit on him.
A housewife **whose husband always comes home late** usually gets suspicious.
Astrology, **which is mere superstition,** nevertheless holds sway over millions of people in this enlightened country.

These adjective clauses are dependent because the subordinating connectives (relative pronouns) *who, whose,* and *which* keep them from standing alone as sentences. The antecedents of the pronouns are *Rufus Goode, housewife,* and *astrology.*

    The **broad-reference dependent clause,** always introduced by *which,* is traditionally called an adjective clause. Its distinguishing characteristic is that it modifies a whole idea rather than a single noun. Examples, with the adjective clauses in boldface:

We made reservations a month in advance, **which assured us of receiving the best suite.**
Growing a beard at age seventeen, **which is an ambitious undertaking,** can impress sixteen-year-old girls.

The *which* clause in the first example modifies the whole idea of the independent clause. In the second example, it modifies the idea of growing a beard at age seventeen. Such clauses are really sentence modifiers rather than adjectivals, though the distinction in terminology need not concern us. Chapter 20 will deal with adjective clauses as sentence expansions.

2. Adverb clauses. An adverb clause is one introduced by one of the subordinating conjunctions listed in Chapter 7 under the heading **Subordinating Conjunctions.** Examples, with the adverb clauses in boldface:

> **Since the weather was bad on election day,** the voter turnout was light.
> **Unless we reduce the arms race with Russia,** the world is in danger of complete destruction.
> This history text is suspect, **because its author is a known Communist.**

Adverb clauses usually function as sentence modifiers, though a few grammarians maintain that they modify single verbs and thus are adverbials. We are not interested in such grammatical technicalities but only in the use of the clauses as sentence expansions. We will study them in that role in Chapter 21.

3. Noun clauses. Noun clauses are dependent because they are introduced by subordinating connectives that prevent them from standing alone as simple sentences. Most often they function as subjects or objects, as illustrated in Chapter 7 on subordinating connectives. We will not be concerned with those functions of noun clauses. However, a noun clause can function as an appositive (see next section), which is a sentence expansion. Here is an example, with the noun clause in boldface:

> Professor Snoolie's most absurd assertion—**that the Aztecs were the lost tribe of Israel**—caused his students to laugh outright.

The connective *that* prevents the noun clause, which contains a full idea, from standing as a simple sentence. In the next section and in Chapter 14 you will learn more about using noun clauses as appositives.

APPOSITIVES

An **appositive** or **appositive phrase** is a noun repeater in that it tells what a noun is. It is said to be **in apposition to** that noun. Various constructions can be appositives. Here are a few examples, with the appositives in boldface:

> The Natchez Trace, **a pioneer trail leading from Kentucky to Mississippi,** is now a superhighway.
> Jane's first love—**drinking brandy before breakfast**—proved to be her destruction.
> My second suggestion—**that English become an elective subject**—was rejected by the administration.

The appositives, which clearly carry full ideas and thus are sentence expansions, are in apposition to *Natchez Trace, first love,* and *second suggestion.* The first is a noun phrase; the second, a verb phrase; and the third, a noun clause. Putting a form of the verb *to be* (*is, was,* and so on) between the appositive and the noun it is in apposition to makes an independent clause. Example:

> The Natchez Trace **was** a pioneer trail leading from Kentucky to Mississippi.

Chapter 14 will give you practice in using appositives as sentence expansions.

PLACEMENT OF MODIFIERS

In composing sentences, be sure to place each of your modifiers so that the reader will instantly know which word or word group it goes with (or modifies). Examples:

misplaced modifier: We were taught how to ask for a date **in junior high.**
properly placed modifier: **In junior high** we were taught how to ask for a date.

misplaced modifier: I realized that many people are dishonest **just recently.**
properly placed modifier: I **just recently** realized that many people are dishonest.

misplaced modifier: We will discuss how the stock market rapidly fluctuates **today.**
properly placed modifier: **Today** we will discuss how the stock market rapidly fluctuates.

properly placed modifier: We will discuss **today** how the stock market rapidly fluctuates.

PROPER MODIFIER FORMS

Use adverb forms to modify intransitive and transitive verbs (see Chapter 2) and adjective forms to function as predicate adjectives following linking verbs (see Chapters 2 and 4). Examples:

incorrectly used adjective form: I did **good** on that test.
correctly used adverb form: I did **well** on that test. (The adverb *well* modifies the verb *did.*)

incorrectly used adjective form: Joey was breathing **normal** by noon.
correctly used adverb form: Joey was breathing **normally** by noon. (The adverb *normally* modifies the verb *was breathing.*)

incorrectly used adjective form: Bimbo talks **harsh** to his wife.
correctly used adverb form: Bimbo talks **harshly** to his wife.

incorrectly used adverb form: I feel **badly** about Hugh's losing his job.
correctly used adjective form: I feel **bad** about Hugh's losing his job. (*Bad* is a predicate adjective following the linking verb *feel* and modifying *I.*)

incorrectly used adverb form: Jeff feels **gladly** not to have been caught.
correctly used adjective form: Jeff feels **glad** not to have been caught. (*Glad* is a predicate adjective modifying *Jeff.*)

EXERCISE 9
Identifying Word Groups

Directions: Each of the following sentences has an italicized word group in it. Without referring to Chapter 9, unless you just have to, write in the blank in front of each sentence **PP** if the italicized word group is a complex prepositional phrase, **INF** if it is an infinitive phrase, **PRE-P** if it is a present-participial phrase, **PAST** if it is a past-participial phrase, **ADJ** if it is an adjective clause, **ADV** if it is an adverb clause, **N** if it is a noun clause, and **APP** if it is an appositive. If a word group fits two categories (that is, if it is an appositive and one of the other word groups), enter both symbols in the blank.

1. _____ The Comstock, *once the richest silver mine in the world,* is now closed.

2. _____ Professor Kreap, *with revenge written all over his face,* began to pass out the exam.

3. _____ The Rams gave up hope of making the play-offs, *having lost their last three consecutive games.*

4. _____ *That I could learn so much about English* surprised me.

5. _____ The man *in whose hands the peace of the Middle East now rested* was the Shah of Iran.

6. _____ These exercises should be easy for all students, *once they get the hang of performing them.*

7. _____ My wife, *to be perfectly honest with you,* earns more money than I do.

8. _____ *Billed as the strongest man in the world,* The Great Biceps drew large crowds to his sideshow.

9. _____ My greatest ambition—*to have a poem published in a national magazine*—has never been realized.

10. _____ The contention *that I am guilty* is absurd. ·

11. _____ *Across the bay in the Melrose Casino,* our enemies were enjoying themselves.

12. _____ Professor Baarff, *since he did not have tenure,* was afraid to oppose the regents' plan.

13. _____ Ernest Hemingway, *who was tremendously famous in the '30s,* has suffered a decline in his literary reputation.

14. _____ *In spite of the numerous get-rich-quick opportunities I've seized,* I am poorer than ever.

15. _____ A light year, *which is the distance that light travels in a year at 186,000 miles per second,* is a distance not easily conceivable by the human mind.

16. _____ Neutron stars, *collapsed remnants of supernovas,* are so dense that a thimbleful of their substance would weigh millions of tons on the earth.

17. _____ This natural bridge, *created by wind erosion,* is one of the most popular sights in this national park.

18. _____ Marshall Foote, *to keep his wife from spending all their savings,* decided to gamble his share in Las Vegas.

19. _____ *Having been cheated before by solicitors for charities,* I refused to give a dime to the Foundation for Wart Removal.

20. _____ The most absurd suggestion—*that we sell our triple A bonds and buy stock in the Fly-by-Night Oil Company*—came from a member who wanted a tax write-off.

10

Reference in Sentence Structure

We will complete our study of the basic system of English grammar with a chapter on **reference words**. A reference word is one that gets its meaning by referring to another word or whole idea, which might be in the same sentence as the reference word or in a preceding sentence. Pronouns and verb auxiliaries are the main reference words in English.

PRONOUN REFERENCE

In Chapter 5 you were introduced to various kinds of pronouns. Here we will discuss three kinds of **faulty reference of pronouns**.

1. Ambiguous reference. *Ambiguity* means having two possible meanings. Pronoun reference is ambiguous when the writer does not make clear which noun (known as the pronoun's **antecedent**) a pronoun refers to. Example:

> *ambiguous reference:* When the professor berated the student, **he** appeared unruffled.

Since the antecedent for *he* could be *the professor* or *the student,* the reference is ambiguous. In speech, tone of voice might make the speaker's meaning clear; but in writing, the reader would just be confused. And even if context did eventually make clear the antecedent that the writer intended for *he,* the reader would be annoyed at having to pause to make out the writer's meaning. Another example:

> *ambiguous reference:* The dean of instruction and the registrar had a dispute. **He** claimed that **he** falsified a student's record.

The *he's* are ambiguous, and thus the sentence represents careless and unacceptable writing. In your own writing, *think* about your pronouns to be sure their reference is clear.

2. Indefinite reference. Pronoun reference is indefinite when a sentence has no specific noun to serve as a pronoun's antecedent but instead has an

implied antecedent. Such reference is faulty because the reader is forced to supply a noun himself to make the pronoun's reference clear. Example:

> *indefinite reference:* Jane was more beautiful than the other girls, but it did not get her the role in the movie. *[handwritten: pronoun "it" refers to beautiful / should refer to noun]*

In this sentence the *it* refers to the adjective *beautiful;* since in good writing such pronouns are supposed to refer to nouns and not adjectives, the reference is faulty. True, the reader knows what the writer meant; but the writing is nevertheless poor because the writer did not use standard reference for his pronoun. He either should have used the noun *beauty* for *it* to refer to or should have replaced *it* with the noun *her beauty.* Remember that in writing, the excuse "But you know what I meant" is not acceptable.

Another example:

> *indefinite reference:* When I traveled around Russia, I was amazed at their apparent backwardness.

The reference in this sentence is indefinite because the pronoun *their* should refer to the noun *Russians,* but that noun is not in the sentence (and presumably not in the preceding sentence). The reader is forced to supply the antecedent for *their.* Again, the reader knows what the writer meant, but the writing is poor because of the writer's careless use of a pronoun. The writer should have used *the natives'* instead of *their* or should have phrased his sentence in some other acceptable way.

3. Faulty broad reference. Broad reference means that a pronoun refers to a whole idea rather than to just one noun. The chief broad-reference pronouns are *it, which, this,* and *that.* Broad reference is perfectly acceptable when it is wholly clear and not confusing. Examples:

> *correct broad reference:* Whenever the Senator attacked his opponents, he did it with vehemence.
> *correct broad reference:* The manager of Brock's installed several closed-circuit television cameras. This made detection of shoplifters much easier.

In these sentences the *it* and the *this* refer to whole ideas, not individual nouns, but their reference is completely clear and thus the writing is acceptable.

But when a broad-reference pronoun is used so that its reference is not immediately clear or is ambiguous or indefinite, the writing is bad. Faulty broad reference is more common in student writing than the kind of ambiguous and indefinite reference discussed above. Example:

> *faulty broad reference:* The odds are that such youngsters will drop out of school eight or ten years later with little to show for it but the experience of failure.

The *it* in this sentence represents faulty broad reference because the reader has to pause to determine whether it refers to the dropping out of school (which seems to be the reference) or to the years spent in school (which is the reference the writer intended).

Another example:

faulty broad reference: Any food you buy that you do not like or use reduces the amount of your savings, **which** after all is the main purpose of our plan.

The writer of this ad seems to be saying that his company's purpose is to reduce the amount of your savings, whereas he really meant to say the opposite. The broad reference of *which* is indeed faulty.

Another example:

faulty broad reference: Yesterday's paper reported that an army colonel suggested that the draft age be lowered to 16. **This** is completely absurd as it has no sound basis.

The news reporter who wrote this sentence (some years ago) so misused the broad-reference *this* as to make his writing absurd; we are not sure what it was that he thought absurd.

Another example:

faulty broad reference: When someone mentions voter apathy, most people think of minority groups. **This** is not true.

The student-writer of this sentence used the broad-reference *this* with such indefiniteness that the reader could not avoid pausing to try to puzzle out the meaning.

So: Be very careful in your use of the broad-reference pronouns *it, which, this,* and *that.* They are very easily and quite often misused.

REFERENCE IN VERB AUXILIARIES

Verb auxiliaries, which are discussed in Chapter 3, may also be reference words. For example, in such sentences as *John could, You didn't!,* and *Can you?,* the meanings of the auxiliaries *could, did,* and *can* must come from reference to verbs in preceding sentences. Occasionally, such reference is ambiguous or ungrammatical. Examples:

ambiguous reference: How many people would fail to play the king in this position? Well, Sam Fry, Jr., **didn't.**

Didn't what? Play the king or fail to play the king? The author of this sentence was careless with the reference of her auxiliary.

ungrammatical reference: I hope that at any time I can be of further assistance, it will be possible to **do so.**

Now *do* or *do so* can be used with clear reference. Example:

correct: "Can I participate in the campaign?" "I hope you **do.**"

Here the reference of *do* to *participate* is crystal clear. But in the ungrammatical sentence above, the *do so* has no verb to refer to, and thus the writing is very bad. (According to the *AAUP Bulletin,* the sentence was written by a college president to an instructor he had fired.)

Sometimes faulty reference of auxiliaries can be humorous. Here is a sentence that was flashed on a movie screen some decades ago.

Will those who have seen the entire program please pass out so that others may
do so.

Literate people in the audience must have howled with laughter when that notice
appeared on the screen.

Chapters 8 and 10 have been included in Part 1 rather than Part 4 because
they deal with matters directly connected with the basic system of English
grammar rather than with errors in conventional usage, as defined in Chapter 1.

EXERCISE 10A
Identifying Reference Words

Directions: In the following passages underline each reference word and be prepared to explain what each refers to. Some of the words you underline will have
specific nouns as antecedents; others will refer to whole ideas or actions.

1. And now the astonishing and perturbing suspicion emerges that perhaps
   almost all that had passed for social science, political economy, politics, and
   ethics in the past may be brushed aside by future generations as mainly
   rationalizing. John Dewey has already reached this conclusion in regard to
   philosophy. Veblen and other writers have revealed the various unperceived
   presuppositions of the traditional political economy, and now comes an Italian
   sociologist, Vilfredo Pareto, who, in his huge treatise on general sociology,
   devotes hundreds of pages to substantiating a similar thesis affecting all the
   social sciences. This conclusion may be ranked by students of a hundred years
   hence as one of the several great discoveries of our age. It is by no means
   fully worked out, and it is so opposed to nature that it will be very slowly
   accepted by the great mass of those who consider themselves thoughtful. As
   a historical student I am personally fully reconciled to this newer view.
   Indeed, it seems to me inevitable that just as the various sciences of nature
   were, before the opening of the seventeenth century, largely masses of
   rationalizations to suit the religious sentiments of the period, so the social
   sciences have continued even to our own day to be rationalizations of un-
   critically accepted beliefs and customs. *It will become apparent as we proceed
   that the fact that an idea is ancient and that it has been widely received is
   no argument in its favor, but should immediately suggest the necessity of
   carefully testing it as a probable instance of rationalization.*
        This brings us to another kind of thought which can fairly easily be
   distinguished from the three kinds described above. It has not the usual
   qualities of the reverie, for it does not hover about our personal complacencies
   and humiliations. It is not made up of the homely decisions forced upon us
   by everyday needs, when we review our little stock of existing information,
   consult our conventional preferences and obligations, and make a choice of
   action. It is not the defense of our own cherished beliefs and prejudices just
   because they are our own—mere plausible excuses for remaining of the same
   mind. On the contrary, it is that peculiar species of thought which leads us to
   change our mind. [James Harvey Robinson, "On Various Kinds of Thinking"]
2. An insect, therefore, is not afraid of gravity; it can fall without danger, and can
   cling to the ceiling with remarkably little trouble. It can go in for elegant and
   fantastic forms of support like that of the daddy longlegs. But there is a force
   which is as formidable to an insect as gravitation to a mammal. This is surface
   tension. A man coming out of a bath carries with him a film of water of about
   one-fiftieth of an inch in thickness. This weighs roughly a pound. A wet mouse

has to carry about its own weight of water. A wet fly has to lift many times its own weight and, as every one knows, a fly once wetted by water or any other liquid is in a very serious position indeed. An insect going for a drink is in as great danger as a man leaning out over a precipice in search of food. If it once falls into the grip of the surface tension of the water—that is to say, gets wet— it is likely to remain so until it drowns. A few insects, such as water beetles, contrive to be unwettable; the majority keep well away from their drink by means of a long proboscis. [J. B. S. Haldane, "On Being the Right Size"]

3. Perhaps because of my unorthodox view of cops, I do not consider the crime problem which currently plagues our cities nearly so insoluble as is generally believed. I blame the prevailing despair in large measure on what may be called the social-work approach to crime prevention.

This is the approach favored by many public administrators and civic leaders—and the more enlightened ones at that. Its central theme is the importance of attacking the crime problem "at its roots." By roots they mean those social injustices and inequities which frequently turn the less fortunate members of our imperfect society into its enemies. This is unquestionably a human position. At first sight it seems logical too. Admittedly, crime flourishes amid poverty, slums, and discrimination. What better way, then, to deal with criminal behavior than by striving for decent housing, equal opportunity, phychiatric and other social services for all who need them?

As an old, passionate New Dealer I do not dispute the merit of such programs. They are valuable ends in themselves. What I do question is the wisdom of regarding social services as crime-prevention measures—as practical methods of making our city streets and park paths safe at night. They are no such thing. [Richard Dougherty, "The Case for the Cop," *Harper's*, April 1964, p. 129.]

PART 2

SENTENCE EXPANSIONS
AND SENTENCE COMPOSITION

11
Introduction to Sentence Composition

Most of the writing that you will do in college and in any occupation you enter that requires writing will be of paragraph length or longer. Part 3 of this text, some of which you may already have studied, provides instruction in organizing whole papers and in developing paragraphs. But, as was explained in Chapter 1, the sentence is really the heart of all composition. Anyone who can write mature, well-formed sentences has an easy time with organization and paragraph development. Thus Part 2 provides instruction in sentence composition, instruction that can benefit almost every college student. We cannot overemphasize the importance of the sentence in effective writing.

Many composition teachers and students find that an elementary understanding of the basic system of English grammar is very useful in learning to write sentences (and thus longer passages) that in effectiveness and quality can be considered of college level. Part 1 has, we hope, provided you with an understanding of the aspects of grammar that can serve as a useful tool in studying sentence composition. In the following nine chapters this tool will be used to help you learn to write more effective sentences than you perhaps now write. However, in studying these chapters, you will not need to keep constantly in mind small details of English grammar. Basically, you will just need to see how large sentence parts fit together in mature, well-formed sentences. But you will find an understanding of basic grammar very useful.

A large sentence part attached to an independent clause is called a **sentence expansion**,[1] because it adds to the independent clause (or basic simple sentence) a whole idea that could be expressed in another basic simple sentence. For example, suppose someone writing a paper on the nature of sentence composition wants to express these three ideas:

[1] Actually, any sentence part added to a core, basic independent clause is a sentence expansion. For example, if we change the sentence *the professor is lecturing* to *the professor is lecturing brilliantly,* we have added a sentence expansion in the form of the adverb *brilliantly*. However, in this text we are using the term *sentence expansion* to refer only to a construction that expresses a whole idea that could be expressed in an independent clause, or simple sentence.

1. An appositive is a useful sentence expansion.
2. An appositive in a sense functions as a definition of a noun.
3. An appositive permits a whole idea to be expressed briefly.

If our hypothetical writer uses three simple sentences to express these three ideas, his readers will think his style is childish. But if he himself knows how to use sentence expansions effectively, he will be able to express all three ideas in one well-formed sentence containing an independent clause and two sentence expansions. He will not need to think consciously about what kind of sentence expansions he will use nor say to himself, "Now this is my independent clause"; but he will need to have the syntactical maturity (see Chapter 1) to compose a sentence something like this:

> An appositive, which in a sense functions as a definition of a noun, is a useful sentence expansion, since it permits a whole idea to be expressed briefly.

Then his readers will not think his style childish but will think that he writes quite effectively.

In studying the following chapters you will consciously use particular sentence expansions, which will be defined and illustrated for you and which you will understand better because of your study of Part 1. We should emphasize, however, that the grammatical terminology used is of secondary importance and that no great harm will be done if you compose, say, an adjective clause when you are asked to compose an appositive phrase (they are similar). Though the following chapters will each deal with just one kind of sentence expansion, we will also make the chapters somewhat cumulative so that in, say, Chapter 16 you may be asked to use the sentence expansion explained in that chapter plus one from a previous chapter.

We should make it clear, however, that what we want to be the chief end result of your study of this part of the text is not your ability to identify types of sentence expansions but your ability to use them unconsciously but effectively in your future writing. Remember: no good writer consciously thinks about the specific grammatical structure of his sentences as he writes them (except when he is practicing by performing exercises), but he must have a subconscious command of mature sentence structure if his writing is to be of college-level quality. After your study of this text, we hope you will have such a subconscious command of the various sentence expansions. Your study of this text is **analysis** (the breaking of a whole into its parts) for later **synthesis** (the arranging of parts into a whole). This study is somewhat like analyzing the syllabic construction of a medium- or long-length word in preparation for pronouncing and spelling the word naturally and correctly in your later use of it. When you have full command of a word like *approximately*, you do not think about its syllables. Similarly, when you have full command of the pattern of a well-formed sentence, you do not think about its parts.

12

Compound Sentences

An independent clause is a simple sentence, not a sentence expansion. But two independent clauses not only may be but very often are joined together to form a **compound sentence,** which is defined as a sentence consisting of two (or more) independent clauses. Thus, though Part 2 is devoted to sentence expansions, we need first to discuss compound sentences briefly. Writers frequently join two independent clauses[1] to make one sentence because the ideas in two clauses may be so closely related that the writer wants to make their relationship to each other crystal clear. Usually, one of the coordinating connectives discussed in Chapter 6 is used to join the independent clauses of a compound sentence, though sometimes such clauses are separated by a semicolon with no connective between them.

When the relationship between two independent clauses in a compound sentence is one of **addition** or **accumulation,** one of the following connectives usually joins the clauses: *and, also, besides, moreover,* and *furthermore.* Examples:

> Most African countries have now recovered their independence, **and** the common experience of having achieved this as a hard struggle is a powerful bond between them.
> In his public performances Faulkner read too fast; **also** his breathing became a problem.

Each of the composers of these sentences felt that his two ideas belonged in the same sentence with a connective to express the relationship of accumulation of ideas. When *and* is the connective, a comma is usually the proper mark of punctuation between the two clauses; with the other connectives of accumulation (conjunctive adverbs), a semicolon is required. Of course, the relationship of accumulation is very common in most kinds of writing.

When the relationship between two independent clauses in a compound sentence is one of **time,** one of the following connectives usually joins the clauses: *afterward(s), earlier, later,* and *then.* Examples:

[1] Of course, a compound sentence may also have sentence expansions in addition to the independent clauses. This kind of sentence structure will be explained in Chapter 22.

Initially Mr. Farago agreed with the charges against Eisenhower; **later** he praised both Eisenhower and Bradley for their foresight.

Patton first refused to answer the telephone; **then** he ordered his aides to shut off the walkie-talkies.

In all compound sentences with connectives of time, a semicolon is the proper mark of punctuation; a comma would produce the error known as a comma splice.

When the relationship between two independent clauses in a compound sentense is one of **cause and result,** one of the following connectives usually joins the clauses: *accordingly, consequently, for, hence, so, therefore, thus,* and sometimes *and.* This long list of connectives shows that cause and result is a common relationship between the ideas in two independent clauses. Examples:

The struggle for economic justice has taken on a different aspect, **for** today we face a new kind of poverty.

A poet is sensitive to the intended effects of his poems; **hence** I like to hear a poet read his own poetry.

With the connectives *and, so,* and *for,* a comma suffices as punctuation for a compound sentence; with the other connectives listed, a semicolon is necessary. For practice, see how many of the listed connectives could be used in each of the two example sentences.

When the relationship between two independent clauses in a compound sentence is one of **contrast** (which includes **opposition, paradox, contradiction,** and so on), one of the following connectives usually joins the clauses: *but, however, nevertheless, still, yet,* and sometimes *otherwise.* This long list shows that contrast is a common relationship between the ideas in two independent clauses. Examples:

Some people disliked Eliot's High Church voice and manner, **but** everything about his reading seemed right for his poems.

In theory these immigrants had been repatriated to their ancestral continent; they seemed, **however,** alien to the land.

With the connectives *but* and *yet,* a comma suffices as punctuation; with the other connectives listed, a semicolon is required. As explained in Chapter 6, most of the conjunctive adverbs can be shifted to the interior of the second clause, as illustrated in the second example sentence. For practice, see how many of the connectives listed could function in the two example sentences.

When the relationship between two independent clauses in a compound sentence is one of **condition,** one of the following connectives usually joins the clauses: *otherwise, or, or else,* and *either . . . or.* Examples:

Uganda must reduce its tribal rivalries; **otherwise** it cannot make democratic progress.

South Africa must resolve its race problems, **or** the blacks will eventually revolt.

The relationship of condition is the *if* relationship. For practice, rewrite each of the two example sentences with an *if* clause. *Otherwise* requires a semicolon; the other connectives require just a comma; the correlative *either . . . or* may be used with no mark of punctuation.

The relationship of **alternative choices** (or lack of them) is expressed by *or, nor, either . . . or,* and *neither . . . nor.* Example:

> You may purchase a copy of *Rip-Off* at your local bookstore **or** we will ship you a copy COD.

With short independent clauses joined by a coordinating conjunction (*and, but, yet, or, nor, for,* and *so*), the comma may be omitted. But a comma before *or* in the above example sentence would also be correct.

Sometimes a writer will use a semicolon but no connective between the independent clauses of a compound sentence. Various relationships can be understood though not verbally expressed in such sentences. Examples:

> *relationship of accumulation:* South of the desert barrier lies a Christian Negro Africa; north of it lies a Moslem Arab Africa.
> *relationship of cause and result:* Bradbury doesn't even drive; he keeps a full-time chauffeur.

Such sentence structure is rather sophisticated and is not a pattern you need to cultivate extensively.

Short simple sentences have an important place in good writing, but such compound sentences as we have illustrated in this chapter contribute to maturity of style.

EXERCISE 12A
Writing Compound Sentences

Directions: Write a compound sentence with the relationship of cause and result expressed between the two independent clauses. Then rewrite the sentence as many times as you can, using a different connective each time. Then do the same for the relationship of contrast.

1. Cause and result: _____

_____

_____

_____

_____

_____

_____

_____

_____

_____

2. Contrast: _____

_____

_____

_____

_____

_____

_____

EXERCISE 12B
Punctuating Compound Sentences

Directions: The following compound sentences are written without marks of punctuation. Explain what mark of punctuation, if any, would serve best in each sentence, and also explain whether an alternative mark of punctuation would be acceptable. Identify the relationship expressed between the two independent clauses in each sentence, and suggest other connnectives that could have been used.

1. The liquidation of colonialism is not just an African phenomenon it is a worldwide one.
2. Robert Frost was constantly reading his poetry aloud and he read it as it should be read.
3. Bradbury's characters speak for themselves they do not react to each other in dramatic terms.
4. Dylan Thomas's reputation has declined since the hero-worship of the period just before and after his death but I think he will be remembered as a good poet.
5. W. H. Auden did not have the pleasantest voice in the world but he knew what he meant and he read illuminatingly.
6. At times his lack of balance bordered on the psychotic he also had a constant need to prove his bravery to himself.
7. The rush to get a radio station has grown so frenzied that in 1974 the FCC announced a partial freeze on new licenses still 14,000 Americans filed license applications in 1975.
8. It is hard to cite the precise moment when radio's fortunes started to turn upward it is less difficult however to establish the reason for its survival.
9. The city fathers of Baltimore last year banned the loud playing of transistor radios on public transportation thus they placed this abominable addiction in the same category of public nuisance as spitting on the sidewalk.
10. Radio will continue to flourish for the teen-age market will continue to grow.
11. The camel may be the "ship of the desert" nevertheless the Sahara remains today a greater obstacle to travel than the Mediterranean Sea.
12. Ethiopia is a Christian country but it is not a Negro country.
13. I like to hear a poet read his own poetry for he always gives some insight into his intentions.
14. The book obviously suffered from censorship besides the author did not have access to some important documents.
15. You will mend your ways or you will be expelled.

13

Sentence Expansion: Compound Constituents

COMPOUND CONSTITUENTS

A sentence constituent is simply a unified sentence part, from single words that function as subjects, objects, adjectivals, and so on to all kinds of word groups, as defined in Chapter 9. One of the simplest methods of expanding a simple sentence is through the use of **compound constituents**—that is, through using two or more similar constituents in a series rather than expressing each in a simple sentence. Such compounding reduces wordiness and makes writing more effective. Only the coordinating conjunctions (except *for* and *so*) and the correlatives (see Chapter 6 for a list of both groups) can be used to compound sentence constituents.

Here are some examples of two or more simple sentences being transformed into one sentence with compound constituents. In order, the following constituents are compounded: (1) whole subjects, (2) whole predicates, (3) verbs, (4) complements of verbs, (5) adjectives as modifiers, (6) verb phrases as modifiers, (7) objects of prepositions, and (8) objects of nonfinite verbs. The compound constituents are in boldface.

1. The public man is usually an extrovert. His assistant is usually an extrovert.
   Both **the public man** and **his assistant** are usually extroverts.
2. A master of ceremonies will rise on a podium. He will introduce the administrative assistant as "the man who really does all the work our Congressmen take credit for."
   A master of ceremonies will **rise on a podium** and **introduce the administrative assistant as "the man who really does all the work our Congressmen take credit for."**
3. In a bitter campaign, Doby ran against Brady. Doby defeated Brady.
   In a bitter campaign, Doby **ran against** and **defeated** Brady.
4. The speech may draw laughter from the audience. It may draw applause from the audience.
   The speech may draw **laughter** and **applause** from the audience.
5. A beautiful secretary may earn up to $10,000 a year. An inefficient secretary may earn up to $10,000 a year.
   A **beautiful** but **inefficient** secretary may earn up to $10,000 a year.

6. Blinded by ambition, they all accepted the offer. Not questioning **my authority,** they all accepted the offer.

   Blinded by ambition and **not questioning my authority,** they all accepted the offer.
7. The Congressman's time must be shared with party leaders. It must be shared with lobbyists. It must be shared with reporters. It must be shared with constituents.

   The Congressman's time must be shared with **party leaders, lobbyists, reporters, and constituents.**
8. It was child's play to convert their talents to my candidate's cause. It was child's play to convert their energies to my candidate's cause. It was child's play to convert their positions to my candidate's cause. It was child's play to convert their bank accounts to my candidate's cause.

   It was child's play to convert their **talents, energies, positions,** and **bank accounts** to my candidate's cause.

Many variations of these kinds of compounding could be cited, but the main lines of this kind of sentence expansion are illustrated above.

Compound constituents, which are very common in writing, produce not only economy of phrasing, and thus less wordiness, but also a pleasing rhythm in sentences because of the parallelism of their structure. Carefully reread some of the above examples, and note the rhythm produced by the balanced structure of the compound constituents.

PUNCTUATING COMPOUND CONSTITUENTS

The normal method of punctuating compound constituents is *not* to separate with a comma two constituents joined by a coordinating conjunction, but to separate three or more constituents. Unless confusion would result from its omission, the comma before the conjunction in a series of three or more constituents may be omitted. Both versions of the following sentence are correctly punctuated:

   A considerable number of teachers, businessmen, preachers, and public-relations types were hired.
   A considerable number of teachers, businessmen, preachers and public-relations types were hired.

Many writers prefer the comma before the conjunction just to be sure there will be no confusion.

Occasionally, a comma may separate only two constituents in a series, especially two long predicates with one subject. Examples, with the constituents in boldface:

   A Congressman **often must spend as much as half of his working time for less than one percent of his constituents,** and **then often finds them unappreciative.**
   The administrative assistant may be called upon **to turn away a group of lobbyists,** or **to discourage some agitated mystic with a scheme for ending poverty.**

A comma between two constituents joined by a conjunction will normally be used only when the writer wants a distinct pause between the two parts, as though the second is almost an afterthought. Such writing is rather sophisticated, and in general you should stick to the rule that two constituents in a series are not separated with a comma but that commas are used to separate three or more constituents in a series.

Sometimes compound constituents are separated by semicolons rather than commas. Such punctuation is used only when the constituents are long or have internal punctuation of their own. Then semicolons help clarify the sentence structure. Example:

> If one has eaten sheep's eyeballs with Arabs; or has relished grubs with the tribesmen of Uganda; or has nibbled on snails in a fashionable Paris restaurant; or has savored a pidong, a 1000-day-old egg, in China; or has chewed heartily on humble pie with the Laplanders—if one has engaged in all these gastronomic adventures, then he can call himself a gourmet.

With elaborate sentence structure of this kind, semicolons are needed for clarity. Commas would only confuse.

The word *not* is often used as a connective between two compound constituents. Example, with the constituents in boldface:

> Julia is **a kleptomaniac,** not **an ordinary shoplifter.**

Similarly, when *but* is followed by *not,* the two words together function as a connective. Example:

> Roquefort is **moronic** but not **dangerous.**

In such sentences, the *not* expresses negation and also serves as a connective.

PUNCTUATING COORDINATE ADJECTIVALS

Coordinate adjectivals (a kind of compounding) that come before the noun they modify are separated by commas. The easiest test to tell whether adjectivals are coordinate is to see whether *and* between them sounds natural. If *and* does sound natural, the adjectives are coordinate and should be separated by a comma. Examples, with the coordinate adjectivals in boldface:

> a **rusty, dented** tin cup (*Rusty and dented tin cup* sounds natural; thus a comma is needed.)
> a **bright-eyed, eager** student (*A bright-eyed and eager student* sounds natural; thus a comma is needed.)

But when *and* does not sound natural between adjectivals, the adjectivals are not coordinate and should not be separated by a comma. Examples, with the adjectivals in boldface:

> **interesting political** intrigue (*Interesting and political intrigue* does not sound natural; thus no comma separates the adjectivals.)
> **beautiful open** countryside (*Beautiful and open countryside* does not sound natural; thus no comma separates the adjectivals.)

The test is simple and reliable.

EXERCISE 13A
Punctuating Compound Constituents

Directions: Identify the compound constituents in the following sentences by underlining the constituents in each compound structure and encircling the conjunction, if any. No marks of punctuation are included to separate any of the constituents in compound structures; suggest what marks of punctuation should be entered. An example sentence illustrates the procedure.

> Programmed instruction is quite a different kind of learning from <u>reading a sentence</u> (and) <u>hoping to remember it</u>. (The compound constituents are objects of the preposition *from.*)

1. We need a federal agency to retrain the jobless educate immigrant illiterates and reeducate high school dropouts.

   _____

   _____

2. The community college is adequate for most vocational training and provides good lower-division instruction in liberal-arts education.

   _____

   _____

3. Our college's standards are high but not impossibly so.

   _____

4. Professor Willard is a firm taskmaster yet gentle at the same time.

   _____

5. I wanted a marriage not an alliance.

   _____

   _____

6. Intelligent but unlearned, the immigrant found the school admirably suited to his needs and inexpensive enough for his modest means.

_____

_____

_____

7. He must present the top banana in the best possible light always be faithful to curtain time speak his assigned lines on cue and never, even under the most exceptional circumstances, upstage the hero.

_____

_____

_____

8. We must continue negotiations with Russia or risk world war.

_____

_____

9. General education should stress the ability to read with good comprehension to conduct simple experiments in the various sciences and to participate in democratic government.

_____

_____

_____

10. His behavior was in no way dictatorial but completely permissive.

_____

_____

EXERCISE 13B
Correcting Faulty Parallelism

Directions: Refer to Chapter 6 to refresh your memory as to the error in sentence structure known as faulty parallelism. Then in each of the following sentences underline the constituents in faulty parallelism, encircle the conjunction, and suggest a satisfactory revision. An example sentence illustrates the procedure.

> He said that the process would cut the necessary bulbs from 30 to 19, (and) yet the light would be brighter. (dependent and independent clauses)
> Revision: He said that the process would reduce the necessary bulbs from 30 to 19 (but) would produce a brighter light. (compound predicate)

1. An anarchic protester is one who does not want law and order nor interested in reform.

   _____

   _____

   _____

2. A poor teacher is one who doesn't really want to understand his students nor cares what their capabilities are.

   _____

   _____

   _____

3. We were suspicious of his resolve to study every night, to attend class regularly, and his attitude toward his professors.

   _____

   _____

   _____

4. Every time you open a newspaper you read of war, murder, earthquakes, divorce, or a woman is raped.

   _____

   _____

   _____

5. This book will not only teach you to relax, but you will also learn how to enjoy hobbies.

_____

_____

_____

6. Christian living requires more than just tolerance, but you must also give positively of yourself to others.

_____

_____

_____

7. The flu epidemic gradually declined and reaching a low of ten cases a week in March and April.

_____

_____

_____

8. We will receive praise not by winning but if we play with good sportsmanship.

_____

_____

_____

9. We tried to find out how much the burglar stole, did he force entry, and his past record.

_____

_____

_____

10. Teaching helps young Americans to learn not only the basic subjects, but they also learn how to get along in the modern world.

_____

_____

_____

EXERCISE 13C
Forming Compound Constituents

Directions: In the first five items below, combine the simple sentences in each item into one sentence with compound constituents. An example item illustrates the procedure. In item 6 combine the simple sentences into one sentence with two independent clauses, one of which has compound constituents.

The Capitol Hill community consists of some 6,000 displaced souls.
They include elevator operators.
They include waiters.
They include mailmen.
They include page boys.
They include carpenters.
They include cops.
The Capitol Hill community consists of some 6,000 displaced souls, including elevator operators, waiters, mailmen, page boys, carpenters, and cops.

1. I returned to my room.
   I turned on the TV.
   I settled down to study.
   Only then I remembered my date.

   _____

   _____

   _____

2. I was confused.
   I was interested.
   I entered into the conversation.
   I became greatly enlightened about the election.

   _____

   _____

   _____

3. I regretted my impolite remark.
   Yet I did not wish to apologize.
   I mumbled something about an appointment.
   I hurried away.

   _____

   _____

   _____

4. The professor asked us to review the last four chapters.
He made no new assignment.
He did not specifically say we would have a test.

_____

_____

_____

5. An Action worker must be facile at learning languages.
He must be adaptable to new modes of living.
He must be patient in teaching slow learners.
He must be willing to endure hardships.

_____

_____

_____

_____

6. Judge Sirica often took the defense lawyers' bait.
Judge Sirica made prejudicial statements.
The Appeals Court did not invalidate the trial.

_____

_____

_____

_____

14

Sentence Expansion: Appositives

Compound sentences are formed through **coordination** of independent clauses, and compound constituents are formed through coordination of various kinds of sentence constituents. Such coordination is explained in Chapter 6 and in the preceding two chapters. The remaining chapters in this part will deal with sentence expansions that are **subordinate** constructions, as explained in Chapter 7.

NOUN AND NOUN-PHRASE APPOSITIVES

The **appositive** or **appositive phrase** is a simple and useful sentence expansion but one infrequently used by student writers. You can improve your style considerably through a close study of this chapter. Usually, an appositive is a noun or noun phrase that defines, identifies, or describes another noun, which the appositive is said to be **in apposition to.** The appositive is a sentence expansion because it adds to its sentence a whole idea that could be expressed in a simple sentence.

Here are some examples of two simple sentences being transformed into one sentence with an appositive. The appositive is in boldface, and the noun it is in apposition to is italicized.

1. William Faulkner was a writer of prose fiction. He is considered by many to be America's greatest author.
   William Faulkner, **a writer of prose fiction,** is considered by many to be America's greatest author.
2. At about three months hair starts to form on the fetus's head. The fetus's head is the part of the body that develops first.
   At about three months hair starts to form on the *fetus's head,* **the part of the body that develops first.**
3. The whale is a completely naked mammal. It is adapted to living in polar waters by a thick layer of insulating blubber.
   The *whale,* **a completely naked mammal,** is adapted to living in polar waters by a thick layer of insulating blubber.

4. John Wilkinson is the skillful and enthusiastic translator of this horrifying book. He is himself a scientist.

   John Wilkinson, **the skillful and enthusiastic translator of this horrifying book,** is himself a scientist.

5. Man is in many ways built like his furrier relatives. They are the gorilla, the orangutan, and the chimpanzee.

   Man is in many ways built like his furrier *relatives*—**the gorilla, the orangutan, and the chimpanzee.**

The greater effectiveness of the sentences with the appositives should be clear to you.

Almost always an independent clause results when a form of *to be* (*is, was, are, were*) is placed between the appositive and the noun it is in apposition to. Examples, with the appositives in boldface and the nouns they are in apposition to italicized, follow:

> *John Milton,* **an important politician in Cromwell's regime,** wrote his greatest poetry after he became blind at 43.
> John Milton **was** an important politician in Cromwell's regime.
> *Robert Frost,* **a kindly father figure to many lovers of poetry,** was in fact a cantankerous, devious man.
> Robert Frost **is** a kindly father figure to many lovers of poetry.

To contain a full idea, an appositive draws meaning from another part of the sentence, as these examples show.

Sometimes an appositive is introduced by an **appositive conjunction,** such as *that is, namely, such as,* and *or.* Examples, with the appositives in boldface and the nouns they are in apposition to italicized, follow:

> There are indications that unusual skin markings may be associated with congenital *brain abnormalities,* such as **mental deficiency and epilepsy.**
> Nearly all mammals have long, sensitive *vibrissae,* or **whiskers,** around the muzzle.
> I inherited a *fortune,* that is, **rights to the formula of a popular patent medicine.**

No mark of punctuation comes after *such as* or *or* (many students incorrectly put a semicolon after *such as*), but a comma comes after *that is* and *namely.*

OTHER APPOSITIVE CONSTRUCTIONS

Occasionally, **noun clauses** and **verb phrases** function as appositives, and as such they are sentence expansions containing full ideas that could be expressed in simple sentences. Here are examples of noun-clause appositives, with the appositive in boldface and the noun it is in apposition to italicized:

> The best *suggestion*—**that we adjourn**—came an hour too late.
> The first established *fact*—**that the burgular had been a female**—was all the police had to go on.
> Mervin's latest *misconception,* **that the Socialists had taken over the PTA,** received only ridicule.

Noun-clause appositives almost always are in apposition to such nouns as *belief, suggestion, idea,* and so on. The above examples can be shown to be appositives by placing a form of *to be* between the appositive and the noun it is in apposition to. Examples:

> The best suggestion **was** that we adjourn.
> The first established fact **was** that the burglar had been a female.

Usually, dashes are used to set off noun-clause appositives, but commas may sometimes be used, as the third example above illustrates.

Verb phrases can also function as appositives. Examples, with the appositive in boldface and the noun it is in apposition to italicized, follow:

> My abiding *ambition*—**to become an expert mountain climber**—has cost me three broken legs.
> My roommate's silliest *habit*—**getting up at 4:00 A.M. to study**—is preventing me from getting enough sleep.

Again, an independent clause results if a form of *to be* is placed between the verb-phrase appositive and the noun it is in apposition to. Example:

> My roommate's silliest habit is getting up at 4:00 A.M. to study.

Verb-phrase appositives are almost always set off by dashes.

PUNCTUATING APPOSITIVES

For the purpose of punctuation, appositives are called either **essential** or **nonessential**. These are grammatical terms; a nonessential appositive may in the writer's mind carry information that is absolutely essential to his purposes. Grammatically, an appositive is nonessential when it is not needed to identify the noun it is in apposition to; that is, the noun is already fully identified. The nonessential appositive just gives additional information about an already-fully-identified noun. This means that if the nonessential appositive is removed from the sentence, a fully meaningful sentence will remain. For example, if the boldface appositive is removed from

> Shakespeare, **an Englishman,** is considered by most experts to have written the world's greatest plays,

the remaining sentence will be fully clear, for the noun *Shakespeare* is fully identified as the name of an individual. Since a nonessential appositive can be removed and leave a fully meaningful sentence, it is set off by commas or dashes. All of the appositives given as examples so far in this chapter are nonessential and thus are set off by commas or dashes. You should review some of these to see that they just give additional information about a noun already fully identified and that they, therefore, need to be set off by commas or dashes.

Some appositives, however, are **essential** because they are necessary to identify the nouns they are in apposition to. Removal of an essential appositive will leave a sentence indefinite and not fully meaningful. Essential appositives are most often (though not always) titles or persons' names. Examples, with the essential appositives in boldface:

correct: The novel ***The Reivers*** was Faulkner's last book.
correct: Poe's poem **"To Helen"** was written when he was fifteen.
correct: The British novelist **Colin Wilson** became a politician.
correct: The great chemist **Linus Pauling** won two Nobel Prizes.

The appositives in these examples are essential to identify which novel, poem, novelist, and chemist are under discussion. That is, unless a previous sentence has already identified the book under discussion, the sentence *The novel was Faulkner's last book* would be indefinite and not fully meaningful, for we would not know which novel was meant. And so with the other three examples. If in the last two examples commas were used to set off *Colin Wilson* and *Linus Pauling*, the sentences would mean that there is only one British novelist and only one great chemist, for the appositives would then be nonessential; that is, they would just give additional information about nouns presumably already fully identified.

The error of setting off essential appositives with commas is so common that further illustration is needed. For example, the following sentences are incorrectly punctuated because Conine has written hundreds of editorials and Faulkner wrote more than a dozen novels.

incorrect: Ernest Conine's editorial, **"How to Feed the World,"** was reprinted in the *New York Times.*
incorrect: William Faulkner's novel, ***Sanctuary,*** has sold over a million copies.

As punctuated, these sentences mean that Conine has written only one editorial and that Faulkner wrote only one novel, since punctuating the titles as nonessential means that *editorial* and *novel* are already fully identified.

On the other hand, when a name or title is a nonessential appositive, it must be set off by commas. Example:

correct: Don's wife, Carol, is a former Miss America.

The word *Don's* fully identifies the noun *wife,* and thus *Carol* is a nonessential appositive because it just gives additional information about a fully identified noun. Without the commas, the appositive *Carol* would be essential, which would mean that it is needed to identify which of Don's wives is under discussion, which would mean that Don has more than one wife. Thus the punctuation of appositives can very definitely affect meaning. Further examples:

only one son: Mr. Moxie's son, **Toby,** has entered medical school.
more than one son: Mr. Moxie's son **Toby** has entered medical school.

You should study all these examples until you fully understand the difference between a title or a name as an essential or nonessential appositive.

15
Sentence Expansion: Adjective Phrases

In Chapter 4 you learned that a noun phrase is a unified group of words with a noun (or noun substitute) as its **headword** and with the rest of the words attached in some way to the headword. An example is

> all the **students** on the Dean's List,

in which *students* is the headword. Such noun phrases serve chiefly as subjects, objects, and appositives.

ADJECTIVE PHRASES

An **adjective phrase** is a construction that has an adjective as its headword; it functions as a modifier (an adjectival) and thus is usually a sentence expansion rather than an integral part of an independent clause, as a noun phrase usually is. Here are some examples of adjective phrases with the adjective headwords in boldface:

> extremely **afraid** of his colleagues
> more **intelligent** than a chimpanzee
> **classifiable** as abstract art
> not **old** enough to know his own mind
> especially **happy** about winning first prize

In a sentence, an adjective phrase usually modifies a noun, and in conjunction with that noun it expresses a whole idea. Therefore the adjective phrase is a sentence expansion used to avoid composing too many short sentences in a sequence. For example, here are two simple sentences:

> Professor Muddlemind was extremely afraid of his colleagues. He seldom engaged in conversation with them.

Changing the first simple sentence into an adjective-phrase expansion produces more mature sentence structure:

*Extremely **afraid** of his colleagues,* **Professor Muddlemind** seldom engaged in conversation with them.

The adjective phrase is in italics, and both the headword of the phrase and the noun the phrase modifies are in boldface. The adjective phrase is a sentence expansion carrying a full idea, as is made clear in the example simple sentences. Like an appositive, an adjective phrase becomes an independent clause when a form of *to be* (*is, was, were,* and so on) is placed between it and the noun it modifies.

Here are some other examples of adjective phrases helping to create mature, well-formed sentences. The adjective phrases are in italics, and the headwords of the phrases and the nouns they modify are in boldface:

Mrs. Jacobs, *unhappy with the urban renewal program,* argues that a slum can "unslum" itself.

Insignificant compared to his brother's novels, John Faulkner's **fiction** is nevertheless popular.

*More **handsome** than clever,* **Jacobs** attempted to swindle only widows and spinsters.

Lost in the desert, **we** asked directions of a Navaho woman.

The inexperienced **hunter,** *oblivious of the danger,* continued to stalk the deer.

The **Cannes Festival,** *not **easy** to coordinate because of government interference,* is a formidable undertaking.

Note that if a form of *to be* is placed between the adjective phrase and the noun it modifies, an independent clause is formed. The noun will, of course, be the sentence subject.

The connective *though* is often used to introduce an adjective phrase when a relationship of contrast is expressed between the idea in the adjective phrase and the idea in the independent clause or word group that contains the modified noun. For example, here are two simple sentences:

Mr. Trimble was bitter about his defeat. He pledged his support to his victorious opponent.

The first sentence can be transformed into an adjective phrase introduced by the connective *though* to express the relationship of contrast:

*Though **bitter** about his defeat,* **Mr. Trimble** pledged his support to his victorious opponent.

The adjective phrase is italicized, and its headword and the noun the phrase modifies are in boldface.

The connective *when* often introduces an adjective phrase when a time relationship is expressed. Examples:

*When **upset** by my failure to make a good grade,* **I** deliberately stay home on Saturday night to read a book.

*When **pleased** with his wit,* **Grumman** usually displays his conceit disgustingly.

The adjective phrases are italicized, and the headwords and the words the phrases modify are in boldface.

The connective *if* sometimes is used to introduce an adjective phrase when a relationship of condition is expressed. Example:

> *If unhappy because her husband neglects her,* **Mrs. Pouty** will often go on a shopping spree.

When any connective is used to introduce an adjective phrase, a sentence will not result if a form of *to be* is placed between the phrase and the noun it modifies. For example,

> *Mrs. Pouty is if unhappy because her husband neglects her

is not grammatical. But if the connective is removed, a grammatical sentence results.

PUNCTUATING ADJECTIVE PHRASES

Like appositives, adjective phrases can be **nonessential** or **essential.** If an adjective phrase is nonessential, the noun it modifies is fully identified without the phrase, and the phrase is therefore set off by a comma or commas. For example, in

> **Marty,** *more knowledgeable about astrophysics than the rest of his classmates,* greatly impressed his astronomy professor,

the noun *Marty* is fully identified as a person's name, and thus the adjective phrase modifying it is nonessential and is set off by commas. All the other example adjective phrases given so far in this chapter are nonessential. You should review them to increase your understanding of their punctuation.

But if an adjective phrase is essential, it is needed to identify the noun it modifies; that is, without the phrase the noun would be indefinite and its sentence not fully meaningful. Thus essential adjective phrases are *not* set off by commas. Here are examples of essential adjective phrases, with the phrase italicized and its headword and the noun the phrase modifies in boldface:

> The **student** *happiest with her report card* is Trina Russell.
> A **parent** *pleased with his teen-age children's behavior nowadays* is rare.

Without the adjective phrases, the nouns *student* and *parent* would not be fully identified and the sentences would be indefinite and not fully meaningful. For example,

> A parent is rare

is an indefinite sentence. The essential adjective phrase in the example sentence tells which parent is under discussion.

If a form of *to be* is placed between an essential adjective phrase and the noun it modifies, the resulting sentence may not be meaningful or may not express the writer's intended meaning. For example,

> The student is happiest with her report card

may be a grammatical sentence but it is not a meaningful one.

137

16

Sentence Expansion:
Absolute Phrases;
Infinitive Phrases

In Chapter 9 we defined and illustrated three broad categories of verb phrases: (1) those with an infinitive (the *to* form of a verb), such as *to be a sure winner* and *not to have understood the question;* (2) those with a present participle (*ing* form) in the verb, such as *being rich as Croesus* and *not having been understood by his audience;* and (3) those whose verb form is a single past participle, such as *broken into a thousand pieces* and *invented for the specific purpose of killing wolverines.* Infinitive, present-participial, and past-participial phrases function in various ways in sentences, but we shall consider them only in their function of modification, in which they function as sentence expansions that contain full ideas that could be expressed in simple sentences. For ease of study, we will devote a separate short chapter to each.

There is also another kind of verb phrase, known as an **absolute phrase.** It is a phrase in which some nonfinite verb form has a subject, and it always functions as a sentence modifier. We will consider the absolute phrase in this chapter with the infinitive phrase.

ABSOLUTE PHRASES

A variation of the present- and past-participial phrases is known as an **absolute phrase.** It has a subject, but since its verb form is nonfinite it cannot stand alone as a sentence. Here are two examples:

the **delivery** of the mail **having been delayed**
the **solution** to the puzzle not **being** immediately clear

The simple subjects and the verb forms are in boldface. As you can readily see, such phrases are not sentences. They function as sentence modifiers.

The absolute phrase is a sentence expansion in that it allows the writer to avoid writing a sequence of simple sentences and thus to achieve a more mature style. Here are some examples of two simple sentences being transformed into one sentence with an absolute phrase. The absolute phrase is italicized and its subject is in boldface.

1. The trial did not go to the defense lawyer's liking. He resorted to histrionics in his summation.

   The trial not having gone to his liking, the defense lawyer resorted to histrionics in his summation.
2. This is a case of life imitating art. The real becomes synthetic.

   This is a case of life imitating art, *the real becoming synthetic.*
3. There are remains of old Spanish forts everywhere. Their adobe walls are dissolving poetically into the dust they came from.

   There are remains of old Spanish forts everywhere, *their adobe walls dissolving poetically into the dust they came from.*
4. The meal was finished. Now we were ready to talk business.

   The meal finished, we were now ready to talk business.

Your ear should tell you that the sentence with the absolute-phrase expansion is more pleasing stylistically than a sequence of simple sentences. Absolute phrases are always set off by commas.

INFINITIVE PHRASES

As a modifier, an **infinitive phrase** can be either an adverbial, an adjectival, or a sentence modifier. For example, in

   Joe waited **to buy a ticket.**

the boldface infinitive phrase is an adverbial modifying the verb *waited.* And in

   The man **to solve this problem** is Buck Tuth,

the boldface infinitive phrase modifies the noun *man* and is thus an adjectival. But the kind of infinitive-phrase sentence expansion that we are interested in is a sentence modifier. Here are some examples of two simple sentences being transformed into one sentence with an infinitive phrase as a sentence expansion.

1. Mr. Jackson wanted to avoid antagonizing his student audience. He avoided completely the issue of reinstituting the draft.

   Mr. Jackson, **to avoid antagonizing his student audience,** avoided completely the issue of reinstituting the draft.
2. A gourmet cook wants to serve a perfect gourmet meal. He must keep all hot dishes piping hot till the moment of serving.

   To serve a perfect gourmet meal, a gourmet cook must keep all hot dishes piping hot till the moment of serving.
3. The Town Bank's vice-president wanted to cover his extensive embezzlements. He kept juggling deposits made by big retail stores.

   The Town Bank's vice-president, **to cover his extensive embezzlements,** kept juggling deposits made by big retail stores.

Infinitive phrases of this sort express a relationship of purpose; therefore when such a phrase is converted into a simple sentence, a noun from the independent clause must serve as the sentence subject with the sentence verb usually being *wants.* The infinitive phrase does, however, contain a full idea, which is expressed more briefly and with better style than when it is a separate sentence. All sentence-modifier infinitive phrases are nonessential and are set off by a comma or commas.

EXERCISE 16A
Composing Sentences
with Absolute and Infinitive Phrases

Directions: Combine each of the following pairs or triplets of sentences into one well-formed sentence with either an absolute phrase or an infinitive phrase. In the last two items also have either an appositive or an adjective phrase.

1. Ted Broxton wanted to take full advantage of his scholarship. He had to work all summer and save his money.

_____

_____

_____

2. The last guest had left. Rosa began to clean up the house.

_____

_____

3. The firemen wanted to contain the brush fire threatening a subdivision. They cleared a fire lane fifty feet wide and several hundred yards long.

_____

_____

_____

4. I wanted to understand this textbook better. I asked my smart sister to help me with the difficult parts.

_____

_____

_____

5. The school year was over. I looked for a summer job.

_____

_____

6. Robert wanted to assure himself of admission to med school. He went to a good university for his undergraduate work and tried to make all A's.

_____

_____

_____

7. The police were stumped. No motive for the murder had been found.

_____

_____

8. The professor's explanation was not clear. We turned to our class leader for help.

_____

_____

_____

9. We wanted to get a better view of the Devil's Gorge. The Devil's Gorge is the most popular area of Glen Canyon. We edged closer to the rim.

_____

_____

_____

10. No remedy for Ms. Chatworth's illness was known. Ms. Chatworth was not unhappy to be out of her misery. Ms. Chatworth prepared herself for death.

_____

_____

_____

EXERCISE 16B
Composing Sentences
with Absolute and Infinitive Phrases

Directions: In the first five of the following items combine each of the three sets of sentences into one sentence with either an absolute or infinitive phrase and also either a compound constituent or an appositive or an adjective phrase. In the last five items either add an absolute or infinitive phrase of your own creation or transform the simple sentence into one of those two phrases and add an independent clause of your own.

1. Gus Sanguine's grades were excellent. Gus was a premed student. He expected no difficulty in gaining admission to a med school.

   _____

   _____

   _____

2. Rufus Lightthrottle wanted to get better gas mileage. He was an expert mechanic. He advanced the spark in his car's ignition system. He added small amounts of water to his gasoline.

   _____

   _____

   _____

   _____

3. Romeo McHaystack's car was washed and polished. Romeo called for his date. His date was an easily impressed farm girl.

   _____

   _____

   _____

   _____

4. Combid was eager to meet Marilyn. He wanted to make certain of meeting her properly. He bribed Rancid to introduce him to her.

_____

_____

_____

5. We put politics out of our mind. We returned to pleasurable pursuits. The election was over.

_____

_____

6. We decided to be honest with our professors.

_____

7. The old Cranford house had burned down.

_____

8. I want to learn to read at the rate of 600 words per minute.

_____

9. My bout with tuberculosis was over.

_____

10. I bought spare parts from a junkyard.

_____

_____

17

Sentence Expansion:
Present-Participial
Phrases

PRESENT-PARTICIPIAL PHRASES

Present-participial phrases are the most commonly used verb-phrase sentence expansions. Here are some typical examples, with the verb form in boldface:

thinking the matter was settled
having driven at a high rate of speed
not **understanding** the issues involved
having been expelled from a boarding school

As sentence expansions, such phrases are always adjectivals, modifying a noun or pronoun in an independent clause or in some other part of a complex sentence. They function just like the adjective phrases discussed in Chapter 15, carrying a full idea that could be expressed in a separate simple sentence. To form such a separate simple sentence, the nonfinite present-participial verb form must be transformed into a finite verb form and the noun the phrase modifies must serve as the sentence subject. Example of a present-participial phrase being transformed into a simple sentence:

Nine conservative Congressmen, **speaking before 200 businessmen,** charged that the Urban Renewal Act is "taxing the needy to benefit the greedy."
Nine conservative Congressmen spoke before 200 businessmen. They charged that the Urban Renewal Act is "taxing the needy to benefit the greedy."

The boldface present-participial phrase becomes a sentence by having the nonfinite verb *speaking* changed to the finite verb *spoke* and by having the modified noun phrase (*nine conservative Congressmen*) serve as the sentence subject.

The process we have just illustrated is the opposite of the process we want you to learn. In the preceding three chapters we have first given two simple sentences and then showed how one could be changed into an appositive or adjective phrase or infinitive phrase. We thought that approaching the process from the opposite direction in this section might increase your understanding of sentence expansions.

The purpose of the present-participial phrase as a sentence expansion is to allow the writer to compose a mature, well-formed sentence rather than a sequence of simple sentences, a kind of style that often sounds childish. In effect, all but one of the sentence expansions we have studied so far, and some more to come, allow for the meaning of a noun or noun phrase to be delivered twice in a sentence but expressed only once. That provides brevity of style and better sentence rhythm too.

Here are some examples of two simple sentences being transformed into one sentence with a present-participial phrase. The phrase is italicized, and the verb form and the noun it modifies are in boldface.

1. The committee underestimated the scope of their task. They oversold the Urban Renewal program as a cure-all for city ills.
   Underestimating the scope of their task, the **committee** oversold the Urban Renewal program as a cure-all for city ills.
2. Urban renewal originated as a simple real-estate venture. It brought into view the extent of poverty in the slums.
   Originating as a simple real-estate venture, **Urban renewal** brought into view the extent of poverty in the slums.
3. At the east end of town are the Sandia Mountains. They glow red at sunset.
   At the east end of town are the **Sandia Mountains,** *glowing red at sunset.*
4. The present-participial phrase is only one of many kinds of sentence expansions. It does not occur in writing with high frequency.
   The **present-participial phrase,** *being only one of many kinds of sentence expansions,* does not occur in writing with high frequency.
5. Senator Will Wright was not reelected in the Democratic landslide. He was forced to take a low-paying job in business.
   Senator Will Wright, *not having been reelected in the Democratic landslide,* was forced to take a low-paying job in business.

The majority of present-participial phrases like the above express the relationship of cause and result between the idea in the phrase and the idea in the independent clause it is attached to. For instance, in the first example the cause is the committee's underestimating the scope of their task, and the result is their overselling the urban renewal program. Sometimes, however, the relationship is simply one of accumulation, as in the second and third examples. That is, *and* could be placed between the two simple sentences in each to make a compound sentence (though the compound sentence would sound childish). And occasionally, as will be explained below, a relationship of contrast or of time is expressed between the present-participial phrase and the independent clause.

Connectives are sometimes used to introduce present-participial phrases. *Thus, thereby,* and *by* express the relationship of cause and result. Examples, with the present-participial phrase italicized and its verb and the noun the phrase modifies in boldface, follow:

Cranford concentrated his campaign in the heavily populated eastern side of his district, *thereby getting a large majority of the ethnic vote.*
The **Saddleback Knights** won all ten of their football games, *thus assuring themselves a place in the play-offs.*

By lowering the speed limit on open highways, the **government** has lowered gasoline consumption.

When used with the connectives *thereby* and *thus,* present-participial phrases usually come last in a sentence; when used with the connective *by,* the phrase usually comes first.

Though expresses the relationship of contrast. Example, with italics and boldface as usual:

Though **growing** *increasingly bored,* the **Senator** appeared to be interested in his constituent's problems.

There is a contrast or opposition between the idea in the phrase and the idea in the independent clause.

After, before, when, while, and *since* express a relationship of time. Examples:

When **dating** *a new girl friend,* I take extra precautions to be polite and considerate.
After **growing** *some marijuana plants,* I was afraid to keep them.

The time relationship between the two ideas in each sentence is clear, but also a relationship of cause and result is suggested. *Besides* expresses a relationship of accumulation. Example:

Besides **working** *part time to stay in college,* I also make some money by writing short stories for cheap magazines.

The connective *besides* shows that one idea is added to another; that is, if both ideas were expressed in independent clauses, the conjunction *and* would join them.

PUNCTUATING PRESENT-PARTICIPIAL PHRASES

Present-participial phrases may be **nonessential** or **essential.** A nonessential phrase is not needed to identify the noun it modifies but only gives additional information about an already-fully-identified noun. Such a phrase is set off by a comma or commas. All the present-participial phrases illustrated so far in this chapter are nonessential. You should review them in order to increase your understanding of their proper punctuation.

An essential present-participial phrase is needed to identify the noun it modifies. If the phrase is removed from its sentence, the noun it modifies becomes indefinite and the remaining sentence not fully meaningful. Here are examples of essential present-participial phrases, with the phrase italicized and its verb and the noun the phrase modifies in boldface:

The **car** *carrying the criminals* was driven by a deputy sheriff.
The **confusion** *surrounding the issues* caused a light voter turnout.

The present-participial phrases are needed to tell which car and which confusion are under discussion. That is, unless the car is identified in a previous sentence, the sentence

The car was driven by a deputy sheriff

is not fully meaningful because the car is unidentified. Such an essential present-participial phrase always follows the noun it modifies. It is so much a part of the independent clause that it is not really the same kind of sentence expansion that we are studying in this part of the text.

EXERCISE 17A
Composing Sentences with Present-Participial Phrases

Directions: Combine each of the following pairs of sentences into one well-formed sentence with a present-participial phrase.

1. The judge threw the case out on a technicality. He thus freed Crossman for the third time.

2. The school board met secretly. It decided that some way must be found to fire the principal.

3. The Buena Vista School District employs two clinical psychologists. It thereby makes mental health services available to all its children.

4. We are letting 98 percent of mentally disturbed children slip through our fingers. We thereby condemn them to lives of futility and anguish.

5. Our mental health centers cooperate with the schools and courts. They offer a variety of services to children.

6. Three months later Billy was in a Brooklyn police station. He was confessing to a horrendous catalogue of sex crimes.

_____

_____

_____

7. A juvenile judge deals day in and day out with delinquents. He has an excellent opportunity to spot mentally disturbed youngsters.

_____

_____

_____

8. Woodstein was sure that more scandal was to be uncovered. He renewed his efforts to get information from his contacts.

_____

_____

_____

9. Morton refused to answer the question. He was not sure that his own safety was not in danger.

_____

_____

_____

10. Gerstein had not heard the latest news of the scandal. He continued to talk candidly to Woodstein.

_____

_____

_____

EXERCISE 17B
Composing Sentences with Present-Participial Phrases

Directions: In the first five of the following items combine each of the three sets of simple sentences into one well-formed sentence with a present-participial phrase and either an absolute phrase, an infinitive phrase, an adjective phrase, or an appositive. In the last five items, expand the simple sentence either by adding a present-participial phrase of your own creation or by converting the simple sentence into a present-participial phrase and adding an independent clause of your own.

1. Mr. Butts's complete stock of shoes had been sold. He closed up his shoe store for the rest of the week. He hoped to take a vacation.

_____

_____

_____

_____

2. Mrs. Neerbroak wanted to make ends meet. She did not have a working husband. She earned money as a seamstress.

_____

_____

_____

_____

3. Miss Bilt was pleased with her success at courtship. She felt the need to celebrate. She bought a whole case of champagne.

_____

_____

_____

_____

4. Fannie Foxx was a nightclub stripper. She jumped from the moving car. She feared that she might be arrested.

_____

_____

_____

5. Mr. Shrooddeeler knew that the stock market was about to collapse. He was a heavy investor in Orient Petroleum. He quietly sold all his stock.

_____

_____

_____

6. Mr. Lastflinger withdrew all his savings.

_____

_____

7. For nearly a century *Huckleberry Finn* has been a popular novel.

_____

_____

8. Physics is a difficult subject.

_____

_____

9. The East Dorm is nearly empty.

_____

_____

10. Fraternities are making a comeback.

_____

_____

18

Sentence Expansion: Past-Participial Phrases

PAST-PARTICIPIAL PHRASES

The past participles of regular verbs in English end in *ed,* such as *talked, climbed, burned,* and so on. The past-tense form of such verbs is the same, but that fact poses no problem for us. The past participles of irregular verbs take various forms, sometimes the same as the past-tense form and sometimes not. They are forms that go with the auxiliary *has* (and some others), such as (*has*) *broken,* (*has*) *sung,* (*has*) *brought,* and so on. Phrases that have only a past participle with no auxiliaries are **past-participial phrases.** They almost always modify nouns[1] and thus function as adjectivals. Here are some examples, with the past participles in boldface:

> not **understood** by most of his audience
> **published** in an expensive edition
> **sung** by a choir of 1,200
> **brought** from Texas by his uncle

Such past-participial phrases contain full ideas and may be used as sentence expansions.

Here are some examples of two simple sentences being transformed into one sentence with a past-participial phrase. The phrase is in italics, and the past participle and the noun it modifies are in boldface.

1. The rare orchid was carefully nurtured by its owner. It bloomed profusely.
   *Carefully **nurtured** by its owner,* the rare **orchid** bloomed profusely.
2. A condensation of Herter's book was published in the *Reader's Digest.* It emphasized the increase of crime in our cities.
   A **condensation** of Herter's book, *published in the Reader's Digest,* emphasized the increase of crime in our cities.

---

[1] Of course, these phrases, when the verb is the same as the past-tense form, can function as sentence predicates, and any verb phrase can function as a predicate if its verb form is made finite. But we are not concerned now with that aspect of grammar.

3. Throckmorton's personal card was printed in gold ink. It became a collector's item.

Throckmorton's personal **card, *printed in gold ink,*** became a collector's item.

4. The on-duty police were angered by the shouted obscenities. They began to use their clubs.

Angered by the shouted obscenities, the on-duty **police** began to use their clubs.

Such past-participial phrases function just like the adjective phrases discussed in Chapter 15. They permit full ideas to be expressed briefly and in a more pleasing style than that of a sequence of simple sentences.

Past-participial phrases are sometimes introduced by the connectives *though,* expressing contrast; *if* and *until,* expressing condition; and *when,* expressing a time relationship. Examples:

Though **printed** *clearly,* the **book** was hard to read because of its small type.

If **cooked** *thoroughly,* **pork** cannot cause trichinosis in one who eats it.

When **played** *by two pianists,* this **piece** by Mozart is especially beautiful.

The past-participial phrases are italicized, and the past participles and the nouns they modify are in boldface.

PUNCTUATING PAST-PARTICIPIAL PHRASES

All of the past-participial phrases in the preceding section are **nonessential;** they just give additional information about nouns already fully identified. Therefore they are set off by commas. Such a phrase is **essential** when it is needed to identify the noun it modifies. That is, if the phrase is removed from the sentence, the noun becomes indefinite and the sentence not fully meaningful. Here are examples of essential past-participial phrases, with the phrase italicized and the past participle and the noun it modifies in boldface:

The **gift** *promised to me by my father* was a Jaguar sports car.

The **phrase** *printed in italics* was not in the original edition.

The **food** *brought to the picnic by the Berrys* was spoiled.

The phrases are needed to identify which gift, phrase, and food are under discussion. They are, therefore, essential and not set off by commas.

DANGLING MODIFIERS

Nonessential verb and adjective phrases are particularly subject to an error in sentence structure known as the **dangling modifier.** A modifier is said to dangle when it seems to modify the wrong noun or no noun at all. Here is an amusing example of a dangler:

Having numerous dangerous curves, Jane drove very carefully over the mountain road.

The participial phrase is supposed to modify *the mountain road,* but since it appears to modify *Jane,* it dangles. The sentence can be recast to eliminate the dangler:

Jane drove very carefully over the mountain road, because it had numerous dangerous curves.

Now the dangler is eliminated.

Though most danglers are participial phrases, adjective phrases can also dangle. Examples:

When dejected, the dial-a-prayer service may help.
Happy to have been invited, the party seemed a great deal of fun.

In the first example, the dial-a-prayer service seems to be dejected, and in the second the party seems to be happy. The sentences can easily be rewritten to eliminate the danglers:

When dejected, you may receive comfort from the dial-a-prayer service.
Happy to have been invited, John was having a great deal of fun at the party.

Of course, the incorrect sentences could be corrected in other ways.

To help you get a better understanding of the nature of danglers, here are some other examples, with revisions. The danglers are italicized.

dangler: The Sherman Country Inn was nowhere in sight, *having apparently taken the wrong road some miles back.*
correct: Since I apparently took the wrong road some miles back, the Sherman Country Inn was nowhere in sight.
dangler: Not understanding the text or the lectures well, my exam received a poor grade.
correct: Not understanding the text or the lectures well, I made a poor grade on my exam.
dangler: Though well potted, I cannot get my African violets to bloom.
correct: Though my African violets are well potted, I cannot get them to bloom.
dangler: The offer was turned down, *not being one to speculate recklessly.*
correct: Not being one to speculate recklessly, I turned the offer down.
dangler: Though friendly, quarrels aplenty arose to reduce the goodwill he had enjoyed.
correct: Though friendly, he engaged in so many quarrels that the goodwill he had enjoyed was reduced.

The better you understand sentence structure, the less likely you are to write dangling modifiers.

EXERCISE 18A
Punctuating Verb Phrases

Directions: The following sentences have some nonessential and some essential verb phrases. Set off with commas those that are nonessential. Underline each verb-phrase expansion.

1. John's message written on the back of an envelope was in code.

2. A sweater worn by Barbara Eden was auctioned off for $200.

3. In his passing, Churchill may have served his nation as he did in life toughening its fiber and raising its spirits.

4. Usually sponsored by churches on a nonprofit basis these inner-city housing developments are given low-cost financing.

5. The contender in the fight to gain time because of his many hurts ran from the champion as much as he could.

6. A man committed to a cause is a happy man.

7. The notes containing the heart of Maxwell's speech were lost.

8. I could see the brief notes from which he spoke consisting only of lead sentences and transitions.

9. The official center of the Cannes Festival abundantly equipped with projection rooms is a nondescript modern building.

10. Patton was a first-class field general towering over all others on the western front.

11. The Mayor of Cleveland to increase the use of public transportation suggested reduced fares with city subsidies.

12. We saw a play written by one of my students.

13. Mr. Shepard stopped by all his worker's desks helping them to understand the company's newest policy statements.

14. Art films often precariously financed have to earn their money back as fast as possible.

15. The man feeding the pigeons sat very still not wanting to alarm the birds.

16. Professor Lerned concerned about the high dropout rate in his classes decided to make his tests easier.

17. The score at half time being 36 to 0 our team seemed to have no chance of winning.

161

18. Our quarterback having been thoroughly briefed during half time was able to confuse our opponent's defense so that we won 37 to 36.

19. The cheetah almost hunted to extinction makes a very docile pet.

20. The cheetah photographed by my uncle was a full-grown but young male.

21. My driver's license having expired I drove very carefully to the Department of Motor Vehicles.

22. A man being only human often gives in to temptation.

23. A man newly converted to a religion often makes an offensive display of his new piety.

24. There lay my toast burned to a crisp.

25. Maria not having understood the directions made a very low score on her final exam in chemistry.

EXERCISE 18B
Composing Sentences with Past-Participial Phrases

Directions: Combine each of the following pairs of simple sentences into one well-formed sentence with a past-participial phrase.

1. Mr. Garner was given a false diagnosis by his family physician. He decided to consult a specialist.

_____

_____

_____

2. The ploy was favored by a majority of the committee members. The ploy was to agree to a settlement on impossible terms.

_____

_____

_____

3. Willie Sutton was already convicted on a robbery charge. He now faced a charge of manslaughter.

_____

_____

_____

4. Desert dwellers are denied a full measure of reality. They get even by talking about the horrors of life in New York.

_____

_____

_____

5. The execution of Absabid was a last-ditch measure. It was intended to frighten the guerrillas.

_____

_____

_____

6. The sheriff was disturbed by the distant gunfire. He sent a deputy to investigate.

_____

_____

7. This book is printed on the finest paper and bound in the finest leather. It is one of only one hundred copies of a special edition of *Science and Health with Keys to the Scriptures*.

_____

_____

_____

8. The star Cygnus Y is located in the constellation Sagittarius. It is thought to be accompanied by a black hole.

_____

_____

_____

9. Knoxite is known to be a deadly poison. It must be handled with extreme care.

_____

_____

10. Jim Null was fired for incompetency. He decided to appeal to his union leaders for help.

_____

_____

_____

EXERCISE 18C

Composing Sentences with Past-Participial Phrases

Directions: Combine the three simple sentences in each of four of the first five of the following items into one well-formed sentence with a past-participial phrase and one of the five kinds of sentence expansions discussed in Chapters 14 through 17. In one of the five, have two independent clauses and a past-participial phrase. In the last five items either add a past-participial phrase of your own or change the simple sentence into a past-participial phrase and add an independent clause of your own.

1. Anthony was judged to be sane. He was eventually returned to his mother. This started again a vicious circle of mental derangement.

_____

_____

_____

_____

2. The players were accused of not trying their best. They sat silent in their seats. They were obviously unhappy and angry.

_____

_____

_____

3. Judge Sirroco was often called Maximum John. He seemed more restrained than usual. He was apparently not sure of the action he should take.

_____

_____

_____

_____

4. Julius had been informed about threats against his father. His father was a patrolman in a rough neighborhood. Julius decided to try to get his father a transfer.

_____

_____

_____

5. The students were constantly amazed at Professor Smartfeller's learning. They dared not cut his class. They knew that every class period was important.

_____

_____

_____

6. The school board was forced to raise its teachers' salaries.

_____

_____

7. Judge Roy Bean found the defendant innocent.

_____

_____

8. The newspaper strike came to an end.

_____

_____

9. Al Hodad's hostages were allowed to exercise.

_____

_____

10. Professor Smallie was applauded by his students.

_____

_____

EXERCISE 18D
Revising Dangling Modifiers

Directions: Each of the following sentences has a dangling modifier. Revise each. sentence to eliminate the dangler. A sample sentence illustrates the procedure.

By not playing his best, the golf tournament was lost.
By not playing his best, Nick Lowse lost the golf tournament.

1. By applying a tourniquet, the blood stopped flowing.

_____

_____

_____

2. Most miscarriages take place when three months pregnant.

_____

_____

_____

3. While answering the first fire alarm, arsonists set another house afire.

_____

_____

_____

4. Being shy by nature, dates often were uncomfortable affairs.

_____

_____

_____

5. Coming just after a severe illness, I was unable to take advantage of the good opportunity.

_____

_____

_____

6. Although authorized by the chief of police, the demonstrators tried to give the impression that the authorities were against them.

_____

_____

_____

7. Besides being quite educational, children also enjoy "The Saturday Morning Doodlers."

_____

_____

_____

8. The reefers are usually put out when satisfied.

_____

_____

_____

9. By conducting open meetings, the citizens can better judge the effectiveness of the County Supervisors.

_____

_____

_____

10. The party was especially exciting, not having been to an acid bash before.

_____

_____

_____

19

Sentence Expansion: Complex Prepositional Phrases

A simple prepositional phrase is one that begins with a preposition and has a simple object (usually a noun) with perhaps one or more modifiers of the object. An example is *in the bright sunshine,* which could come at the beginning, within, or at the end of a sentence and could modify a noun or a verb. Simple prepositional phrases, which usually are adjectivals or adverbials, occur with great frequency in our language.

A **complex prepositional phrase** is one that begins with a preposition but becomes complex in structure because its object is a word group rather than a noun or because its object is extensively modified, perhaps by a word group such as a dependent clause or verb phrase. Here are some examples, with the prepositions, some of them compound, in boldface:

> **because of** his growing concern for his father's health
> **contrary to** the best estimates of the experts
> **without** looking back toward the accident
> **with** no intention of giving up his hard-earned money
> **aside from** wasting money that is needed for food

You need not be concerned with analyzing the grammatical structure of such complex phrases, but you should understand their unity and see that they can function as sentence expansions, expressing full ideas. When such prepositional phrases function as sentence expansions (of the sort we are studying in this part), they usually are sentence modifiers and not adjectivals or adverbials.

Here are examples of two simple sentences being transformed into one sentence with a prepositional-phrase expansion. The phrase is italicized and its preposition is in boldface.

1. Maureen did not have a dollar left in her bank account. She was desperate for a job.
   Without *a dollar left in her bank account,* Maureen was desperate for a job.
2. I could have been badly beaten by the thugs trying to rob me. A passerby courageously intervened.

But for the courageous intervention of a passerby, I would have been badly beaten by the thugs trying to rob me.

3. The base could be closed immediately. Headquarters planned instead to phase it out slowly.

Rather than close the base immediately, headquarters planned instead to phase it out slowly.

4. Brom Bones was in a state of shock because of his accident. He was unable to explain what had happened.

Brom Bones, *in a state of shock because of his accident,* was unable to explain what had happened.

5. Science has come a step closer to understanding plant chemistry. This step is due to the achievement of the first artificial synthesis of cell wall material.

With the achievement of the first artificial synthesis of cell wall material, science has come a step closer to understanding plant chemistry.

6. Judge Renchy would not reduce Major Hoople's sentence. Major Hoople received favorable testimony from many character witnesses.

Judge Renchy would not reduce Major Hoople's sentence, *despite the favorable testimony of many character witnesses.*

Like other sentence expansions, complex prepositional phrases allow writers to avoid sequences of simple sentences that might sound childish.

Also the preposition in such complex phrases as those illustrated often makes clearer the relationship between two full ideas. For example, the preposition in the first example above makes clear the cause-and-result relationship between the idea in the phrase and the one in the independent clause. With the simple sentences, a connective such as *therefore* would be needed. Various other relationships are also made clear by various prepositions.

Such complex prepositional phrases usually come first in a sentence, but, as examples 4 and 6 show, they can come within or at the end of a sentence. They are always set off by commas.

Sometimes a simple prepositional phrase may function as a sentence expansion of the sort we are studying in this part. Examples, with the prepositional phrases italicized and the preposition in boldface:

There was a downpour. The game continued.
Despite the downpour, the game continued.

There was a strike. Christmas was bleak for the miners.
Because of the strike, Christmas was bleak for the miners.

When such a simple prepositional phrase can be a sentence expansion, the idea contained in the phrase can be expressed in a very simple sentence, as illustrated. Note how the prepositions *despite* and *because of* express the relationships of contrast and of cause and result.

Many prepositional phrases serve not as sentence expansions nor as simple modifiers within a sentence but as transitional phrases between sentences. Their function is very similar to that of the coordinating connectives discussed in Chapter 6. The phrases provide smooth movement from one sentence to another. Here are some examples:

as a matter of fact	with this in mind
for example	contrary to that
on the other hand	in contrast
in addition	by extension
in fact	for the most part

Such transitional prepositional phrases do not contain full ideas that could be expressed in simple sentences, and thus they are not sentence expansions. However, they are very important in the same way that coordinating and subordinating connectives are.

EXERCISE 19A
Composing Sentences
with Complex Prepositional Phrases

Directions: Combine each of the following pairs of sentences into one sentence with a prepositional phrase set off by a comma or commas. To help you get started, we will tell you that a good preposition to start the first sentence with is the compound preposition *in addition to.*

1. Marilyn was caused pain by her injury. She had to worry about how to pay her medical bills.

   _____

   _____

   _____

2. Gary had revenge on his mind. He began buying components for making homemade bombs.

   _____

   _____

   _____

3. The administration revised the dormitory rules for coeds. The administration showed itself to be enlightened and not tradition-bound.

   _____

   _____

   _____

   _____

4. Ruby's behavior toward the uninvited guests was uncivil. In contrast, Gloria treated them courteously and prevented possible quarrels.

   _____

   _____

   _____

   _____

5. There was a three-hour delay. Then the troop train started out once again.

_____

_____

6. Miss Broadstreet gave a sigh of relief. She reported the happy news to her boyfriend.

_____

_____

_____

7. We went by Greyhound bus. We did this for the purpose of economy.

_____

_____

8. There was a high demand for money. Therefore the Federal Reserve Board raised the discount rate.

_____

_____

_____

9. I spent a day in the woods. I felt in better spirits.

_____

_____

10. There was a power failure. We had to use candles.

_____

_____

EXERCISE 19B
Composing Sentences
with Complex Prepositional Phrases

Directions: In the first five items below convert the simple sentences in each into one sentence with one independent clause, one prepositional-phrase expansion, and any one of the other sentence expansions we have studied so far. In the second five items, complete a prepositional-phrase expansion of your own, and compose an independent clause that will complete a meaningful sentence.

1. Mr. Lookman felt a great sense of relief.
   He was the owner of the liquor store.
   He watched the shady-looking characters leave.

   _____

   _____

   _____

2. I am not being regarded as just another nonintellectual woman.
   I am regarded as a professional.
   That is a reputation that I enjoy.

   _____

   _____

   _____

   _____

3. Changes in courses and textbooks might be anticipated.
   Courses and textbooks are always sensitive to social change.
   Courses and textbooks reflect the increased number of women in law school.

   _____

   _____

   _____

   _____

   _____

4. Since the turn of the century, changes have occurred in the operation of prisons.
A new code of social philosophy has slowly eroded punitive attitudes towards wrongdoing.
This new code has brought more rehabilitation of prisoners.

_____

_____

_____

_____

_____

5. I had no one to turn to for help.
I started my own program of rehabilitation.
I was determined to become respectable again.

_____

_____

_____

6. In spite of _____

_____

7. Because of _____

_____

8. For lack of _____

_____

9. Aside from _____

_____

10. Except for _____

_____

20
Sentence Expansion: Adjective Clauses

ADJECTIVE CLAUSES

An **adjective clause** is one of the three kinds of dependent clauses discussed in Chapter 9. Being a clause, it has a subject and predicate and thus contains a full idea. Since it is dependent, it cannot stand alone as a sentence and is therefore a sentence expansion (because, unlike a noun clause, it cannot be a subject or object but must be a modifier). Adjective clauses are introduced by **relative pronouns** (*who, whom, whose, which, that, who(m)ever,* and *whichever*), which are **subordinating connectives,** as explained in Chapter 7.

An adjective clause usually modifies a noun, noun phrase, or pronoun and thus is an adjectival by function. It is also similar to the appositive phrase, discussed in Chapter 14, in that it identifies, defines, or in some way describes the noun it modifies. In fact, sometimes an adjective clause can be changed to an appositive. Example, with the clause and the appositive in boldface:

> *adjective clause:* Joseph Barnes, **who is a Southerner,** is thought by strangers to speak like an Englishman.
> *appositive:* Joseph Barnes, **a Southerner,** is thought by strangers to speak like an Englishman.

In such cases, the appositive is preferable because of its economy of expression. But most adjective clauses cannot be changed to appositives. They are sentence expansions in their own right, allowing a writer to avoid too many simple sentences in a sequence and thus to achieve a more pleasing and mature style.

Here is a sentence containing an adjective clause, with the clause italicized and its relative pronoun and the noun the clause modifies in boldface:

> The greatest growth in college enrollment in the 60s was in the **two-year community college,** *which is usually controlled by a local school board.*

A relative pronoun functions as a subject, object, or, in the case of *whose,* a determiner in its own clause. In the example above, the *which* is the subject of the clause. If the noun, noun phrase, or pronoun that the adjective clause modifies replaces the relative pronoun of the clause, an independent clause will result. For example, in the above example such replacement converts the adjective clause into this sentence:

The two-year community college is usually controlled by a local school board.

Thus the adjective clauses does not contain unexpressed[1] meaning that is drawn from another part of the sentence, as verb phrases and some other expansions do. For example, in

The two-year community college, *usually controlled by a school board,* is . . . ,

the italicized verb phrase draws unexpressed meaning—that is, unexpressed in the verb phrase—from the boldface noun phrase that it modifies. But a pronoun is expressed in an adjective clause, though it gets its meaning from its antecedent. Also no such relationship as cause and result, contrast, condition, and so on is expressed between the idea in the adjective clause and another idea in the sentence. Instead, the clause usually just makes a comment about a noun.

Here are some examples of two simple sentences being transformed into one sentence with an adjective-clause expansion. The clause is italicized and its relative pronoun and the noun the clause modifies are in boldface.

1. Hauptman masterminded the whole illegal intelligence-gathering operation. He received the heaviest sentence of all the convicted conspirators.
   Hauptman, *who masterminded the whole illegal intelligence-gathering operation,* received the heaviest sentence of all the convicted conspirators.
2. The last remaining covered bridge in the area was destroyed by arsonists. The local Historical Society had wanted to preserve it.
   The last remaining **covered bridge** in the area, *which the local Historical Society had wanted to preserve,* was destroyed by arsonists.
3. Our most distinguished professor has been invited to the University of Cambridge to give a series of lectures. The Nobel Committee once nominated him for the prize in physics.
   Our most distinguished **professor,** *whom the Nobel Committee once nominated for the prize in physics,* has been invited to the University of Cambridge to give a series of lectures.
4. The Lamont Mutual Fund has become bankrupt. Hundreds of our citizens had invested in it.
   The **Lamont Mutual Fund,** *which hundreds of our citizens invested in,* has become bankrupt.
5. Urban renewal has brought into public view multitudes of people. They are in themselves walking slums.
   Urban renewal has brought into public view multitudes of **people** *who are in themselves walking slums.*

[1] However, when the relative pronoun in an adjective clause functions as an object in the clause, it may often be omitted and just understood. For example, in

The candidate *I vote for* always loses,

the italicized adjective clause has the relative pronoun *whom* or *that,* which is the object of *vote for,* understood. *Candidate* is the antecedent of the understood relative pronoun. Such omissions are very common but are not of especial interest to us in studying composition, because the construction is one you unconsciously understand and use well enough.

6. We stumbled on a cache of rare coins. They had been stolen.
   We stumbled on a cache of rare **coins** *that had been stolen.*
7. We were searching for an eagle. We wanted its lifetime mate to have been killed.
   We were searching for an **eagle** *whose lifetime mate had been killed.*

The greater syntactical maturity of the sentences with the adjective clauses should be clear to you.

In an adjective clause the relative pronoun can sometimes be preceded by a preposition, which is a part of the adjective clause. Examples, with the clause italicized and the preposition in boldface:

I'm in a jam **for** *which I have only myself to blame.*
There's the crooked solicitor **to** *whom I gave a charitable donation.*

In such sentences the preposition can also come last in the adjective clause. Examples:

I'm in a jam *which I have only myself to blame* **for.**
There's the fellow (*whom*) *I sold a gold brick* **to.**

The adjective clauses are italicized and the prepositions in boldface. *It is not wrong to end such a sentence with a preposition,* and in fact sometimes a sentence sounds more natural and less stilted with the preposition at the end. In either case, the relative pronoun is the object of the preposition. The relative pronoun in such a sentence can often be omitted, as the parentheses show in the last example.

SENTENCE-MODIFIER ADJECTIVE CLAUSES

One kind of dependent clause that is for convenience called an adjective clause is really a sentence modifier, since it modifies a whole idea expressed in an independent clause or word group. This type of clause is always introduced by the broad-reference pronoun (see Chapter 10) *which.* Here are three examples of two simple sentences being transformed into one sentence with an adjective clause modifying the whole idea of each sentence's independent clause. The adjective clauses are in boldface.

New Mexicans are proud of their Spanish heritage. This seems only natural.
New Mexicans are proud of their Spanish heritage, **which seems only natural.**
The Confederate troops planned to attack after dark. This seemed to be the best strategy.
The Confederate troops planned to attack after dark, **which seemed to be the best strategy.**
The soldiers' rations were cut in half. This infuriated them.
The soldiers' rations were cut in half, **which infuriated them.**

Adjective clauses that function as sentence modifiers, as in the preceding three examples, are always nonessential and thus set off by commas.

PUNCTUATING ADJECTIVE CLAUSES

Like appositives and verb and adjective phrases, adjective clauses are either **essential** or **nonessential.** When the clause is nonessential, it modifies an already-fully-identified noun and just gives additional information about it. Therefore the clause is set off by a comma or commas. For example, in

> Our governor, **who took bribes from horse-racing organizations,** was indicted and convicted,

the noun *governor,* which the adjective clause modifies, is fully identified by *our,* and thus the clause, being nonessential, is set off by commas. The term *non-essential* is a grammatical one and has nothing to do with whether the writer considers his information necessary or not.

When an adjective clause is needed to identify the noun it modifies, it is grammatically essential and thus is not set off by commas. If the clause is removed from the sentence, the noun it modifies (unless it has been fully identified in a previous sentence) becomes indefinite and the sentence not fully meaningful. For example, in

> Students *who form good study habits and set regular study hours* make much better grades than disorganized students,

the adjective clause is needed to identify which students are meant. Removal of the clause leaves *students make much better grades than disorganized students,* which is nonsense. The adjective clause is essential and thus not set off by commas.

For further understanding of punctuation of adjective clauses, reinspect the examples above in which two sentences are combined to form one. The adjective clauses in the first four examples are nonessential, for the nouns or noun phrases *Hauptman, last . . . bridge, our . . . professor,* and *Lamont Mutual Fund* are fully identified without the clauses, which therefore must be set off by commas. The adjective clauses in the last three examples are essential, for they are needed to identify the nouns *people, coins,* and *eagle.* Thus the clauses must not be set off by commas.

One good tip to remember is that an adjective clause introduced by *that* is always essential and thus not set off by commas. Since *that* can refer to things or people, you can test an adjective clause that is introduced by *who, whom,* or *which.* Examples:

> We wanted to find a garage *which had a fuel-injection mechanic.*

Since *that* will sound natural in place of *which,* the italicized adjective clause is essential.

> We continued to converse with Professor Sherman, *who is very amusing.*

Because

> We continued to converse with Professor Sherman, *that is very amusing*

is wholly unnatural, the clause in the original sentence is nonessential and must be set off by a comma. For practice, try this test on other example sentences in this chapter.

EXERCISE 20A
Punctuating Adjective Clauses

Directions: Each of the following sentences contains an adjective clause without punctuation. Enter a comma or commas to set off nonessential clauses; of course, you should not set off essential clauses. Underline the adjective clause once and the noun, noun phrase, or pronoun that it modifies twice. You should have no trouble identifying each adjective clause, for it will be introduced by a relative pronoun (though the relative pronoun can be preceded by a preposition that is a part of the clause) and will have a subject and predicate. An example sentence illustrates the procedure.

Albuquerque, which could have been a beautiful city, has submitted to wholesale vulgarization.

1. The Cochiti Corn Dance which I had witnessed twelve years ago had not changed significantly.

2. To me, the symbol of the Indians was a young Navaho who worked as a groundsman at the university.

3. New Mexico is unlike California whose history has largely been erased by developers.

4. In town there is one art movie which wobbles uncertainly between the real thing and nudie trash.

5. We visited the caves of the Manzano Range in whose deep recesses nuclear weapons are stored.

6. I inspected a jagged chunk of the plane's propeller which my host had laboriously carried down from the mountainside.

7. The Cannes festivals have given art movies opportunities that they otherwise would not have had.

8. Joseph Strick who made the American film *The Balcony* recently praised the Cannes festivals.

9. There is no doubt that commercial producers whose films represent a large investment look on the festivals with mistrust.

10. In 1949 Mme. Georges Bidault whose husband is now a fugitive from French justice was a member of the jury.

11. The Joint Commission on Mental Health and Illness whose studies laid the groundwork for that legislation lacked the funds even to study the problem of emotionally disturbed children.

12. Judge Benchley who knew nothing of Anthony's past psychiatric record released him on $500 bond.

13. Here are the salient facts which I think are worth restating and pondering.

14. His physical ills put him under the wing of Dr. Otto who observed and treated his emotional ills also.

15. Why should teaching be the only important function in our society that is not subject either to criticism or to the appraisal of the market?

16. The Grand Coulee Dam which is located in eastern Washington delivers power to three states.

17. I own a grammar book in which the author actually says that we should say "somebody's else pencil."

18. The movie *Gone with the Wind* which won ten Oscars has been released six times.

19. Television which has been trying to get *Gone with the Wind* feels that it should have a legal right to any movie over ten years old.

20. The beauty contest entrant who seemed most poised was Miss Red China.

21. The giant sequoia tree which is the largest living thing grows only in the Sierra Nevada mountain range.

22. The sequoia tree that I like best is called the General Sherman tree.

23. My Datsun averaged 29 miles per gallon on one trip which is good mileage for any car.

24. My cat Blue which is half Siamese is blue in color and probably could originate a new breed.

25. I read *The Return of the Native* in one sitting which is a record for me.

EXERCISE 20B
Composing Sentences with Adjective Clauses

Directions: Combine each of the following pairs of sentences into one sentence with an adjective clause. In your sentence underline the adjective clause once, and underline twice the noun, noun phrase, or pronoun the clause modifies. Be sure to punctuate properly by distinguishing between essential and nonessential clauses. An example sentence illustrates the procedure.

> Psychic phenomena are human experiences. These experiences seem contrary to the known laws of science.
> Psychic phenomena are human experiences which seem contrary to the known laws of science.

1. The Jews received their family names from Gentile authorities. These authorities wished to keep the census and police register accurate.

   _____

   _____

2. The student's parents are angry about the extent of inept teaching. The parents are taxpayers and targets of fund-raising campaigns.

   _____

   _____

3. Part of the blame lies with the faculty. The faculty no longer has much contact with students outside the classroom.

   _____

   _____

4. Many professors argue that most students would vote for the merely entertaining lecturer. I have discussed teacher-rating with these professors.

   _____

   _____

5. The students have at hand some powerful tools. They have just begun to use these tools.

   _____

   _____

6. Some college students want to enroll only in certain courses. These courses are those that are relevant to the world they live in.

_____

_____

_____

7. Other college students enjoy such academic courses as Ancient Greek and Pre-Columbian Art. These courses seem far removed from our day-to-day living.

_____

_____

_____

8. Professor Gordon was selected by the president as his special assistant. He has a sympathetic understanding of the students' problems.

_____

_____

_____

9. The police were called in only when fighting broke out. They were instructed to treat the students gently.

_____

_____

_____

10. One policeman apparently had an uncontrollable temper. He suddenly began wielding his billy club savagely.

_____

_____

_____

EXERCISE 20C
Composing Sentences with Adjective Clauses

Directions: In each of the first five items below combine the three sentences into one sentence with one independent clause, one adjective clause, and one of any of the other sentence expansions you have studied. In the second five items add an adjective clause of your own to compose a meaningful complex sentence.

1. Jack Casey had no thought that he could be defeated.
   He had campaigned vigorously in earlier campaigns.
   He virtually ignored the voters in his last campaign.

   _____

   _____

   _____

   _____

2. Angus McDonald was a Scotsman.
   He saved every penny he could.
   This practice eventually made him rich.

   _____

   _____

   _____

   _____

3. One policeman apparently had an uncontrollable temper.
   He suddenly began wielding his billy club savagely.
   He seemingly did not care that his victims were mostly innocent.

   _____

   _____

   _____

   _____

185

4. Milos Valvich enjoys a literary reputation outside Russia.
   He was educated at Genstad University.
   Genstad University is a favorite gathering place for aspiring writers.

   _____

   _____

   _____

   _____

5. The rebellious students have some powerful tools at hand.
   The rebellious students are much concerned about social injustices.
   The rebellious students have just begun to use the tools they have at hand.

   _____

   _____

   _____

   _____

6. Mr. Buffle picked up a hitchhiker.

   _____

   _____

7. Orchid corsages are popular with young girls.

   _____

   _____

8. Miss Othmar took a trip to Diamond Head.

   _____

   _____

9. The Puritans settled in Massachusetts.

   _____

   _____

10. Cosmology is Professor Witter's specialty.

    _____

    _____

21

Sentence Expansion: Adverb Clauses

ADVERB CLAUSES

Like the adjective clause, the **adverb clause** is one of the three kinds of dependent clauses discussed in Chapter 9. Because it has a subject and predicate, it must contain a whole idea; and because it always functions as a modifier (not as a subject or object, as a noun clause most often does), it is a sentence expansion. The adjective clause is introduced by a relative pronoun and, usually, defines, identifies, or in some way describes a noun. An adverb clause is introduced by a **subordinating conjunction,** which prevents it from standing alone as a sentence. The subordinating conjunction expresses a relationship between the idea in the adverb clause and the idea in an independent clause or some other word group outside the adverb clause.

Here is an example, with the adverb clause italicized and the subordinating conjunction in boldface:

The defendant pleaded guilty, **because** *the evidence against him was overwhelming.*

The subordinating conjunction *because* expresses a relationship of cause and result between the idea in the adverb clause (the cause) and the idea in the independent clause (the result). In Chapter 7 under the heading **Subordinating Conjunctions,** there is a list of the subordinating conjunctions and a division of them into the six broad kinds of relationship that they express beween ideas. You should briefly review those pages; here we will just illustrate the use of adverb clauses as sentence expansions.

Adverb clauses almost always function as sentence modifiers, for they express a relationship between two whole ideas rather than between the idea in the adverb clause and a single verb. That is, adverb clauses do not usually modify single verbs, as adjective clauses modify single nouns. Here are six examples of two simple sentences being transformed into one sentence with an adverb clause. The adverb clause is italicized, and its subordinating conjunction is in boldface.

See if you can tell the exact relationship expressed between the adverb clause and the independent clause in the single sentences.

1. We now controlled the conservative vote. We were confident that our candidate would win.
   Now that we controlled the conservative vote, we were confident that our candidate would win.
2. Mrs. Gurley argued vehemently against federally sponsored slum clearance. The Senators were unimpressed.
   Though Mrs. Gurley argued vehemently against federally sponsored slum clearance, the Senators were unimpressed.
3. We can save many of these disturbed children. We must identify their problems early enough.
   We can save many of these disturbed children *provided we identify their problems early enough.*
4. We studied for the final exams. We thought our careers depended on them.
   We studied for the final exams *as though our careers depended on them.*
5. Our relatives arrived on Sunday. We were not ready for them.
   Our relatives arrived on Sunday, *before we were ready for them.*
6. I established a tax-deferred annuity. I wanted my retirement to be financially secure.
   I established a tax-deferred annuity *so that my retirement would be financially secure.*

Now, for practice, refer to the list in Chapter 7 under the heading **Subordinating Conjunctions,** and see how many other subordinating conjunctions will fit with reasonable meaningfulness the slots occupied by *now that, though, provided, as though, before* (allowing for different times), and *so that* in the sentences above. You may reverse or alter the clauses so long as you do not change the meaning.

PUNCTUATING ADVERB CLAUSES

It is impossible to codify exact rules for the punctuation of adverb clauses. Unlike adjective clauses, they do not fall neatly into essential and nonessential categories. One general rule is that an introductory adverb clause is usually set off by a comma, unless it is very short. Example:

Because the diplomatic issue was so sticky, the Ambassador was for once in his life indecisive.

Such use of a comma usually clarifies sentence structure.

An internal adverb clause is also usually set off on both sides by commas. Example:

The General, **after he had briefed his subordinates,** circulated among the troops themselves.

If you hear distinct voice pauses before and after internal adverb clauses, you should set them off by commas.

For adverb clauses coming at the end of a sentence you must just depend on your ear for punctuation. If you detect no voice pause, you should not use a comma. Example:

The Ambassador refused to act **until he received instructions from Washington.**

But if your ear detects a voice pause, then use a comma to set off the adverb clause. Example:

The Ambassador finally released the data, **although he did so with much reluctance.**

In no other aspect of punctuation is the writer so much on his own as in the punctuation of adverbial clauses. Few clear-cut rules exist. The best advice is to use commas when distinct voice pauses accompany adverb clauses.

EXERCISE 21A
Identifying and Punctuating Adverb Clauses

Directions: Each of the following sentences contains an unpunctuated adverbial clause. In each sentence underscore the entire adverbial clause, encircle the subordinating conjunction, and enter a comma or commas only if clarity will be improved. Be prepared to explain the relationship expressed by the subordinating conjunction. A sample sentence illustrates the procedure.

(Now that) the foreign troops have been removed, Santo Domingo is gradually returning to normal. (relationship of cause and result)

1. Although the waves were over 30 feet high the little ship weathered the storm.

_____

_____

2. I lost rapidly whereas I had expected my roulette system to work perfectly.

_____

_____

3. When the car's radiator began to boil over we pulled into a turnout and stopped.

_____

_____

4. The children began to pass notes as soon as the teacher's back was turned.

_____

_____

5. After the incident was over we realized how foolishly we had acted.

_____

_____

6. Unless the president relented the college might be closed for weeks.

_____

_____

7. The students behaved as though they owned the school.

_____

_____

8. When the heat became too oppressive our tempers became frayed.

_____

_____

9. The natives always slowed down their work as soon as their foreign straw bosses turned their backs.

_____

_____

10. We were unable to ferret out real news inasmuch as the head officers were all secretive and closemouthed.

_____

_____

EXERCISE 21B
Composing Sentences with Adverb Clauses

Directions: Combine each of the following pairs of sentences into one, using an adverb clause as a sentence expansion in each. Punctuate accurately, and be prepared to explain the relationship expressed by the subordinating conjunction you use. A sample sentence illustrates the procedure.

> Pornography is seldom of much importance. It may be of considerable interest. *Though pornography is seldom of much importance, it may be of considerable interest.* (relationship of contrast)

1. Some modern theologians do not believe in the virgin birth of Christ. That belief is still at the core of Christianity.

_____

_____

_____

2. Competition incites people to better performance. The capitalistic system strongly depends on it.

_____

_____

_____

3. The line of succession was not clear in case of presidential death or disability. Congress added an amendment to the Constitution stipulating the exact line of succession.

_____

_____

_____

4. Twenty million dollars was poured into one 10-block square in St. Louis's slums. Little change was noted in living conditions.

_____

_____

_____

5. Professor Gilbert is a very learned man. He is a mediocre teacher.

_____

_____

6. The building's roof had already collapsed. Therefore the fire department could do little to prevent complete destruction.

_____

_____

_____

7. The Shogunate might have allowed political opposition. Then the revolution might not have occurred.

_____

_____

_____

8. There is a special problem raised by realism. It aims to present people as they actually are.

_____

_____

_____

9. Kennedy might have lived longer and had time to do more. Then he would have sought more outside advice.

_____

_____

_____

10. I visited Moscow last fall. The threat of war seemed to worry the Soviet high command.

_____

_____

_____

EXERCISE 21C
Composing Sentences with Adverb Clauses

Directions: In each of the first five items below combine the three simple sentences into one sentence with one independent clause, one adverb clause, and one sentence expansion of some other type. In each of the second five items add an adverb clause of your own to create a meaningful sentence.

1. Methanol can be used to power cars.
   Methanol can be made from coal.
   We should be able to overcome our gasoline shortage.

   _____

   _____

   _____

   _____

2. The price of copper could continue to rise.
   Copper is an element in short supply.
   We may be forced to use a less efficient substitute in electrical products.

   _____

   _____

   _____

3. My mother is easily converted to any passing fad.
   She claims she is retaining her youth.
   She uses Royal Jelly in several different ways.

   _____

   _____

   _____

   _____

4. The supervisor was gone for the day.
   We boys on shift 12 slowed our work greatly.
   We felt we had been overworked recently.

   _____

   _____

   _____

   _____

5. You may slice baloney in any way.
   Baloney is a mild sausage.
   Baloney is still baloney.

   _____

   _____

   _____

6. The circus did not open.

   _____

   _____

7. The final exam covered only the last half of the course.

   _____

   _____

8. My term paper was late.

   _____

   _____

9. The students peaceably dispersed.

   _____

   _____

10. The cost of the party was higher than expected.

    _____

    _____

22
Complex Sentences in General

In the previous chapters of this part you have studied the chief kinds of **sentence expansions** in the sense we are using the term: a word group containing a full idea that could be (and often is in childish writing) expressed in a simple sentence but that in a complex sentence functions as a modifier. You may have become adept at identifying and naming such expansions, or you may just have improved your writing skill somewhat without feeling secure in trying to attach the proper name to a particular expansion, such as an appositive. It is certainly worthwhile for a person to know something about the structure of his language, but much more important is one's ability to write mature, well-formed sentences and effective longer passages. Thus if you write effectively (or even adequately), do not feel that you are a poor English student just because you cannot attach proper labels to sentence parts.

In the past chapters you have been asked to understand various kinds of sentence expansions and to compose sentences containing specific kinds of expansions. But no writer thinks about grammatical labels *as he writes.* The good writer unconsciously and by habit uses various sentence expansions as he formulates ideas and composes effective sentences. *Thus our whole purpose in Part 2 has been to give you conscious practice in composing sentences in hopes that this practice will be converted into unconscious habit* (though a good writer must, as he rereads and revises his writing, be aware of sentence structure even if he cannot analyze the specific grammatical structure of each sentence). The exercises in this chapter are intended to give you additional practice in composing sentences.

We should, however, repeat that short, simple sentences are often effectively used in the best writing and that composing a long sentence just for the sake of its being long is foolish (unless you're just playing with language). But it is also true that the majority of sentences in good writing are complex, with various sentence expansions helping to prevent a childish style and to produce a mature style.

In the exercises for this chapter you will not be directed to use any particular sentence expansion. Each sentence you compose must, of course, have at least one independent clause, but the remaining ideas may be in any kinds of expansions that seem suitable to you. The point is for you to try to compose well-formed, effective sentences, as further practice in the composing process. There may be several ways to convert a set of simple sentences into one well-formed, mature sentence, and thus two students may have different structures for one sentence but with both versions being excellent.

In class discussion of the exercises, your instructor may want you to identify expansions and to suggest different ways of combining several ideas into one sentence.

EXERCISE 22A
Composing Complex Sentences

Directions: Make one sentence out of each of the following groups of short sentences. Do not be concerned with grammatical labels for sentence constituents or expansions—at least not until after you have composed your sentences. To help you, the sentence that should be the independent clause is italicized. A sample sentence illustrates the procedure.

    a. *The urban renewal proponents often have had no experience with slum life.*
    b. Most of the urban renewal proponents are well-meaning people.
    c. Slum life has its own peculiar set of mores.
The urban renewal proponents, most of whom are well-meaning people, often have had no experience with slum life, which has its own peculiar set of mores.

1. a. Jack was not especially heavy.
    b. *Jack was wiry and fast.*
    c. His being wiry and fast added to his athletic abilities.

   _____

   _____

   _____

   _____

2. a. *Three of the books were required reading.*
    b. These three included *Moby-Dick.*
    c. The other seven were simply suggested reading.
    d. The other seven included two of nonfiction.

   _____

   _____

   _____

   _____

3. a. Mr. Pierre voted early.
    b. Mr. Pierre was a candidate for a municipal judgeship.
    c. *He went home to await the election returns.*

   _____

   _____

   _____

   _____

4. a. Employment among minority groups in New York has risen recently.
   b. *There is still an unemployment rate of 12 percent.*
   c. This is a condition that causes continued bitterness.

---

5. a. Harriman was unawed by the magnitude of the task.
   b. *Harriman continued to pursue the peace talks.*
   c. He hoped that the enemy would eventually listen to reason.

---

6. a. Deacon Jones was fatigued.
   b. Deacon Jones was one of the Fearsome Foursome.
   c. *Deacon Jones continued to hit savagely.*
   d. Deacon Jones dropped the quarterback six times in all.

---

7. a. Miss Othmar was on the verge of tears.
   b. Miss Othmar was the second grade teacher.
   c. *Miss Othmar asked Linus to be sure to bring the eggshells next week.*
   d. Miss Othmar expected him to forget again.

---

8. a. Not all slum children become delinquent.
   b. *The proportion who do is high.*
   c. This fact leads sociologists to attribute much delinquency to slum conditions.

   _____

   _____

   _____

   _____

9. a. The evidences of maladjustment in Oswald might have led to his being given early treatment.
   b. *He might have overcome his instabilities.*
   c. He might have overcome them at least sufficiently to lead a nearly normal life.

   _____

   _____

   _____

   _____

10. a. *The University of New Mexico is in most respects excellent.*
    b. The university is a state-supported institution of some 10,000 students.
    c. The university has been upgraded by the settling of electronics industry in Albuquerque.

    _____

    _____

    _____

    _____

11. a. *The Tri-State Corporation was awarded the contract to build the Black Canyon Dam.*
    b. The corporation is the largest construction company in the world.
    c. The corporation submitted the lowest bid.

    _____

    _____

    _____

    _____

12. a. *Carbon has an amazing capacity to form chainlike molecules of enormous size.*
    b. Carbon is an element.
    c. The element carbon is found in all organic compounds.
    d. The element carbon is found in some fossils.

    _____

    _____

    _____

    _____

13. a. The Allies seemed on the brink of defeat in early 1942.
    b. *Winston Churchill refused to be disheartened.*
    c. Winston Churchill was the great English War Prime Minister.

    _____

    _____

    _____

    _____

14. a. Racial discrimination is not virulent in New Mexico.
    b. *There exists some prejudice against citizens of Spanish descent.*
    c. Many of these citizens of Spanish descent consider themselves the elite of the state.
    d. They rightly consider themselves the elite.

    _____

    _____

    _____

    _____

EXERCISE 22B
Composing Complex Sentences

Directions: Make one sentence out of each of the following groups of short sentences. Some of your sentences will have only one independent clause, but some will have two or more. You must decide for yourself which sentences should be kept as independent clauses and which should be used as sentence expansions.

1. a. Professor Snoally did not realize that he had mistaken an adjective clause for an appositive.
   b. Professor Snoally seldom makes a mistake in grammatical analysis.
   c. Professor Snoally confused his students.

   _____

   _____

   _____

   _____

2. a. The trial ended with a hung jury.
   b. The defendant had hired the best lawyers.
   c. The defendant felt that the state might not order a new trial.

   _____

   _____

   _____

   _____

3. a. The movie *Dark Victory* has elements of humor.
   b. The movie *Dark Victory* has an impressive moral.
   c. The moral is that we must be idealistic.
   d. We must be idealistic if we are not to be overcome with despair.

   _____

   _____

   _____

   _____

4. a. The *Atlantic* is a magazine with a rather small circulation.
   b. It contributes to the thinking of a very influential group of people.
   c. It gives them news.
   d. It gives them discussion.
   e. It gives them imaginative literature.

   _____

   _____

   _____

   _____

5. a. Not many young men choose military service as a career.
   b. Military service has several disadvantages.
   c. The fact that military service restricts one's freedom of movement is not
      its least disadvantage.
   d. Military service offers many advantages.
   e. Some of these are financial security and opportunity for rapid promotion.

   _____

   _____

   _____

   _____

6. a. I read *Frown No More*.
   b. It received good reviews.
   c. I found the book disgusting.
   d. It had a low moral tone.

   _____

   _____

   _____

   _____

7. a. The Republican candidate wanted to appeal to the lower-class voters.
   b. He was himself a rich man.
   c. He promised to enact tax reforms.
   d. They would close loopholes.
   e. These loopholes favored the rich.

   _____

   _____

   _____

   _____

8. a. The easiest way to wealth is through real estate speculation.
   b. That is the easiest way aside from inheriting money.
   c. The amount of land doesn't increase.
   d. The population does.
   e. This causes a constant increase in the demand for land.

   _____

   _____

   _____

   _____

9. a. Neither the United States nor Russia appears to want war.
   b. The complexity of our weapons systems makes it possible for war to start accidentally.
   c. Some minor official might push the wrong button in panic.
   d. Or he might push it by mistake.

   _____

   _____

   _____

   _____

10. a. I completed all the requirements for my major.
    b. I decided to enroll in Samoan Folkways for fun.
    c. I had traveled in the South Pacific.
    d. I knew some of the Samoan language.

    _____

    _____

    _____

    _____

11. a. Mr. Sorreltop had umpired in the major leagues for five years.
    b. Mr. Sorreltop was given a disability pension.
    c. The pension was for poor eyesight.

    _____

    _____

    _____

    _____

12. a. *Harper's* magazine has fiction.
    b. Nevertheless it is of much interest to politicians.
    c. It carries many articles on world and domestic affairs.

    _____

    _____

    _____

    _____

13. a. We went to the jail window to tease Mr. Brightbeak.
    b. He was in jail again for drunkenness.
    c. We were chased away by the sheriff.
    d. The sheriff felt sympathy for the old man.

    _____

    _____

    _____

    _____

23

Developing Sentence Judgment

In the preceding chapters you have been given practice in the art of composing well-formed sentences. You have learned that just getting two, three, or four ideas into one sentence is not enough: you must phrase and arrange the parts of the sentences in an effective, stylistically pleasing way. For example, the following two sentences contain the same information but are quite different in the effectiveness of their structure:

> *poor composition:* The so-called brush wars may continue and if they do the United States might become bankrupt because we do not have a controlled economy, and Russia does have a controlled economy.
> *effective composition:* If the so-called brush wars continue, the United States might become bankrupt, because we do not have a controlled economy as Russia does.

If you have well-developed sentence judgment, you will immediately see the marked superiority of the second sentence over the first. We hope that your study of the past chapters has improved your sentence judgment, and thus it seems appropriate that we close Part 2 with some exercises to test your sentence judgment. In all of the sets of four versions of one sentence in the following exercises, the structure of one sentence is distinctly superior to that of the others, though occasionally a second sentence might be acceptable. Your task is to choose the most effectively constructed sentence in each group of four. This practice should reinforce what you have learned about composing sentences of your own.

Your instructor may want to use one or more of the exercises in this chapter early in the course as an initial diagnosis of your sentence judgment. In fact, some of the exercises could be used at the beginning of the course and the remainder at the end of your study of Part 2 to see to what degree your sentence judgment has improved. Class discussion of why certain sentences are faulty or poorly constructed might also be profitable.

EXERCISE 23B
Developing Sentence Judgment

Directions: In each of the following sets of four sentences, encircle the letter of the sentence you think most effectively constructed. Follow any other directions your instructor gives you.

1. a. The study of grammar, which I did, was helpful in learning to write better, as you can see.
   b. The study of grammar, which I pursued, was helpful in learning, as you see, to write better.
   c. My study of grammar helped me learn to write better, as you can see.
   d. As you can see, the study of grammar which I did helped me to write better.

2. a. By working hard and eschewing vice was how my grandfather became a success.
   b. By working hard and eschewing vice my grandfather became a success.
   c. By working hard and eschewing vice was the way my grandfather became a success.
   d. Hard work and avoidance of vice was how my grandfather became a success.

3. a. The influence of politics on the lawyer is much greater than the teacher.
   b. The influence of politics on the lawyer is much greater than in teaching.
   c. The influence of politics on the lawyer is much greater than its influence on the teacher.
   d. The influence of politics on the lawyer is much greater than on the teacher's.

4. a. The soil must be adequately prepared before planting the slips.
   b. The soil must be adequately prepared when planting the slips.
   c. The soil must be adequately prepared prior to planting the slips.
   d. The soil must be adequately prepared before the slips are planted.

5. a. Physics is when you study the properties of matter and energy.
   b. Physics is when the properties of matter and energy are studied by you.
   c. Physics is you're studying the properties of matter and energy.
   d. Physics is the study of the properties of matter and energy.

6. a. Ruth finds it hard to accept the possibility that another soprano may have abilities comparable or even greater than her own.
   b. Ruth finds it hard to accept the possibility that another soprano may have abilities comparable to or even greater than her own.
   c. Ruth finds it hard to accept the possibility that another soprano may have abilities comparable or greater even than her own.

d. Ruth finds it hard to accept the possibility that another soprano may have abilities comparable to her own, even greater.

7. a. I am looking for a remedy to relieve a headache with a peculiar brand name.
   b. I am looking for a remedy to relieve a headache having a peculiar brand name.
   c. I am looking for a remedy with a peculiar brand name to relieve a headache.
   d. I am looking for a headache remedy with a peculiar brand name.

8. a. Our car broke down after attending the party.
   b. After attending the party, our car broke down.
   c. After we attended the party, our car broke down.
   d. Subsequent to attending the party, our car broke down.

9. a. An obligation to his sister which Fairfield, I discovered, could not fulfill.
   b. Fairfield owed an obligation to his sister which, I discovered, he could not fulfill.
   c. There being an obligation to his sister which Fairfield, I discovered, could not fulfill.
   d. An obligation owing to his sister which Fairfield, I discovered, could not fulfill.

10. a. When beginning the hobby of photography, expensive equipment seemed important to me.
    b. Upon beginning the hobby of photography, expensive equipment seemed important to me.
    c. When I began the hobby of photography, I thought expensive equipment was important.
    d. Beginning the hobby of photography, expensive equipment seemed important to me.

EXERCISE 23C
Developing Sentence Judgment

Directions: In each of the following sets of four sentences, encircle the letter of the sentence you think most effectively constructed. Follow any other directions your instructor gives you.

1. a. The lessons of art and history will enable us to understand future problems and how we can cope with them.
   b. The lessons of art and history will enable us to understand future problems and to cope with them.
   c. The lessons of art and history will enable us to understand future problems and how they can be coped with by us.
   d. The lessons of art and history will enable us to understand future problems and in coping with them.

2. a. She had all the qualities that I admired: honesty, sincerity, responsibility, witty, and pleasant.
   b. She had all the qualities that I admired: honesty, sincerity, responsibility, and was witty and pleasant.
   c. She had all the qualities that I admired: honesty, sincerity, responsibility, wit, and a pleasant attitude.
   d. She had all the qualities that I admired: honesty, sincerity, responsibility, witty, and pleasantry.

3. a. Teaching the fundamentals in high school is the wrong place for them.
   b. To teach the fundamentals in high school is the wrong place for them.
   c. Fundamentals teaching in high school is the wrong place.
   d. High school is the wrong place for teaching fundamentals.

4. a. Having launched the rocket in the morning, the loudspeakers were not used again that day.
   b. The rocket having been launched in the morning, the loudspeakers were not used again that day.
   c. The loudspeakers, after launching the rocket in the morning, were not used again that day.
   d. In the morning, after launching the rocket, the loudspeakers were not used again that day.

5. a. After the liner had put to sea, is when the captain discovered the stowaways.
   b. After the liner had put to sea, is the time when the captain discovered the stowaways.
   c. After the liner had put to sea, was when the captain discovered the stowaways.
   d. After the liner had put to sea, the captain discovered the stowaways.

6. a. After leaving the cakes in the pantry for a month, mold was discovered on them by the cook.
   b. After leaving the cakes in the pantry for a month, a discovery of mold on them was made by the cook.
   c. After leaving the cakes in the pantry for a month, they had mold on them, the cook discovered.
   d. After leaving the cakes in the pantry for a month, the cook discovered mold on them.

7. a. Professor Eisenkopf said that by demonstrating the existence of many freedoms in a particular society, that society was not proven free.
   b. Professor Eisenkopf said that by demonstrating the existence of many freedoms in a particular society did not prove that society free.
   c. Professor Eisenkopf said that demonstrating the existence of many freedoms in a particular society did not prove that society to be free.
   d. Professor Eisenkopf said that demonstrating the existence of many freedoms, a society was not proven free.

8. a. His friends agreed about John's having courage but that, at the same time, he was rather foolhardy.
   b. John's friends agreed that he had courage but felt that, at the same time, he was rather foolhardy.
   c. His friends agreed that John had courage but feeling that, at the same time, he was rather foolhardy.
   d. His friends agreed that John was courageous but disagree that, at the same time, he was rather foolhardy.

9. a. Every evening there is a gigantic traffic jam of homeward-bound commuters, thus showing the inadequacy of our freeways.
   b. A gigantic traffic jam of homeward-bound commuters every evening thus showing the inadequacy of our freeways.
   c. The fact that every evening a gigantic traffic jam of homeward-bound commuters shows the inadequacy of our freeways.
   d. Every evening a gigantic traffic jam of homeward-bound commuters shows the inadequacy of our freeways.

10. a. The insistence of mediation taking place between the parties involved by the government quickly ended the steel strike.
    b. The government's insistence that the parties involved mediate their dispute quickly ended the steel strike.
    c. The insistence by the government on the necessary mediation of the dispute between the parties involved quickly ended the steel strike.
    d. The government's insistence on the necessity of mediation of the involved parties' dispute quickly ended the steel strike.

EXERCISE 23D
Developing Sentence Judgment

Directions: In each of the following sets of four sentences, encircle the letter of the sentence you think most effectively constructed. Follow any other directions your instructor gives you.

1. a. When running for public office, tactful is what you should be, since people are easily offended.
   b. When running for public office, you should be tactful, people being easily offended.
   c. When you run for public office, be tactful, for people being easily offended.
   d. When running for public office, be tactful, for people are easily offended.

2. a. Without a knowledge of the world of finance, one should avoid investing large sums, unless carefully consulting investment experts.
   b. Without a knowledge of the world of finance, large sums of money should not be invested without careful consultation with investment experts.
   c. Without a knowledge of the world of finance, one should avoid investing large sums until he consults investment experts.
   d. One without a knowledge of the world of finance, should not invest large sums except with consulting of investment experts.

3. a. One often sees articles on advances in delicate, complex heart surgery in the daily newspapers.
   b. One often sees articles on advances in the daily newspapers in delicate, complex heart surgery.
   c. One often sees articles in the daily newspapers on advances in delicate, complex heart surgery.
   d. One in the daily newspapers often sees articles on advances in delicate, complex heart surgery.

4. a. By teaching new skills to the poor, these socially deprived people may benefit.
   b. By teaching new skills to the poor, these socially deprived people may be benefited.
   c. By us teaching new skills to the poor, we may benefit these socially deprived people.
   d. By teaching new skills to the poor, we may benefit these socially deprived people.

5. a. By using suspect patent medicines, they may impair the health of the people who use them.
   b. By using suspect patent medicines may impair the health of the people who use them.
   c. Suspect patent medicines may impair the health of the people who use them.

d. Their use of suspect patent medicines which may impair the health of the people who use them.

6. a. When in danger, all a cat's abilities come into play as it seeks to escape.
   b. When threatened by danger, a cat's abilities all come into play as it seeks to escape.
   c. Being in danger, all of a cat's abilities come into play as it seeks to escape.
   d. When a cat is threatened by danger, all of its abilities come into play as it seeks to escape.

7. a. In some societies, everyone being considered as equal at all times, they do not need to fight for equality.
   b. In some societies, everyone being considered equal at all times, the people do not need to fight for equality.
   c. In some societies, everyone is considered equal at all times, and they do not need to fight for equality.
   d. In some societies, everyone is considered as equal at all times, and in addition their people do not need to fight for equality.

8. a. Since Doris wanted to be a cheerleader, this caused her to practice leaping about and to study the art of screaming.
   b. Since Doris wanted to be a cheerleader, she decided to practice leaping about and studying the art of screaming.
   c. Since Doris wanted to be a cheerleader, she decided to practice leaping about and to study the art of screaming.
   d. Since Doris wanted to be a cheerleader, this caused her to practice leaping about and study the art of screaming.

9. a. Despite the poverty in southern Spain, they seem a fairly happy people.
   b. Despite the poverty in southern Spain, they seem a fairly happy group of people.
   c. Despite the poverty in southern Spain, happiness seems to be fairly common among them.
   d. Despite the poverty in southern Spain, the people there seem fairly happy.

10. a. If the cat will not eat its food, put it through the meat grinder once more.
    b. If the cat will not eat its food, you should put it through the meat grinder once more.
    c. If the cat will not eat food, put it through the meat grinder once more.
    d. If the cat will not eat its food, put the food through the meat grinder once more.

EXERCISE 23E
Developing Sentence Judgment

Directions: In each of the following sets of four sentences, encircle the letter of the sentence you think is most effectively constructed. Follow any other directions your instructor gives you.

1. a. When applying for admission to a medical school, an interview with the director of admissions should be requested, because they do not like to base decisions only on grades and test scores.
   b. When applying for admission to a medical school, one should request an interview with the director of admissions, because most such directors do not like to base decisions only on grades and test scores.
   c. When applying for admission to a medical school, the director of admissions should be asked for an interview, because he may not like to base his decisions on grades and test scores only.
   d. The director of admissions should be asked for an interview when you apply for admission to a medical school, because he may not like to base his decisions on grades and test scores only.

2. a. Being easygoing, the tricks played on Frank did not bother him as they did his mother.
   b. Being easygoing, Frank was not bothered by the tricks played on him, which bothered his mother.
   c. Being easygoing, Frank, unlike his mother, was not bothered by the tricks played on him.
   d. Being easygoing, unlike his mother Frank was not bothered by the tricks played on him.

3. a. When tipsy, the police should be called to drive you home, which they will do.
   b. When you are tipsy, you should call the police to drive you home, which they will be glad to do.
   c. When you are tipsy, the police should be called, because they are willing, to drive you home.
   d. When tipsy, don't drive home until the police have driven you there, which they will be glad to do.

4. a. After the ship went down in mid-ocean, the survivors were left in despair in an open boat which caused them to panic.
   b. After the ship went down in mid-ocean, the survivors were left in an open boat that caused some to panic and others to despair.
   c. After the ship went down in mid-ocean, the survivors were left in an open boat, a plight which caused some to panic and others to despair.
   d. After the ship went down in mid-ocean, the survivors were left in an open boat which caused some to panic and others to despair.

5. a. Because Henry James failed as a playwright did not cause him to lose faith in his ability as a writer.
   b. Because of Henry James's failure as a playwright did not cause him to lose faith in his ability as a writer.
   c. Since Henry James failed as a playwright did not cause him to lose faith in his ability as a writer.
   d. The fact that Henry James failed as a playwright did not cause him to lose faith in his ability as a writer.

6. a. In order to see the forest clearly, an excessively close examination of the trees must be avoided.
   b. In order to see the forest clearly, an excessively close examination of the trees must be avoided by us.
   c. In order to see the forest clearly, we must avoid an excessively close examination of the trees.
   d. In order to see the forest clearly, the trees must not be too closely examined.

7. a. The truck struggled up the hill in the rain loaded with dynamite.
   b. The truck in the rain struggled up the hill loaded with dynamite.
   c. The truck struggled up the hill loaded with dynamite in the rain.
   d. The truck loaded with dynamite struggled up the hill in the rain.

8. a. The president told the secretary to attend the meetings regularly, take down every motion carefully, and he should record each vote.
   b. The president told the sectretary to attend the meetings regularly, take down every motion carefully, and to record each vote.
   c. The president told the secretary to attend the meetings regularly, take down every motion carefully, and record each vote.
   d. The president told the secretary to attend the meetings regularly, take down every motion carefully, and that he should record each vote.

9. a. The gift consisted of goat cheese made and imported from Portugal.
   b. The gift consisted of goat cheese made by and imported from Portugal.
   c. The gift consisted of goat cheese made in and imported from Portugal.
   d. The gift consisted of goat cheese made by Portugal and imported from them.

10. a. Mary studied Sanskrit during the summer, and her leisure hours were devoted to alchemy.
    b. Mary studied Sanskrit during the summer and devoted her leisure hours to alchemy.
    c. Mary studied Sanskrit during the summer, and alchemy was her leisure pleasure.
    d. Mary studied Sanskrit during the summer, and alchemy was studied in her leisure hours.

EXERCISE 23F
Developing Sentence Judgment

Directions: In each of the following sets of four sentences, encircle the letter of the sentence you think is most effectively constructed. Follow any other directions your instructor gives you.

1. a. When the Santa Ana winds blow, fire danger is extreme, being so dry in the brush country.
   b. When the Santa Ana winds blow, fire danger, since it is so dry, is extreme in the brush country.
   c. When the Santa Ana winds blow, fire danger is extreme because the brush country is so dry.
   d. Fire danger, when the Santa Ana winds blow, is extreme, being very dry in the brush country.

2. a. The flight was anything but pleasant, because of the stiff wind, the sputtering of the engine, and I got worried.
   b. The flight was unpleasant with my getting worried and the engine sputtering in the stiff wind.
   c. The wind was stiff and the engine sputtered; I became worried and so the flight was unpleasant.
   d. Because of the stiff wind, the sputtering engine, and my worry, the flight was unpleasant.

3. a. The fact that he was well acquainted with the field of logistics helped him to become a good student in it.
   b. He was well acquainted with the field of logistics, causing him to become a good student in it.
   c. He was well acquainted with the field of logistics, thereby enabling him to become a good student in it.
   d. Being well acquainted with the field of logistics, he became a good student in it.

4. a. Coming down in the jungle, desert, or arctic, certain things are necessary for you to do to get along on your own.
   b. Whether you are forced down in the jungle, the desert, or the arctic, you must follow certain procedures to get along on your own.
   c. Due to a forced landing in the jungle, the desert, or arctic regions, certain procedures must be complied with by all concerned to get along on your own.
   d. As a result of making a forced landing in jungle country, desert areas, or arctic regions, to survive on your own you must follow certain procedures.

5. a. The text of this message will be written with as few words as possible, maintaining clarity, without making the message vague or ambiguous.

219

b. With as few words as possible, maintaining clarity, without making the message vague or ambiguous, the text of this message will be written.

c. The text of this message will be brief and clear, not wordy and vague.

d. The text of this message will be clear and as brief as possible, at the same time it will not be vague or ambiguous.

6. a. The author was praised for his organization, choice of subject, and because he was brief.

b. The author was praised for the organization of his book, for his choice of subject, and because he was brief.

c. The author was praised for his organization, his choice of subject, and his brevity.

d. The author was praised for his organization, his choice of subject and the book having brevity.

7. a. The store sold expensive silver, china, and pottery, disdaining cheap merchandise.

b. The store sold expensive silver, china, pottery, and was disdainful of cheap merchandise.

c. The store sold expensive silver, china, pottery, and disdained cheap merchandise.

d. The store sold expensive silver, as well as china and pottery, and disdaining cheap merchandise.

8. a. As the hunter explained that he wanted to hire a guide and ride into the wilderness in order to shoot a bear.

b. As the hunter explained that he wanted to hire a guide and to ride into the wilderness in order to shoot a bear.

c. The hunter explained that he wanted to hire a guide and ride into the wilderness in order to shoot a bear.

d. The reason was as the hunter explained that he wanted to hire a guide and ride into the wilderness to shoot a bear.

9. a. His duties include soliciting new business, visiting old customers, and require him to train new salesmen.

b. His duties include soliciting new business, visiting old customers, and that he train new salesmen.

c. His duties include soliciting new business, visiting old customers, and to train new salesmen.

d. His duties include soliciting new business, visiting old customers, and training new salesmen.

10. a. Having refused to meet the press, the newspapers frequently criticized the candidate.

b. Having refused to meet the press, the newspapers criticized the candidate frequently.

c. Having refused to meet the press, criticism of the candidate by the newspapers was frequent.

d. Having refused to meet the press, the candidate was frequently criticized by the newspapers.

EXERCISE 23G
Developing Sentence Judgment

Directions: In each of the following sets of four sentences, encircle the letter of the sentence you think is most effectively constructed. Follow any other directions your instructor gives you.

1. a. P. T. Barnum was hailed both as the "prince of showmen" and the "prince of humbug," but his main effort was to fool all the people all the time—and make them like it.
   b. Hailed alike as the "prince of showmen" and the "prince of humbug," P. T. Barnum tried to fool all the people all the time—and make them like it.
   c. P. T. Barnum, who was hailed by some as the "prince of showmen" and by others as the "prince of humbug," tried to fool all the people all the time and meanwhile making them like it.
   d. Because trying to fool all the people all the time and make them like it was P. T. Barnum's main effort, so he was hailed alike as the "prince of showmen" and the "prince of humbug."

2. a. The American public was curious and gullible regardless of their "Yankee good sense," and would therefore fall for almost any lie that was big enough, and this P. T. Barnum, forerunner of the modern ad man, quickly realized.
   b. As this forerunner of the modern ad man realized, the American public readily falls for almost any lie that is big enough, for they are curious and gullible in spite of their "Yankee good sense."
   c. Although possessing "Yankee good sense," the American public's curiosity and gullibility would make them fall for any lie big enough, as P. T. Barnum, forerunner of the modern ad man, well knew.
   d. This forerunner of the modern ad man realized that the American public, curious and gullible in spite of its "Yankee good sense," would fall for almost any lie that was big enough.

3. a. His first success was the discovery of Joice Heth, a woman who claimed to be 161 years old and to have been the nurse of Washington, whom she called "dear little George."
   b. He made his first success by discovering Joice Heth, a woman claiming to be 161 years old and formerly the nurse of Washington, who she called "dear little George."
   c. The discovery of Joice Heth, a woman who claimed to be 161 years old, was Barnum's first success, because she said she had been Washington's nurse, whom she called "dear little George."
   d. The discovery of Joice Heth, Barnum's first success, was a woman who claimed she was 161 years old and had been the nurse of Washington, whom she called "dear little George."

221

4. a. Finally his audiences began to dwindle, and then Barnum announced Joice not to be alive at all, but a dummy made out of whalebone, rubber, and springs.
   b. When his audiences began to dwindle, Barnum told them Joice was not alive at all, but a dummy of whalebone, rubber, and with springs.
   c. When his audiences began to dwindle, Barnum announced that Joice was not alive at all, but merely a dummy made of whalebone, rubber, and springs.
   d. Barnum's audiences began to dwindle, and he then said that Joice, not being alive at all, was merely a dummy made out of rubber, whalebone, and springs.

5. a. Thousands came back again, even though they had already seen her, in order to discover whether they had been cheated, but never finding out, Barnum became still richer.
   b. Although when thousands who had already seen her came back to discover whether they had really been cheated and departed no wiser, Barnum became richer still.
   c. Thousands who had already seen her came back to discover whether they had really been cheated; they departed no wiser than before, but left Barnum much richer.
   d. Thousands of people who had already seen her came back to discover whether they had really been cheated; their departing no wiser than before made Barnum much richer.

6. a. Though "the prince of humbugs," Barnum showed many bona fide, interesting exhibits, and one was Jumbo.
   b. Barnum, though "the prince of humbugs," showed Jumbo, and he showed other bona fide, interesting exhibits too.
   c. Though "the prince of humbugs," Barnum showed many bona fide, interesting exhibits, such as Jumbo.
   d. Jumbo was showed by Barnum as one of his bona fide, interesting exhibits, though he was "the prince of humbugs."

PART 3
ORGANIZATION AND PARAGRAPH DEVELOPMENT

24
Organizing a Short Composition

As Part 2 demonstrates, a sentence is a composition in miniature. For it to be effective, its parts must be assembled properly so that the whole sentence will read smoothly and express its ideas clearly. Similarly, paragraphs and whole papers should have effective form, or arrangement of parts, so that the reader can easily grasp the information being conveyed and also be pleased with the smoothness of the writer's style. In this chapter we will give you brief but adequate guidance in planning, or organizing, a short paper, usually, in a composition class, called a theme or essay.

ORGANIZING EXPOSITORY THEMES

Most writing required in college and in important jobs that require writing is called **exposition** or **expository writing**, which is writing intended to inform by presenting the reader with facts, ideas, and opinions. Though, strictly speaking, exposition does not include **persuasion,** in actual fact the two kinds of writing are very often mixed, and thus in this section we will be dealing with writing intended to inform or to persuade or both. For example, the topic "Discuss how to rebuild the engine of a car" would be purely informative. But such a topic as "Discuss the harmful aspects of our jury system in dispensing justice" would be in part informative but would also be intended to persuade the reader to change his mind and accept new ideas or attitudes. The best method of organizing short papers of either sort is the same, and thus we will explain the organization of informative and persuasive writing as though they are one kind.

In the previous paragraph we used the phrase "the best method of organizing short papers." Of course, there are various ways of organizing informative and persuasive writing, especially long articles; our phrase applies only to the type of short themes usually assigned in composition courses and to essay exam questions in such courses as sociology. For that kind of writing we will stick to our claim that there is one best method of organization. That method is to organize your paper on the basis of three to five **main points.** Each main point will be expressed in a topic sentence (see next chapter) and developed in one paragraph (see following chapters). Mastering the main-point method of organization will prepare you to vary your patterns of organization in your later, and perhaps longer, pieces of writing, such as term papers in college or business reports in your occupation.

The best way to formulate three to five main points for your paper is to state your topic fully and to find in it a stated or implied **plural noun** that in a sense can be divided into main points. It is important for you to understand the difference between a title and a topic. A good title may not reveal the subject matter of the paper and may contain humor, irony, suspense, and so on. The topic reveals the subject matter of the paper. Whether your instructor provides you with a topic or requires you to think of one for yourself, you need it to be stated fully and clearly so that it can guide your organization. Many teachers like a student's composition to be preceded by a **thesis sentence,** which is one general sentence that summarizes the content of the whole paper. An example is "This paper will discuss the dilemma of modern American teen-agers being biologically ready but financially unready for marriage." There is little difference between a thesis sentence and the full and clear statement of the topic of a paper. We will use the term *topic*.

A fully stated topic often contains a plural noun from which several main points can be derived. For example, the topic "Discuss what you consider to be some justifiable uses of lying" contains the plural noun *uses*. To organize a short paper on this topic, you would just need to think of three to five *general* uses of justifiable lying. The plural noun *uses* is your clue to organization. Also we stressed the word *general,* because each main point must be developed into a full paragraph, and that means the point must be a generalization, such as "to avoid hurting people's feelings" rather than a specific, such as "to coax Aunt Martha to give me some money." A generalization covers several or many specifics. A generalization in your basic organization will be expanded into a paragraph through the use of specific details and explanations.

Once you spot your plural noun, such as *uses,* in your fully stated topic, you then jot down in scratch outline form the few uses that will serve as your main points. For example, for the above topic you might jot down these points.

1. Use of lies as compliments that will harm no one
2. Use of lies by doctors to spare terminal patients more mental pain
3. Use of lies to avoid penalties for breaking unjust laws
4. Use of lies to get rid of unwanted guests or salesmen

Now (though you may want to arrange the main points in a different order) you have a basic organization to guide you in writing a good composition of four paragraphs. Of coure, you will learn how to write brief introductions and concluding sentences (see farther on), but the outline of your paper is now clear, which will make your writing easier. You should understand clearly, too, that your scratch outline is for your use only and is not a formal outline to present to your instructor. Therefore you can phrase your main points in any meaningful way that will guide you in writing your paper. For some students, even single words might suffice; for others an extensive expression of the main points might be necessary.

Many, if not most, students can write an adequate short paper once they have their three to five main points clearly in their minds. For further guidance, however, some students like to jot down details under each main point. This is just **expanding the basic organization** for the benefit of the writer who needs such expansion. For example, a student might expand the first point of the above basic organization in this way:

1. Uses of lies as compliments that will hurt no one
   a. thanking my minister for his inspiring sermon
   b. telling my girl friend she looks especially good tonight
   c. passing out words of praise to our mediocre football players
   d. giving encouragement to a new and nervous teacher

You must decide for yourself whether you can develop your paragraph with only the main points jotted down or whether you need to jot down more of your thinking before you begin writing.

Here is one more example of a topic containing a plural noun, with a basic organization derived from that noun:

topic: Discuss the **ways** in which you adjust your language usage to fit different occasions and circumstances.
basic organization expressing five ways:

1. slang, profanity, and bad grammar with my friends
2. less slang and more careful vocabulary in talking to my parents and their friends
3. attempt to be as formal and correct as possible in talking to such people as my minister and college deans
4. breezy style and general carelessness in writing friendly letters
5. semiformal style and high-level vocabulary in writing letters to be read by well-educated people

With general main points such as these, you are ready to write a well-organized paper.

But many topics will not have stated plural nouns from which main points can be derived. Most of these, however, will have **implied plural nouns**, which will serve the same purpose as a stated plural noun. The most common of the implied plural nouns are *reasons, grounds, methods, steps, characteristics,* and *ways.* Here are some examples:

topic: Discuss why the divorce rate in America is so high.
implied plural noun: reasons (why)

topic: Discuss how consumers can best protect themselves from deceptive advertising and faulty merchandise.
implied plural noun: methods *or* ways

topic: Discuss what a person means when he says, "After all, I'm only human."
implied plural noun: characteristics *or* traits

topic: Discuss how you would go about making yourself an expert magician.
implied plural noun: steps

Many topics of the sort assigned in composition courses are most simply and effectively organized on the basis of main points derived from a stated or implied plural noun in the fully stated topic.

We do not need to dwell long on the nature of **introductions** and **conclusions** to informative-persuasive themes. The hoary bit of instruction that tells students to organize their papers on the basis of

I. Introduction
II. Body
III. Conclusion

has led many students to misunderstand the nature of short papers, for that formula seems to give as much space to the introduction as to the content (body) of the paper. But, in fact, most short informative-persuasive themes should have just a brief (usually one sentence) introduction that is a part of the first paragraph and not a separate paragraph. Such an introduction should *usually* be plain, simple, and direct, not cute, folksy, teasing, suspenseful, or startling. We stress the word *usually,* for there are times when an imaginative student can effectively open a paper with some sort of distinctive flourish, such as a brief bit of narration or an anecdote. But our advice is for you to write a straightforward one- or two-sentence introduction *that tells the reader what the topic tells you.* Naturally, though, you want to phrase your introduction in the best style you can muster.

Here are three examples of simple, direct introductions, with an indication of how they can be a part of the first paragraph, which will express the first main point of the paper directly after the introduction:

topic: Discuss the most distinctive characteristics of modern teen-agers.
introduction: Today's teen-agers as a group have several notable characteristics that distinguish them from previous generations. Their most widely discussed characteristic is . . .

topic: Discuss what it means to be "lovable."
introduction: Everyone except a few seriously disturbed people wants to be loved by everybody, but few consciously think about what being "lovable" means. Probably the characteristic that . . .

topic: Explain why most psychologists think that everybody is partly dishonest.
introduction: Most people think of themselves as being honest and are honest most of the time. Nevertheless, it seems that virtually everyone is at times somewhat dishonest. One reason for . . .

One- or two-sentence introductions of this sort are usually best for expository or persuasive themes.

Similarly, the conclusion to a short theme should usually be just a one-sentence ending that makes some reference to the totality of the subject matter of the paper and that sounds a note of finality. It should *not* be a summary of the paper and should usually not be indented as a separate paragraph. For example, the conclusion to the topic about the characteristics of modern teen-agers could be this:

Thus a serious concern about the future seems to be the most notable characteristic of modern teen-agers.

This concluding sentence, which *sounds* like a conclusion, would simply be the last sentence of the paragraph developing the last main point. Note that it makes reference to the topic of the paper but does not summarize it. (A long paper may have a summary of its content as a conclusion.)

ORGANIZING DESCRIPTIVE THEMES

Descriptive writing tells how something looks, smells, tastes, sounds, or feels—mostly looks. Many composition teachers like to assign descriptive themes. Organization of themes of pure description may be, and usually is, much looser than organization of informative-persuasive themes, but nevertheless such a theme must have a detectable organizational pattern if it is to be effective. The simplest method of organizing a descriptive theme is to plan to develop paragraphs on the basis of **units of impression**, which, in a sense, are main points. First, you must understand your topic clearly, which means setting limits to just what you will describe. Then you divide the whole into units of impression, which you will jot down in scratch outline form. You will then compose a short introduction similar to, but perhaps with a little more literary flourish than, the introductions illustrated in the preceding section. Then you will develop one paragraph about each unit of impression.

Here are two examples of this process of organizing a theme of description:

topic: A roving view of the ghost town of Bodie, with emphasis on the deadness of the scene.
units of impression:

1. The whole panorama from the top of the hill south of town
2. A walk along the main street of stores and offices
3. The old schoolhouse with the jail and outhouses nearby
4. The mining works on the side of the hill to the northeast
5. A final panorama from the mining works

topic: The colorful waterfront activity in Ketchikan Bay
units of impression:

1. A passenger steamer just arriving and unloading
2. The fishing boats coming in to unload
3. The floating pier, with many different kinds of boats moored to it
4. The young Indian children and their attempts to earn a little money or make off with objects of some value

Each of the units of impression would be developed into a full paragraph with graphic details. Planning the units of impression is a very important first step in writing a good descriptive theme.

ORGANIZING THEMES OF PERSONAL NARRATIVE

Narration, or **narrative writing**, is storytelling, either fictional or factual. A personal narrative is a little story taken from one's own life. Many composition teachers like to assign themes of personal narrative occasionally because that is the kind of writing students do best. And, of course, training in any kind of writing is educationally desirable. Personal narratives are easier to organize than any other kind of theme, because a story naturally has a beginning, middle, and end. (Flashbacks usually should be avoided in short personal narratives, though occasionally they can be used effectively). Nevertheless, you should plan your personal narrative before you begin writing. You should organize it on the basis of **units of events,** with each unit (except sentences of dialogue) occupying one paragraph, unless it would make an abnormally long or short paragraph. Units of events in personal narratives, however, are much looser than the main points in an expository theme. Mainly, you should start a new paragraph in a personal narrative where there is some perceptible shift of events. Normally, such shifts are rather frequent, and thus you should have paragraphs of between 50 and 125 words (again, except for sentences of dialogue).

For guidance, you should jot down in scratch outline form units of events in your personal narrative. These units need not necessarily form the basis of one paragraph each; for example you may find that just two or three medium-length sentences cover one unit and thus may continue with the next unit before you make a new paragraph indentation. Here is an example:

topic: How I narrowly avoided being arrested for possessing marijuana by out-smarting a policeman

units of events:

1. My decision to make my first purchase of marijuana
2. My sudden fright after the purchase
3. My appearance of being a suspicious character because of my self-consciousness
4. The policeman stopping me
5. My feigning a coughing spell near the curb
6. My being saved by secretely dropping the marijuana into some curbside trash

Jotting down such units of events will help guide you in your writing, though it is true that many students can write stories about their experiences without written notations to guide their organization.

EXERCISE 24A
Organizing Whole Papers

Directions: Plan a basic organization for one or more (as your instructor directs) of the following expository and persuasive topics by jotting down three or four main points for each. Study each topic carefully so that you can think of main points that are generalizations that can be given paragraph development.

1. Discuss some of the main problems that college students face in their first few weeks of college.

   a. _____

   b. _____

   c. _____

   d. _____

2. Discuss some of the disadvantages of "do-it-yourself" projects.

   a. _____

   b. _____

   c. _____

   d. _____

3. Discuss some of the *bad* character traits that participation in varsity sports might develop in athletes.

   a. _____

   b. _____

   c. _____

   d. _____

4. Discuss some ways of improving race relationships in your community or in the whole country.

    a. _____

    b. _____

    c. _____

    d. _____

5. Discuss some of the main arguments for or against federal and state welfare programs.

    a. _____

    b. _____

    c. _____

    d. _____

6. Discuss why you are for or against birth control (either voluntary or compulsory).

    a. _____

    b. _____

    c. _____

    d. _____

EXERCISE 24B
Writing Introductions

Directions: Write a one- or two-sentence introduction for one or more (as your instructor directs) of the topics given in Exercise 24A. If your instructor directs you to, show how an expression of the first main point of the paper could follow directly after the introduction in the same paragraph.

1. _____

_____

_____

_____

_____

_____

_____

2. _____

_____

_____

_____

_____

_____

_____

3. _____

_____

_____

_____

4. _____

5. _____

6. _____

25

Understanding the Paragraph and the Topic Sentence

The term *paragraph* is difficult to define beyond saying that a paragraph is a unit of composition set off by indentation, for paragraphs vary widely according to the kind of writing involved. For example, in dialogue in fiction a new paragraph begins with each new speech, no matter how short. In other kinds of writing, too, paragraphs are likely to be very short. In journalism, for example, short paragraphs are the rule, and in a newspaper article every sentence or two will see the beginning of a new paragraph. Similarly, in various kinds of personal writing, such as friendly letters, very short paragraphs are common. But in other kinds of writing—most college writing, for example—such brief, fragmentary paragraphs are out of place. In effect, no sensible definition of a paragraph can be given to cover all kinds of writing.

But in the kind of expository and persuasive writing college students are called upon to do, a good deal can be said about the nature of the paragraph. Most specifically, it can be said that indentation alone does not necessarily make a paragraph. Instead, in this kind of writing it is a *topic* or *main point* that makes a paragraph. You remember from the last chapter that most college papers are organized around main points. It is what is said about a main point that makes a paragraph in expository writing. So we will define a **paragraph** as *a unit of composition that develops a topic or main point*.

Paragraphs in college writing, then, are likely to be longer than one or two sentences, for it takes more than that to develop most main points. Thus the length of a paragraph is determined by your development of the main point or topic being discussed. An average paragraph in college writing is about one-half to three-quarters of a handwritten page—about 75–125 words. A shorter paragraph is likely to be underdeveloped. A longer paragraph usually needs to be divided into two parts, for overlong paragraphs become fatiguing to a reader, just as overlong sentences do. In college writing, then, you should plan to devote one paragraph to each main point in your organization of your paper, but you should divide a long paragraph into two separate ones at a suitable breaking point.

235

Because a paragraph is a unit of composition developing one topic, it is likely to have a **topic sentence.** This is the main sentence of the paragraph; it states the topic the paragraph will develop. Normally, a topic sentence comes first in a paragraph, for the topic should be announced at the beginning. But not all paragraphs have topic sentences, and occasionally the only sentence that states the topic comes in the middle or at the end of the paragraph. In college writing, however, it is usually best to have a topic sentence for each paragraph and to have that sentence at or near the beginning of the paragraph.

For example, suppose you were assigned the topic "Discuss some improvements that your hometown should make to be a better city." First you would plan your organization by jotting down several main points that you would make, like this:

a. My town needs to improve streets and alleys.
b. My town needs to establish more recreational facilities.
c. My town needs to relieve overcrowded schools.
d. My town needs to hire more competent city employees.

Then you would write a sentence or two of introduction, such as this:

> My hometown is a respectable city, but it needs to make many civic improvements in order to progress with the times.

Now, after such a direct introduction, you would be ready to write paragraphs developing the main points of your organization. Each main point should have one or two paragraphs devoted to it and should have a topic sentence (one topic sentence will serve for a long paragraph arbitrarily divided into two). For example, the sentence following the above introduction should be a topic sentence for the first main point. Thus the second sentence of your paper might be this:

> Many of the streets and alleys, for example, have gradually deteriorated and need various kinds of repairs.

Such a topic sentence is a *general statement* that calls for specific development. The paragraph would be completed with specific examples of repairs needed on the streets and alleys.

Similarly, the other three main points would call for topic sentences, perhaps like these:

b. To make further improvements, my hometown also needs to establish more and better recreational facilities for all age groups.
c. During the past five years our city has grown, but it has not constructed more schools; consequently, we are now faced with overcrowded schoolrooms.
d. No more scandalous situation exists in my hometown than the extensive collection of incompetent city employees.

Each of these topic sentences is a general statement that needs specific development into a full paragraph. Most kinds of college writing—not just English themes—call for the composition of such topic sentences, for it is around such sentences that paragraphs are built. But remember: You must first prepare an organization for your topic before you have main points to turn into topic sentences.

In summary, then, you should understand that a paragraph in college writing is a unit of composition because it deals with just one topic or main point. This main point is given general statement in a topic sentence, which is developed with specific details into a complete, coherent, unified paragraph. The following two chapters will deal more extensively with completeness, coherence, and unity in paragraphs.

EXERCISE 25
Writing Topic Sentences

Directions: Following are two topics that have basic organizations of main points prepared for them. For each main point write a topic sentence that expands and is stylistically more polished than the simple statement of the main point. Be sure that you write topic sentences that can be developed into paragraphs.

1. *Topic:* Discuss ways in which relations between police officers and the citizens of a community might be improved:

   a. Establishment of a civilian review board
   b. A psychological test to be given applicants to see if they are suited to the work
   c. Public service television programs showing the officers' duties and civilian reaction to them
   d. A system providing for a citizen to spend a few hours once a year with a patrolman on duty

   a. _____

   _____

   _____

   _____

   b. _____

   _____

   _____

   _____

   c. _____

   _____

   _____

   _____

   d. _____

   _____

   _____

   _____

2. *Topic:* What are some of the basic rules for conducting oneself on a first date?

    a. Observe all the social amenities.
    b. Don't argue about controversial topics.
    c. Try to discover your date's interests and meet them.
    d. Avoid excessive intimacy.

a. _____

_____

_____

_____

_____

b. _____

_____

_____

_____

_____

c. _____

_____

_____

_____

_____

d. _____

_____

_____

_____

_____

26

Developing the Paragraph: Completeness

One of the most common weaknesses in student writing is underdevelopment of paragraphs. Not even errors in spelling and usage do as much damage to most papers as the incomplete, fragmentary paragraph. The mature writer is one who can sustain a paragraph in order to develop a main point fully.

The problem revolves around the fact that there are generalities and details in expository and persuasive writing. The generalities are the paragraph topics that are made into topic sentences. The details are individual statements that support the generality. Failure to include enough specific details is a conspicuous weakness in student writing. The details are necessary to make the generality seem plausible. A reader has no reason to believe a general statement (topic sentence) unless detailed substantiation is given in the form of particulars.

For example, suppose in writing on the topic "Discuss the characteristics of the modern teen-ager" you should write this paragraph based on one of the points in your organization of the topic:

> A notable characteristic of modern teen-agers is their concern about the future. They want to plan for a secure future.

You might think that you have said all you need to say, but you really have stated only a broad generality without supporting details. The reader is not inclined to believe your general statement just because you made it; he wants to know specifics. A more fully developed paragraph might go like this:

> A notable characteristic of modern teen-agers is their concern about the future. They worry about such things as entering a suitable occupation, making a stable marriage, becoming accepted in their community, and establishing a social and recreational life to match their vocational pursuits. In other words, they are not content just to live from day to day to see what happens; they want to direct their lives. Planning for the future, then, is a conspicuous characteristic of the typical teen-ager. He is not just a happy-go-lucky, will-of-the-wisp character. He is always giving thought to tomorrow.

These details support the general statement in the topic sentence, making a full, complete paragraph—quite different from the fragmentary first example.

Here is another example of a paragraph fragment, with a developed revision:

paragraph fragment:

Another reason why the student body government does not always train for leadership is because some student body officers are only interested in having fun. Some of them treat it as a joke.

developed paragraph:

Another reason why the student body government does not always train for leadership is that some student body officers are interested only in having fun. Instead of providing leadership, these spoilers of student body government provide practical jokes and divert the council and various committees from their real work. For example, when the council once was discussing the important issue of student participation in making college policy, one member set off a stink bomb. Another time we were seriously trying to plan support for campus cultural events, but one loudmouth would only talk about the chances of our football team's becoming champion. Both ignorance and insincerity characterize some members of the student body government, and that diminishes training for leadership.

Learning to write such complete paragraphs is one of the harder tasks of the composition student. To be able to write complete paragraphs, one must be able to concentrate on details and detailed explanations after one has expressed a main point in a topic sentence.

The need to elaborate paragraph topics for paragraph completeness cannot be overemphasized. Dull, colorless, unconvincing writing is the result of fragmentary paragraphs. For example, here are some more incomplete paragraphs as they actually appeared in college papers.

I have had some experience in photographic work from taking a majority of the pictures for the yearbook and the newspaper.

Sociologists seem to think that our family life is breaking up. This is true.

Today's science is at the throat of religion because of its beliefs. What I believe is on the far end of what science believes.

In *Animal Farm* there are many meanings and submeanings. Some of these meanings are easy to comprehend, yet others are more difficult.

These writers totally failed to understand the nature of the paragraph as a unit of composition. Each failed to go into detail about his paragraph topic, leaving an unsubstantiated generality as a paragraph fragment.

To avoid such incomplete paragraphs, first plan your paper around a series of main points. Then express each main point as a topic sentence for a paragraph. Then write a full paragraph by developing the main point with specific details. Do not just let the topic sentence stand by itself as though it alone justifies its main point. Specific details are necessary.

EXERCISE 26
Analyzing Paragraph Fragments

Directions: Each of the following paragraph fragments came from a student paper. Explain why each is incomplete and how it might be developed. Spaces are provided for your notes. Your instructor may want you to develop (using a separate sheet of paper) one or more of these paragraph fragments.

1. The Republican party is good for the country because it spends less money. It gives people more money of their own.

_____

_____

_____

2. The Democratic party is the best for the country because it stands for progress. It tries to help all the people.

_____

_____

_____

3. The novel *Of Human Bondage* gave me a lot to think about. It told how life is, how many conditions are not an individual's fault.

_____

_____

_____

4. The "generation gap" is real. One of the clearest evidences of this is that families don't seek entertainment together any more.

_____

_____

_____

5. The first thing I think should be done to improve the welfare system is to sterilize mothers with illegitimate children. Why should more children just be born to go on relief?

_____

_____

_____

6. My strongest objection to Communism is that it doesn't let you speak your mind. You don't have freedom of expression under it.

_____

_____

_____

7. Law enforcement is a good profession because it is interesting and thrilling and pays a reasonable wage. You need a lot of training to become a law officer.

_____

_____

_____

8. Snake collecting is an interesting hobby. I have been collecting snakes for almost two years now.

_____

_____

_____

9. The family does not love one another as they used to. We do not have fun to-gether anymore.

_____

_____

_____

27

Developing the Paragraph: Coherence and Unity

COHERENCE

A paragraph should not only be complete in its development but should also be **coherent.** This means that the sentences should be so closely connected to one another that they flow smoothly without gaps between them or jumps in logic. The word *coherence* literally means "a sticking together," for it comes from the Latin words *co,* meaning "together," and *haerere,* meaning "to stick." When the sentences of a paragraph flow smoothly, one growing out of the other, the paragraph is said to be coherent. Coherence is the quality of being integrated, logically consistent, and intelligible.

Sentences in a paragraph are coherent when there is a clear *transition* from one to another—that is, when there is a carry-over from one sentence to the next. There are three main methods of transition to achieve coherence.

Transitional Words and Phrases

Perhaps the most common and simple means of transition between sentences in a paragraph is the use of transitional words and phrases. There are dozens of these in English used solely to connect ideas. Some are simple conjunctions, such as *and, but, yet, or,* and *for.* Others are the conjunctive adverbs you studied in Chapter 6, such as *however, nevertheless, therefore, thus, moreover,* and so forth. Still others are connective phrases such as *for example, of course, on the other hand, in addition to, in conclusion,* and so forth. There are several dozens of these connectives in English, and their sole function is to show a relationship between ideas. When used between sentences in a paragraph, they make for coherence, or a smooth flow of ideas.

Here is an example:

A good desk dictionary is the most useful text a student can buy. **But** it is valuable only if it is consistently and intelligently used. **Contrary to what many students think,** the dictionary contains much more information than just spelling and definitions. **For example,** most good dictionaries have a chapter summarizing the rules of punctuation and capitalization. Many **also** have charts on weights and measurements, a gazetteer, a list of famous names with short biographical information, and a list of colleges and universities. **In fact,** the dictionary is a real treasury of all sorts of information. **And in addition, of course,** the dictionary is indispensable for providing information about pronunciation, spelling, and word meanings.

Note how each of the boldface transitional words and phrases leads from sentence to sentence so that there is a smooth flow of ideas. This effect is coherence and is very important in paragraph development. To see how much these transitional devices help, read the paragraph through omitting them. You will see that the effect is disjointed, even though the ideas remain the same. Transitional words and phrases help the reader see immediately the logical relationship between ideas. You should cultivate the use of these devices.

Repetition of Key Words

Transition between sentences for coherence is often effected through the repetition in one sentence of an important word that appears in the previous sentence. The repetition of the word signals to the reader's mind that a train of thought is being continued. Note, for example, the repetition of the word *dictionary* in the example paragraph above. This repetition, as well as the transitional phrases, helps make the paragraph coherent.

Here is another example:

The study of grammar is a worthwhile pursuit in and of itself without regard to utility. **Grammar** may be defined as the total structure of a language and not just as that aspect of language that has to do with correctness of expression. Students of **grammar** divide its study into three parts: phonology, morphology, and syntax. **Phonology** is the aspect of **grammar** that has to do with the sound structure, chiefly the vowel and consonant sounds. **Morphology** is the **grammatical** aspect that has to do with the formation of meaningful units out of individual sounds. For example, not only whole words but meaningful parts such as *ly, er, ed,* and so forth are part of the **grammar** of **morphology.** Finally, **syntax** is that aspect of **grammar** that has to do with the arrangement of words into meaningful patterns. That is, **syntax** has to do with **grammatical** structures. When one studies these three broad aspects of **grammar,** one is indulging in liberal education for its own sake and thus becomes a more educated person. **Grammar** is indeed worthy of study just as a field of knowledge.

The words in boldface in this example paragraph all represent the use of word repetition for coherence; none of them are uselessly repeated (though useless and awkward repetition of a word is possible). Such repetition serves to keep the reader's mind on the proper track so that he can read rapidly without losing his way. Without word repetition or other means of transition, a paragraph is likely to be vague and incoherent.

Pronoun Reference

Similar to repetition of key words is the use of pronoun reference to help effect coherence through transition. The use of a pronoun in one sentence to refer to a noun in the preceding sentence performs the same function as repetition of a key word. The pronoun signals to the reader's mind that a train of thought is being continued.

Here is an example:

> The library is the one indispensable building on a college campus. **It** is both the heart and the brain of the campus. Without **it,** a campus would die shortly. First, the library is essential to the students. **They** find there the materials they need for writing reports and term papers and for doing outside reading. **They** also find **it** the most convenient place to study. Second, the library is the nerve center for teachers. **They** must not only prepare **their** class materials with the aid of the library but must also keep up with new developments in **their** fields. **This** use of the library is so important that any good library must spend thousands of dollars just providing new books and magazines for the faculty to use. No serious student or teacher should regard the library lightly, for **it** is truly the center of the campus.

The boldface pronouns in this paragraph show how pronoun reference is an important transitional device. Each reference literally reaches back to the preceding sentence and ties it closely to the following sentence. Thus coherence is effected.

These three means of transition—the use of transitional words and phrases, the repetition of key words, the use of pronoun reference—are the main ones in effecting coherence. Generally, all three are present in a well-developed paragraph. Coherence can also be effected through more subtle ways, but in an elementary study of composition the above three methods suffice. If you will give more attention to them in your own writing, your paragraphs will be smoother and better developed. The simple clue to this use is to see that each sentence in a paragraph grows out of the preceding one. Any one of these three methods will produce such an effect. The trick is to keep in mind each preceding sentence as you are writing the next sentence. Then you provide a smooth flow of sentences that are coherent.

UNIT — topic sentence (paragraph)

A successful paragraph must not only be complete and coherent in its development but also unified. **Unity,** of course, means oneness, and the oneness that a good paragraph has derives from its development of one central topic, or main point. When a paragraph brings in material that does not relate directly to its topic sentence, it is disunified. Disunity brings a disruption of a paragraph that prevents the reader's mind from following the flow of ideas smoothly.

To maintain unity in your paragraphs, you need to develop an organization of main points. Then you need to develop only one main point in each paragraph. By far the most common source of disunity in paragraphs is the inclusion of more than one main point in one paragraph. The second main point disrupts the unity. Usually, in such a case the writer makes an attempt to develop only one (or even none) of the central ideas, leaving the other as a paragraph fragment within another paragraph. Here is an example based on the topic "Discuss the arguments against capital punishment."

Supporters of capital punishment maintain that it is necessary to deter criminals from committing more capital crimes, but there is no evidence that capital punishment acts as a deterrent. Furthermore, capital punishment is barbaric in its very concept. Deliberate killing for any purpose is vengeful only and is alien to civilized life. Rehabilitation should be the aim of all punishment for crime.

The writer of this paragraph had two main points to consider—capital punishment as (1) a false deterrent and (2) a barbaric vengefulness—but he failed to give them separate paragraph status. Thus he violated the unity of his paragraph. If he had prepared an organization of main points for his paper, he would have known enough to devote one paragraph to each main point.

Note that in this same disunified paragraph neither main point is given sufficient development. Usually, two incomplete paragraphs are merged when paragraph disunity is present. This makes the writing all the worse. The need for full development of paragraph topics cannot be overemphasized.

Maintaining paragraph coherence makes for paragraph unity. When each sentence of a paragraph flows directly from the preceding sentence, there is little opportunity for the writer to become sidetracked and to put in disunifying material. In fact, completeness, coherence, and unity all go together. When one of these aspects is violated, the others usually are also. The best way to protect against such violation is to make a good basic organization for each paper by deciding which main points to develop and then developing each main point fully in one paragraph. Use transitional devices between sentences to preserve paragraph unity by connecting each sentence to the preceding one.

EXERCISE 27A
Identifying Transitional Devices

Directions: The following paragraphs are coherent because of the use of transitional words and phrases, repetition of key words, and pronoun reference. Underline each of the three means of transition for effecting coherence. Be prepared to explain how each word or phrase you underline helps provide paragraph coherence.

1. Do not allow yourselves to be misled by the common notion that an hypothesis is untrustworthy simply because it is an hypothesis. It is often urged, in respect to some scientific conclusion, that, after all, it is only an hypothesis. But what more have we to guide us in nine-tenths of the most important affairs of daily life than hypotheses, and often very ill-based ones? So that in science, where the evidence of an hypothesis is subjected to the most rigid examination, we may rightly pursue the same course. You may have hypotheses and hypotheses. A man may say, if he likes, that the moon is made of green cheese: that is an hypothesis. But another man, who has devoted a great deal of time and attention to the subject, and availed himself of the most powerful telescopes and the results of the observations of others, declares that in his opinion it is probably composed of materials very similar to those of which our own earth is made up: and that is also an hypothesis. But I need not tell you that there is an enormous difference in the value of the two hypotheses. That one which is based on sound scientific knowledge is sure to have a corresponding value; and that which is a mere hasty random guess is likely to have but little value. [T. H. Huxley, "The Method of Scientific Investigation."]

2. Since, then, it is necessary for a prince to understand how to make good use of the conduct of the animals, he should select among them the fox and the lion, because the lion cannot protect himself from traps, and the fox cannot protect himself from the wolves. So the prince needs to be a fox that he may know how to deal with traps, and a lion that he may frighten the wolves. Those who act like the lion alone do not understand their business. A prudent ruler, therefore, cannot and should not observe faith when such observance is to his disadvantage and the causes that made him give his promise have vanished. If men were all good, this advice would not be good, but since men are wicked and do not keep their promises to you, you likewise do not have to keep yours to them. Lawful reasons to excuse his failure to keep them will never be lacking to a prince. It would be possible to give innumerable modern examples of this and to show many treaties and promises that have been made null and void by the faithlessness of princes. And the prince who has best known how to act as a fox has come out best. But one who has this capacity must understand how to keep it covered, and be a skillful pretender and dissembler. Men are so simple and so subject to present needs that he who deceives in this way will always find those who will let themselves be deceived. [Niccolo Machiavelli, *The Prince.*]

3.   This brings us to another kind of thought which can fairly easily be distinguished from the three kinds described above. It has not the usual qualities of the reverie, for it does not hover about our personal complacencies and humiliations. It is not made up of the homely decisions forced upon us by everyday needs, when we review our little stock of existing information, consult our conventional preferences and obligations, and make a choice of action. It is not the defense of our own cherished beliefs and prejudices just because they are our own—mere plausible excuses for remaining of the same mind. On the contrary, it is that peculiar species of thought which leads us to *change* our mind. [James Harvey Robinson, "On Various Kinds of Thinking."]

4.   An insect, therefore, is not afraid of gravity; it can fall without danger, and can cling to the ceiling with remarkably little trouble. It can go in for elegant and fantastic forms of support like that of the daddy longlegs. But there is a force which is as formidable to an insect as gravitation is to a mammal. This is surface tension. A man coming out of a bath carries with him a film of water about one fiftieth of an inch in thickness. This weighs roughly a pound. A wet mouse has to carry about its own weight of water. A wet fly has to lift many times its own weight and, as every one knows, a fly once wetted by water or any other liquid is in a very serious position indeed. An insect going for a drink is in as great danger as a man leaning out over a precipice in search of food. If it once falls into the grip of the surface tension of the water—that is to say, gets wet—it is likely to remain so until it drowns. A few insects, such as water beetles, contrive to be unwettable; the majority keep well away from their drink by means of a long proboscis. [J. B. S. Haldane, "On Being the Right Size."]

5.   The gangster movie, which no longer exists in its "classical" form, is a story of enterprise and success ending in precipitate failure. Success is conceived as an increasing power to work injury. It belongs to the city, and it is of course a form of evil (though the gangster's death, presented usually as "punishment," is perceived simply as defeat). The peculiarity of the gangster is his unceasing, nervous activity. The exact nature of his enterprises may remain vague, but his commitment to enterprise is always clear, and all the more clear because he operates outside the field of utility. He is without culture, without manners, without leisure, or at any rate his leisure is likely to be spent in debauchery so compulsively aggressive as to seem only another aspect of his "work." But he is graceful, moving like a dancer among the crowded dangers of the city. [Robert Warshow, "The Westerner."]

EXERCISE 27B
Analyzing Paragraph Disunity

Directions: Each of the following paragraphs is disunified. First explain why, and then suggest ways the resulting incomplete paragraphs could be made fuller with additional details. Space is provided for you to make notes for your answers.

1. *Topic:* Discuss the most notable characteristics of the so-called generation gap.

   The generation gap really exists. For example, teen-agers have a completely different attitude about sex from that of their parents. The parents are much more conservative. A difference in idealism also separates the generations. Young people are much more idealistic about politics and social problems than their parents.

   _____

   _____

   _____

   _____

2. *Topic:* Discuss the ingredients of pure love.

   Pure love calls for complete unselfishness. One who thinks of himself first cannot be wholly in love. Pure love calls for forgiveness. A devoted lover may momentarily be annoyed by his love's behavior, but he will always forgive it, no matter what it is. Also, as Shakespeare said, "Love is not love which alters when it alteration finds."

   _____

   _____

   _____

   _____

3. *Topic:* Discuss what you think about UFO's (Unidentified Flying Objects).

I feel that UFO's are definitely from another planet. Their speed and means of locomotion are certainly not of this planet, for neither Russia nor the USA has anything remotely resembling their design and speed. Also these objects have been spotted since the eighteenth century, and the earth did not have any flying machines at all back then.

———————————————————————————

———————————————————————————

———————————————————————————

———————————————————————————

4. *Topic:* Discuss your objections to Communism.

Another of my objections to Communism is its drive to bring revolution to other countries. Russia can have the government it wants, but it has no right to force other countries to become Communistic. I don't like their censorship of literature either. Fiction and poetry should be completely free from governmental interference.

———————————————————————————

———————————————————————————

———————————————————————————

———————————————————————————

5. *Topic:* Discuss the thought-provoking aspects of any novel you have read recently.

William Faulkner's *Intruder in the Dust* deals with several aspects of the race problem. Most notably, it shows the great dignity and integrity of Negroes in the character of Lucas Beauchamp. He conducts himself magnificently. It shows the nature of a lynch mob. Even though they have not proved Lucas guilty, the mob is trying to lynch him. The behavior of the mob is skillfully pictured.

———————————————————————————

———————————————————————————

———————————————————————————

———————————————————————————

PART 4

CONVENTIONAL USAGE

28

Sentence Sense and
Sentence Fragments

In Chapter 1 we defined **conventional usage** as that which *custom* dictates is proper for any particular segment of the population. **Standard usage** is the conventional usage considered correct by the educated segment of society. Most so-called **nonstandard usage** is perfectly grammatical and is good language for those who habitually use it in their communication with others who also use it. Nonstandard usage simply belongs to a dialect partly different from the so-called standard dialect, which is highly uniform in writing but which has variations in pronunciation. That is, an educated Alabaman and an educated Rhode Islander will use almost identical conventional usage in their writing but will vary somewhat in their pronunciation of many words. But for basic communication any dialect is as good as any other, for no dialect is linguistically superior to another. For example, *I ain't got no money* communicates just as clearly as *I haven't any money*, and its grammar can be just as easily analyzed.

We use standard conventional usage, then, for *social* and not linguistic reasons. People do make social judgments about the language usage of others, and anyone who departs very far from standard usage will find himself barred from many desirable jobs and perhaps from association with people whose group he would like to belong to. Thus though standard usage is arbitrary and is dictated by custom, its use is important to educated people. Hence this text has a part on conventional usage for use to the extent your instructor thinks necessary.

SENTENCE SENSE

Sentence sense is the ability to distinguish between a construction that is a sentence and thus can "stand alone," beginning with a capital letter and ending with a mark of end punctuation, and a construction that is not a complete sentence but is a fragment, or nonsentence. It might seem that we should have placed this chapter in PART 1: THE BASIC SYSTEM OF ENGLISH GRAMMAR, but since it is conventional to write in sentences, we have placed this chapter in Part 4

255

and will consider an unacceptable sentence fragment an error in conventional usage.

Some people develop sentence sense early and easily; others reach college without having fully developed it. (A study of grammar, such as is presented in Part 1 of this text, can greatly help one develop sentence sense.) A sentence must possess a subject and predicate,[1] but beyond that, sentence sense permits one to recognize the following intuitively:

1. That pronoun reference to a preceding sentence does not prevent a construction from being a sentence. For example, *she threw it to them* is a sentence even though *she, it,* and *them* do not carry their own meaning.
2. That reference of a verb auxiliary to a preceding sentence does not prevent a construction from being a sentence. For example, *I will if she can* is a sentence even though *will* and *can* (and *she,* too) must draw their meaning from a previous sentence.
3. That the reference of *so, thus, then,* and *there* to a preceding sentence does not prevent a construction from being a sentence. For example, *so was old Toby* is a sentence even though *so* must get its meaning from a previous sentence.
4. That beginning a construction with a coordinating connective (see Chapter 6) does not prevent it from being a sentence. For example, *and Sara did too* and *or an adze may be used* are sentences in spite of beginning with the coordinating conjunctions *and* and *or.*

On the other hand, sentence sense permits one to recognize the following intuitively:

1. That a construction without a subject and predicate is not a sentence. For example, *to be free as a bird* and *breaking his leg* are not sentences, though they carry much more meaning than *it could,* which is a sentence.
2. That a clause (which has a subject and predicate) beginning with a subordinating connective (see Chapter 7) is not a sentence. For example, *because Morris was ill* is not a sentence even though it contains much more meaning than *so did he,* which is a sentence. The subordinating conjunction *because* prevents the subject-predicate combination from being a sentence.

It is true that some writers in some kinds of writing use acceptable fragments, or nonsentences, but convention calls for the kind of writing you are studying to be composed in complete sentences. If you write fragments, your instructor is likely to grade your paper down.

SENTENCE FRAGMENTS

Most unacceptable **sentence fragments** in student writing are dependent clauses or phrases detached from sentences they should be attached to. Here are examples, with the sentence fragment italicized and with a corrected version of each:

[1] However, request or command sentences, such as *come inside* and *drink your beer,* do not have subjects. The understood *you* is in direct address, just as *Jane* is in *Jane, come on over.* But this kind of sentence never causes writing problems.

detached clause: I wanted a good report card to show my grandfather. *Because then he would be sure to give me some money.*

correct: I wanted a good report card to show my grandfather, because then he would be sure to give me some money.

detached clause: The scandals caused my father to change his voter registration. *Though he continued to vote for Republicans.*

correct: The scandals caused my father to change his voter registration, though he continued to vote for Republicans.

detached phrase: I would like to be a free spirit. *To soar like a bird.*

correct: I would like to be a free spirit, to be able to soar like a bird.

detached phrase: The chances of a nuclear war are high. *With so many tensions between the superpowers.*

correct: The chances of a nuclear war are high, with so many tensions between the superpowers.

The students who wrote the original sentences were somewhat deficient in sentence sense and thus did not see that they had given sentence status to non-sentences, or fragments.

The great majority of unacceptable fragments are detached phrases or clauses, though two other kinds of fragments occasionally occur. One of these is due to the use of a nonfinite rather than a finite verb form. A finite verb form is one that can function as a sentence verb, such as *has been injured,* and *is coming.* A nonfinite verb form cannot function as a sentence verb; examples are *having gone* and *being defeated.* A fragment occurs if a nonfinite verb form is used when a finite form is demanded. Example, with the nonfinite verb form italicized:

fragment: To keep your job, always be on time and *doing* the routine chores expected of you.

Change the nonfinite *doing* to the finite *do* and the fragment becomes a sentence.

And sometimes fragments occur because the writer lets his sentences become jumbled. Examples:

fragment: Professors, who should assign students independent study, but they don't think the students are capable.

fragment: Most students who cheat, because they are too lazy to study, which hurts them in the long run.

The student who wrote the first example did not provide a predicate to go with the subject *professors,* with a jumbled fragment resulting. He could have just omitted *but they* and produced a sentence. Similarly, the writer of the second example did not provide a predicate for the subject *most students who cheat;* he should have made the *which* clause a predicate, such as *only hurt themselves in the long run.* Students who compose such sentence fragments are either very careless or else are considerably deficient in sentence sense.

coordinating

↳ but, or, so, yet, and

29
The Comma Splice

The **comma splice** is an error in conventional usage often made by people who are deficient in sentence sense. Standard usage calls for a sentence to be ended with a mark of end punctuation (period, question mark, or exclamation point) or for a semicolon to be placed between two independent clauses, each of which could stand as a separate sentence, or for a coordinating conjunction (*and, but, yet, or, nor, for, so*) to join two independent clauses, usually with a comma before the conjunction. But when two independent clauses are separated with just a comma between them and no coordinating conjunction, they form a comma splice. Splicing two independent clauses with a comma is nonstandard usage and usually indicates insufficient sentence sense on the part of the writer. (Under certain circumstances, a comma splice may be acceptable, but rarely in the kind of writing you are studying.)

Quite often the second independent clause in a comma splice begins with *this, that, it,* or one of the conjunctive adverbs (see Chapter 6), for these words lead some writers to believe they are continuing a simple sentence when they are actually beginning a new independent clause. Here are some examples of comma splices:

> *comma splice:* I usually take a nap just after dinner, this then allows me to study late at night when my mind is clear.
> *comma splice:* Professor Knorl told his favorite joke for the fifth time, that made me decide not to take the second semester of his course.
> *comma splice:* A fuel-injection system is very complicated, it can't be worked on by just any mechanic.
> *comma splice:* I saved almost every dollar I made on my summer job, thus I was able to return to college with plenty of cash.
> *comma splice:* My father went on a drunken rampage again, however, this time it was he who left the house.

In each of these examples the comma splice can be corrected by changing the comma (the first comma in the last example) to a semicolon or by changing it to a period and beginning the second sentence with a capital letter. A writer must decide for himself which version produces the better style.

Having fully developed sentence sense is, of course, the best way to avoid writing comma splices. However, there is one good tip that should help you avoid the error when the two independent clauses are joined by one of the conjunctive adverbs. Most of the conjunctive adverbs (*hence, still,* and those expressing time are exceptions) can be shifted to the interior of the second independent clause. For example, the last two examples of comma splices above could be written correctly in this way:

> I saved almost every dollar I made on my summer job; I was **thus** able to return to college with plenty of cash.
>
> My father went on a drunken rampage again; this time, **however,** it was he who left the house.

Anytime such a shift can be made, a comma between the two clauses makes a comma splice. When the conjunctive adverb is shifted, sometimes it is set off on both sides by commas and sometimes not. When there is a distinct voice pause before and after it, it should be set off by commas. Also in such sentences, periods can be used instead of semicolons, with the second sentence then beginning with a capital letter.

Caution: Do not confuse the comma splice with a sentence that correctly has a dependent clause or a phrase set off by a comma. Examples:

> *correct:* Peterson had to find another job, because he was not reelected to the legislature.
>
> *correct: Sanctuary* is a high-quality novel, not just sensational trash.
>
> *correct:* War will break out again in the Near East, unless one side will abandon some of its demands.

The constructions after the commas in these sentences are not independent clauses, and thus no comma splices are created.

30
Spelling

There is less disagreement about spelling than about any other aspect of conventional usage. A few words have two acceptable spellings, but for the most part spelling is fixed and standardized. However, English spelling is to a considerable degree irregular, and thus many people have spelling problems. If you are one of these people, careful study of this chapter should clear up many of your problems.

SPELLING BY SYLLABLES

You can eliminate many of your spelling problems by learning to sound out syllables carefully and individually. Such a practice is particularly useful in spelling long words. For example, instead of thinking of *appropriate* as just a long sequence of letters, think of it as four syllables and spell each of them separately in sequence: *ap-pro-pri-ate*. Then the word will not seem so imposing.

In spelling by syllables, it is often useful to use a *spelling pronunciation*—that is, a pronunciation suited to the spelling rather than the normal pronunciation. For example, consider the word *approximate*. Its normal pronunciation is something like this: *uh-prox-suh-mit*. Such a pronunciation does not tell you that the word has two *p*'s or that the third syllable is an *i* or that the last syllable ends in *ate*. But you can give the word a spelling pronunciation: *ap-prox-i-mate*. And after you get used to exaggerating the pronunciation in order to spell the word, you will spell it correctly from habit and will not have to think about it any more.

Following is a list of frequently misspelled words. Learn them by syllables, as printed. If necessary, deliberately exaggerate the pronunciation for spelling purposes.

ac-cel-er-ate	a-chieve-ment	al-to-ge-ther
ac-ci-dent-al-ly	ac-quaint-ance	am-a-teur
ac-com-mo-date	ad-dress	an-a-lyze
ac-cu-rate	ad-van-ta-geous	a-pol-o-gize

ap-pa-rent
ap-pear-ance
ap-pe-tite
ap-pro-pri-ate
ap-prox-i-mate-**ly**
ar-gu-ment
ar-range-ment
ath-lete
at-tacked
at-tend-ance
au-di-ence
bar-gain
beau-ti-ful
ben-e-fit-ed
breathe
bul-le-tin
ca-len-dar
can-di-date
cat-e-go-ry
cem-e-ter-y
change-able
char-ac-ter-is-tic
col-umn
com-mit-tee
com-pe-ti-tion
com-plete-ly
con-demn
con-quer
con-science
con-sci-en-tious
con-scious
con-trol
con-ven-ience
cor-ner
coun-sel-or
cour-a-geous
cour-te-ous
cri-ti-cism
cur-i-os-i-ty
de-ci-sion
de-fi-nite-ly
de-fi-ni-tion
de-scribe
de-scrip-tion
de-sert
des-pair
des-per-ate

des-sert
de-stroy
dis-ap-pear
dis-ap-point
dis-as-trous
dis-ci-pline
dis-ease
dis-sat-is-fied
di-vi-sion
eas-i-ly
eighth
e-lim-i-nate
em-bar-rass
em-pha-size
en-vi-ron-ment
e-quip-ment
es-pe-cial-ly
ex-ag-ger-ate
ex-cel-ent
ex-haust-ed
ex-is-tence
ex-per-i-ence
ex-pla-na-tion
fas-ci-na-ting
Feb-ru-a-ry
fi-nal-ly
for-eign
for-mal-ly
for-mer-ly
gen-er-al-ly
gov-ern-ment
guar-an-tee
guard
hand-ker-chief
hap-pi-ness
hin-drance
hum-or-ous
i-mag-i-na-tion
im-me-di-ate-ly
in-ci-den-tal-ly
in-de-pen-dent
in-tel-li-gence
in-ter-est-ing
in-ter-fere
in-ter-pret
in-ter-rupt
jeal-ous

know-ledge
lab-or-a-to-**ry**
lei-sure
li-bra-ry
li-cense
light-ning
lit-er-al-ly
lit-er-a-ture
lone-li-ness
main-ten-ance
mar-riage
math-e-ma-tics
med-i-cine
mis-cel-lan-e-**ous**
mis-spell
mus-cle
mys-ter-i-ous
na-tur-al-ly
ne-ces-sar-i-**ly**
nick-el
no-tice-able
now-a-days
ob-sta-cle
oc-ca-sion-al-**ly**
oc-cur-rence
op-er-ate
o-pin-ion
op-por-tun-i-ty
op-po-site
pam-phlet
pa-ral-lel
par-tic-u-lar
part-ner
pas-time
pa-tient
pe-cu-liar
per-form
per-sis-tent
per-suade
phys-i-cal-**ly**
prac-ti-cal-ly
pre-cede
pref-er-ence
pre-ferred
pre-ju-dice
pre-par-a-tion
prin-ci-pal

prin-ci-ple
pri-son-er
pri-vi-lege
pro-ba-bly
pro-ce-dure
pro-ceed
pro-fes-sor
pro-nun-ci-a-tion
psy-cho-lo-gy
pur-sue
qual-i-ty
quan-ti-ty
re-al-ize
re-ceipt
re-ci-pe
re-cog-nize
re-com-mend
re-li-gious
re-mem-brance
re-pe-ti-tion

re-sist-ance
res-tau-rant
rhythm
ri-di-cu-lous
sac-ri-fice
sand-wich
scen-er-y
sched-ule
se-cre-ta-ry
seize
se-mes-ter
ser-geant
ser-vice-able
sev-er-al
se-vere-ly
sin-cere-ly
soph-o-more
spe-ci-men
sta-tion-ary
sta-tion-ery

strength
stretch
suf-fi-cient
su-per-in-ten-dent
sup-press
su-spi-cion
sym-pa-thy
tem-per-a-ment
tho-rough
Tues-day
un-doubt-ed-ly
un-ne-ces-sary
val-ley
val-u-able
va-ri-e-ty
vi-gor-ous
Wed-nes-day (pro-
  nounced as two
  syllables)
weird

SPELLING WORDS WITH PREFIXES AND SUFFIXES

Many of the words in the preceding list have prefixes and suffixes. You can learn to spell them without thinking about the affixes (the word *affix* means both prefixes and suffixes), but you will improve your spelling ability if you are aware that many English words are built out of root words plus affixes. For example, most students can spell the word *usual,* but a surprisingly large percentage misspell the word *unusually.* Those who misspell the word fail to understand that it is built out of a root plus affixes: First you have *usual;* out of that you build *un-usual;* and out of that you build *un-usual-ly.* It is really a simple word to spell if you understand how it is built. And so with many other English words.

The following short list shows how many English words are built:

knowledge—ac-knowledge—ac-knowledg-ment
press—re-press—re-press-ible—ir-re-press-ible
approve—dis-approve—dis-approv-ing—disapprov-ing-ly
collect—re-collect—re-collect-ion
commend—re-commend—re-commend-ation
regular—ir-regular—ir-regular-ly
necessary—un-necessary—un-necessari-ly
lone—lone-ly—lone-li-ness
happy—un-happy—un-happi-ly—un-happi-ness
manner—manner-ly—un-manner-ly
frequent—in-frequent—in-frequent-ly
sufficient—in-sufficient—in-sufficient-ly
employ—employ-ment—un-employ-ment

grace—grace-ful—un-grace-ful—un-grace-ful-ly
person—person-al—person-al-ly—im-person-al-ly
cease—ceas-ing—un-ceas-ing—un-ceas-ing-ly
beauty—beauti-ful—beauti-ful-ly
complete—in-complete—in-complete-ly
advantage—advantage-ous—dis-advantage-ous—dis-advantage-ous-ly
respect—dis-respect—dis-respect-ful—dis-respect-ful-ly

These 20 examples illustrate the process. The more you become aware of the way words are bulit in English, the better you will spell. It is valuable not only to sound out the syllables but also to understand when you are adding affixes to root words.

SPELLING BY RULES

There are five important spelling rules in English. They cover many of the most frequently misspelled words—for the most part simple words. Almost every writer finds these rules indispensable. Therefore if you do not already know them, you should *memorize* and *use* them.

The *ie, ei* rule. *Place i before e when pronounced as ee except after c; place e before i when pronounced as a long a.*

This rule covers the troublesome *ie* and *ei* combinations when the two letters together are pronounced as a long *e* or long *a*. The rule does not cover such words as *science, atheist,* and *foreign,* for the *ie* or *ei* in such words are not pronounced together as a single *e* or long *a*.
Examples:

achieve	conceit	freight
brief	deceit	neighbor
chief	receipt	reins
tier	receive	weight

You can manage five troublesome exceptions to the rule by memorizing this nonsense sentence:

Neither sheik seized weird leisure.

All five words have an *ei* combination pronounced as a long *e* but not preceded by a *c*. (A few other exceptions give no trouble at all.) Exercise 30A lists the most important *ie* and *ei* words.

The dropping-of-the-final-silent-e rule. *Drop a final silent e when adding a suffix beginning with a vowel.*

Here are a few examples of this simple rule:

dine + ing = dining
create + ive = creative
imagine + ative = imaginative
mange + y = mangy

The silent *e* is not dropped when a suffix beginning with a consonant is added. Examples:

like—likeness   safe—safety
fate—fateful   hate—hateful
complete—completely late—lately

Try pronouncing the words without the silent *e*, and you will see that you have pronunciations such as *fat-ful* and *saf-ty*. The following words, however, are exceptions to this part of the rule:

whole + ly = wholly
true + ly = truly
acknowledge + ment = acknowledgment
judge + ment = judgment
awe + ful = awful
argue + ment = argument

The retention-of-the-silent-e rule. *When a word ends in a silent* e *preceded by* c *or* g, *retain the* e *when adding* able *or* ous.

The reason for this rule is that the *e* must be retained in order to keep the soft sound of *c* (that is, *s* instead of *k*) and the soft sound of *g* (that is, *j* instead of *guh*). For example, if the *e* were dropped in *notice + able*, the result would be *noticable*, which would be pronounced *no-tik-able*, instead of the proper *note-iss-able*.

Here are a few examples of the rule being applied:

notice + able = noticeable
peace + able = peaceable
courage + ous = courageous
advantage + ous = advantageous

The y-to-i rule. *Change the* y *to* i *when adding a suffix to a word ending in* y *preceded by a consonant.*

When one follows this rule to make the plural of nouns or the third person singular of verbs, the *y* is changed to *i* and an *es* (or *ed*) is added:

baby—babies   deny—denies—denied
lady—ladies   fry—fries—fried
harpy—harpies   try—tries—tried

The rule operates with many other kinds of suffixes, however. Here are some examples:

busy + ness = business   easy + ly = easily
cry + er = crier   necessary + ly = necessarily
dry + est = driest   lonely + ness = loneliness

The rule does not apply when *ing* or *ist* is added to a word:

study + ing = studying
deny + ing = denying
worry + ing = worrying
copy + ist = copyist

When the final *y* of a word is preceded by a vowel, the *y* is *not* changed when a suffix is added:

annoy + s = annoys
convey + ed = conveyed
valley + s = valleys
donkey + s = donkeys
stay + ed = stayed

There are a number of common exceptions to this part of the rule:

lay + ed = laid
pay + ed = paid
say + ed = said
day + ly = daily
gay + ly = gaily

The *y*-to-*i* rule does not apply in spelling the plural of proper names:

Brady + s = Bradys
Crowly + s = Crowlys
Kennedy + s = Kennedys

The doubling-of-the-final-consonant rule. *When adding a suffix beginning with a vowel to a word accented on the last syllable and ending in one consonant preceded by one vowel, double the final consonant.*

This is the most complicated and probably the most important of the spelling rules. It is based on a very important phonetic principle in English spelling. The principle is this: *In a vowel-consonant-vowel sequence the first vowel, if accented, is long; in a vowel-consonant-consonant or a vowel-final-consonant sequence, the vowel is short.* In the following examples, the vowels in the accented syllables in the first column of words are long, and the vowels in the second column of words are short:

rate	rat
rote	rot
bite	bit
interfere	refer
cured	occurred
scared	scarred
interfered	preferred

The long vowel sounds in the first column are due to the vowel-consonant-vowel sequence. The short vowel sounds in the second column are due to the vowel being followed by two consonants or by one consonant at the end of the word. This phonetic principle accounts for the doubling of the final consonant.

The rule is complicated. You should get all of its parts in mind. These conditions must be present:

1. You must be adding a suffix beginning with a vowel, such as *ing, ed, er, est,* and so forth.
2. The word must be of one syllable or be accented on the last syllable, such as *refér, compél, occúr,* and so on.

3. The word must end in one consonant preceded by one vowel, such as *admit, debar,* and *slap.* If the word ends in two consonants or if the final consonant is preceded by two vowels, the rule does not apply (*equip* is an exception).

When these three conditions are present, you double the final consonant. Here are some examples:

occur + ed = occurred	omit + ing = omitting
refer + ing = referring	red + est = reddest
stop + ed = stopped	scrub + er = scrubber

Note what the pronunciation of the words would be if the final consonants were not doubled. For example, if there were only one *r* in *occurred,* it would rhyme with *cured.* Or if there were only one *r* in *referring,* it would rhyme with *interfering.*

If the last syllable of a word is not accented, the consonant is not doubled when a suffix beginning with a vowel is added: Examples:

banter + ing = bantering
happen + ed = happened
prohibit + ed = prohibited

Similarly, the final consonant is never doubled if a suffix beginning with a consonant is added. Examples:

glad + ness = gladness
sin + ful = sinful

SPELLING BY MNEMONIC DEVICES

Most good spellers use **associational clues** to help them spell troublesome words—that is, they associate the spelling of the word with something they can easily remember. For example, it is easy to remember that *attendance* ends in *ance* if you associate the word with "attending a dance." Clues of this sort that aid our memories are called mnemonic devices, from a Greek word meaning memory. They are valuable aids in spelling troublesome words.

Following is a list of particularly troublesome words with associational clues to help you remember how to spell them. You can also invent private clues for words that happen to give you trouble.

across—Christ died on *a cross.*
a lot—Think of buying a lot; so avoid *alot.*
amateur—Think of *a mate u r.*
attendance—Think of *attend dance* and so use *ance.*
bargain—There is a *gain* in a bargain.
battalion—Think of a *battle* against *a lion.*
breakfast—It is literally to break a fast.
bulletin—Who put a *bullet in* the bulletin?
calendar—Think of calend*ar art.*
courtesy—It is a habit with those who *court.*
definite—It comes from *finite.*

dessert—It has two *s*'s, like strawberry shortcake.

disease—It literally means *dis ease*.

embarrass—Remember two *r*'s and two *s*'s.

familiar—Think of a *fami* (whatever that is) *liar*.

forty—It is not pronounced like *four*.

grammar—The *rammar* part is spelled the same both ways.

handkerchief—You use your hand to pull out your kerchief.

holiday—It comes from *holy* and so has only one *l*.

occurrence—It has *rre* as in *current* event.

peculiar—Think of a *pecu liar*.

principal—The principal of a school is a *pal* to you.

principle—It means rule and ends in *le*.

rhythm—Remember the *rh-th* sequence.

separate—It's hard to spell; therefore there is *a rat* in it.

stationery—It means paper and ends in *er* like *paper*.

tragedy—There is a *rage* in tragedy.

EXERCISE 30A
The *ie, ei* Spelling Rule

Directions: Following the *i-e* spelling rule (and exceptions), fill in the missing letters in the following words.

1. ach_____ve

2. bel_____ve

3. br_____f

4. c_____ling

5. ch_____f

6. conc_____t

7. conc_____ve

8. dec_____t

9. dec_____ve

10. f_____ld

11. fr_____ght

12. gr_____f

13. l_____n

14. inv_____gh

15. inv_____gle

16. l_____sure

17. n_____gh

18. n_____ghbor

19. n_____ce

20. perc_____ve

21. pr_____st

22. rec_____ve

23. rec_____pt

24. r_____gn

25. r_____ns

26. rel_____f

27. rel_____ve

28. s_____ze

29. sh_____ld

30. s_____ge

31. th_____f

32. w_____ght

33. w_____ld

34. w_____rd

35. y_____ld

EXERCISE 30B
The Silent e Spelling Rules

Directions: Build the following words as indicated.

1. write + ing = _____

2. change + able = _____

3. service + able = _____

4. dine + ing = _____

5. come + ing = _____

6. shine + ing = _____

7. arrange + able = _____

8. condole + ence = _____

9. peeve + ish = _____

10. love + able = _____

11. whole + ly = _____

12. argue + ment = _____

13. safe + ly = _____

14. use + ful = _____

15. care + less = _____

16. pursue + ing = _____

17. complete + ly = _____

18. use + ing = _____

19. love + ly = _____

20. guide + ance = _____

21. improve + ment = _____

22. sincere + ly = _____

23. sure + ly = _____

24. trace + able = _____

25. outrage + ous = _____

26. venge + ance = _____

27. argue + ing = _____

28. charge + able = _____

29. fame + ous = _____

30. shine + y = _____

31. scare + ed = _____

32. dine + ed = _____

33. late + ly = _____

34. immediate + ly = _____

35. approximate + ly = _____

36. true + ly = _____

37. awe + ful = _____

38. interfere + ing = _____

39. pure + ly = _____

40. rage + ing = _____

EXERCISE 30C
The y-to-i Spelling Rule

Directions: Following the y-to-i spelling rule, build the following words as indicated.

1. deny + al = _____

2. mercy + ful = _____

3. carry + er = _____

4. carry + ing = _____

5. play + ed = _____

6. rely + ance = _____

7. copy + ed = _____

8. copy + ist = _____

9. try + al = _____

10. modify + er = _____

11. defy + s = _____

12. defy + ing = _____

13. kindly + ness = _____

14. enjoy + s = _____

15. fly + s = _____

16. study + ous = _____

17. delay + ed = _____

18. employ + s = _____

19. lonely + ness = _____

20. busy + est = _____

21. study + ing = _____

22. happy + ness = _____

23. greedy + er = _____

24. lovely + ness = _____

25. necessary + ly = _____

26. pay + ed = _____

27. beauty + ful = _____

28. hurry + ed = _____

29. day + ly = _____

30. busy + ness = _____

31. ready + ness = _____

32. alley + s = _____

33. ally + s = _____

34. worry + ing = _____

35. rely + s = _____

36. worry + er = _____

37. duty + ful = _____

38. bury + ed = _____

39. Grady + s = _____

40. Kennedy + s = _____

EXERCISE 30D
The Doubling-of-the-Final-Consonant Spelling Rule

Directions: Build the following words as indicated. *Both the dropping-of-the-silent-e rule and the doubling-of-the-final-consonant rule are to be followed in this exercise.*

1. occur + ed = _____

2. interfere + ed = _____

3. refer + ed = _____

4. honor + able = _____

5. omit + ing = _____

6. disbar + ed = _____

7. hinder + ed = _____

8. begin + ing = _____

9. come + ing = _____

10. din + ing = _____

11. dine + ing = _____

12. bid + ing = _____

13. bide + ing = _____

14. benefit + ed = _____

15. equip + ing = _____

16. concur + ed = _____

17. note + ing = _____

18. rot + ing = _____

19. confer + ed = _____

20. sin + er = _____

21. big + est = _____

22. big + ness = _____

23. drop + ed = _____

24. droop + ed = _____

25. red + en = _____

26. red + ness = _____

27. abandon + ed = _____

28. firm + er = _____

29. war + ing = _____

30. war + fare = _____

31. bite + ing = _____

32. bit + en = _____

33. fog + y = _____

34. submit + ing = _____

35. differ + ing = _____

36. transfer + ed = _____

37. suffer + ed = _____

38. regret + able = _____

39. offer + ed = _____

40. hate + ing = _____

41. bat + ing = _____

42. stop + ed = _____

31

The Use of
the Apostrophe

The apostrophe is a spelling device, not a mark of punctuation. For the most part it is used in contractions and in certain constructions showing possession. Unlike other aspects of English spelling, it has no irregularities or exceptions in its use. Therefore if you will learn the basic principles of its use, you can avoid misspellings due to faulty use or omission of the apostrophe.

THE USE OF THE APOSTROPHE IN CONTRACTIONS

Using apostrophes correctly in contractions is mostly just a matter of not carelessly omitting the mark. The simple rule is that an apostrophe is entered wherever one or more letters are omitted from a word, as in these examples:

don't	I'd
can't	you've
o'clock	we'll

Dates written in numerals are also often contracted:

I bought a '66 Ford.
The depth of the Depression was reached in '32.

The apostrophe is also used to show omitted letters in constructions that are not true contractions, as in reported dialogue. Example:

"Somethin' funny 'uz goin' on," the hillbilly said.

THE USE OF THE APOSTROPHE IN POSSESSIVE CONSTRUCTIONS

In proper and common nouns. There are two ways to show possession in English: (1) with the so-called possessive construction and (2) with the use of an *of* phrase or *belonging to* phrase. Here are examples:

Bill's car *or* the car belonging to Bill
My mother *or* the mother belonging to me
The dean's office *or* the office of the dean

When we show possession with an *of* or *belonging to* phrase, we do not use an apostrophe. And when we use a personal possessive pronoun, we do not use an apostrophe. But when we use a proper name or a common noun in the possessive construction, we do use an apostrophe. The problem is to learn when to use an apostrophe and where to place it.

Most people usually just learn to sense when the possessive construction is necessary and to know it instinctively. Others have some trouble recognizing it. When in doubt, you can make a test. If the construction you suspect is a possessive can be transformed into an *of* or *belonging to* phrase, it is a possessive and needs an apostrophe (unless a personal possessive pronoun is used). Here are some examples of the transformation:

The teacher's rollbook = the rollbook of the teacher
John's typewriter = the typewriter belonging to John
the car's transmission = the transmission of the car
The President's power = the power of the President
a sheep's fleece = the fleece of a sheep

Since the phrases in the first column can be transformed, they are all possessive constructions and require apostrophes. *You should learn to test all doubtful situations in this way.*

With this test you can tell not only whether an apostrophe is needed but also where to place it. When you make the *of* or *belonging to* phrase transformation, you have a **base noun** at the end of it. In the following examples the base nouns are in boldface:

Helen's new dress = new dress belonging to **Helen**
James' brother = brother of **James**
The dean's office = the office of the **dean**
Mr. Jones' car = car belonging to **Mr. Jones**
The Joneses' house = house belonging to the **Joneses**
the men's mountain party = mountain party of the **men**
a man's watch = watch belonging to a **man**

The rule for spelling possessives, then, is this: *If the base noun (plural or singular) does not end in s, you add an 's to it in a possessive construction. If the base noun (singular or plural) already ends in s, you just add an ' in the possessive construction.* When in doubt, use the simple test and you should never go wrong.

One additional point: If the base noun ends in *s* and is singular, you may add either just an ' or an 's. If the base noun ends in *s* and is plural, then you may add only an '. Examples:

James' (*or* James's)book
Mr. Jones' (*or* Jones's) house
Thomas' (*or* Thomas's) sweetheart
the Joneses' house (*never* the Joneses's house)

Here are some examples of the test in action:

six sheeps fleece = fleece of six **sheep**

Therefore the correct spelling is

six sheep's fleece

since the base noun does not end in *s*.

The watchs minute hand = minute hand of the **watch**

Therefore the correct spelling is

watch's mniute hand

since the base noun does not end in *s*.

James homework = homework belonging to **James**

Therefore the correct spelling is

James' (*or* James's) homework

since the base noun already ends in *s*.

the Thomases children = children belinging to the **Thomases**

Therefore the correct spelling is

the Thomases' children

since the base noun already ends in *s*.

You should be sure to distinguish between making the simple plural of a proper name and the possessive construction. Remember that to make the plural of a noun that already ends in *s* you add *es*. In the following sentence, the proper name is a simple plural.

The Joneses live on Tenth Street.

Note that you have just added *es* to a name already ending in *s* (Jones). Also note that the pronoun you would substitute is *they*, which shows that the word is a simple plural. If the pronoun you would substitute is *their*, then you have a possessive construction, which calls for an apostrophe. For example:

The Joneses' dog visited us.

Note that you would substitute *their*, not *they*. You have first made a name plural by adding *es* and then you have made it possessive by adding an '. The pronunciation does not change, but the spelling does.

Remember that you *never* use an apostrophe with personal possessive pronouns. Following is a list of the possessive pronouns that you might be tempted to spell with an apostrophe. *Never* do so.

yours	its
theirs	whose
hers	ours

You would not use an apostrophe with *his* or *mine*, so you would not use one with the above words, which are equivalent to *his* and *mine*.

Note especially the difference between *its* and *it's* and *whose* and *who's*. *It's* and *who's* are contractions meaning *it is* or *it has* and *who is* or *who has*. It is a very low-level misspelling to confuse these words. You can always test for the contraction. If the meaning is *it is* or *it has* or *who is* or *who has*, then you need an apostrophe for the contraction. If the meaning is possessive (*belonging to it* or *belonging to whom*), then you *do not* need an apostrophe.

In indefinite pronouns. The following words are called indefinite pronouns:

one	anybody
no one	everybody
anyone	somebody
everyone	nobody
someone	

When one of these words shows possession, it is spelled with an 's just like an ordinary noun. You can test with an *of* or *belonging to* phrase:

nobody's business = business of **nobody**

Therefore the correct spelling is

nobody's business

since the base word does not end in s. And so with all of the indefinite pronouns. You can just remember that when the *one* and *body* (except *one* itself) words end in an *s* sound, the spelling should be 's. (There can be exceptions to this, but they will never occur in your normal writing.)

The phrase *somebody else* can also be used in the possessive construction. Then an 's is added to the *else*. Example:

somebody elses car = car belonging to **somebody else**

Therefore the correct spelling is

somebody else's car

since the base word does not end in s.

In words naming periods of time and sums of money. Though, strictly speaking, a period of time or a sum of money cannot own something else, English uses possessive constructions with such words, and apostrophes must be used in the spelling of such constructions. You can use the *of phrase* test for these constructions. Examples:

a months vacation = vacation of a **month**

Therefore the correct spelling is

a month's vacation

since the base word does not end in s.

two months vacation = vacation of two **months**

Therefore the correct spelling is

two months' vacation

since the base word already ends in *s*. Note that the pronunciation is the same but that the spelling is different.

Here are examples with sums of money:

one dollars worth = worth of one **dollar**

Therefore the correct spelling is

one dollar's worth

since the base noun does not end in *s*.

two dollars worth = worth of two **dollars**

Therefore the correct spelling is

two dollars' worth

since the base noun already ends in *s*. Again, the pronunciation is the same, but the spelling is different.

Practice in using the *of* or *belonging to* transformation. The following constructions are mixed. Transform those that are possessive and put an apostrophe in the proper place in the original. Write "No transformation possible" after the constructions that are not possessive. An *es* in parentheses is for pronunciation only and not a part of the spelling.

1. the Harrises distillery _____

2. Mr. Harris(es) moonshine _____

3. the Harrises with the Smiths _____

4. The Harrises children arrived. _____

5. somebody elses fault _____

6. a quarters value _____

7. Februarys weather _____

8. the Munozes horse _____

9. the Bradys supplier _____

10. the Munozes of Tenth Street _____

11. three dollars difference _____

12. a dimes value _____

13. five dollars owed to Joe _____

14. six Tuesdays in a row _____

15. last Tuesdays lesson _____

16. Luis(es) piano _____

17. the Lewises in trouble _____

18. my boss(es) temper _____

19. several bosses at work _____

20. your two cents worth _____

EXERCISE 31
The Use of the Apostrophe

Directions: In the blanks provided write the correct spelling of the word in parentheses beneath the blank.

1. _____ car
      (James)

2. the _____ toys
        (children)

3. one _____ difference
        (nickel)

4. three _____ difference
          (cents)

5. _____ mistake
      (somebody)

6. the _____ roots
        (tree)

7. the _____ leaves
        (trees)

8. _____ coming
      (who)

9. _____ books
      (who)

10. an _____ delay
         (hour)

11. three _____ wait
           (hour)

12. the _____ house
         (Jones)

13. Mr. _____ house
    (Jones)

14. the _____ are waiting
    (Jones)

15. _____ book
    (someone)

16. _____ niece
    (Betty)

17. the _____ end
    (year)

18. _____ friend
    (anybody)

19. _____ enemy
    (no one)

20. the _____ of the company
    (boss)

21. the _____ boss
    (company)

22. three _____ cubs
    (lioness)

23. Mr. _____ office
    (Gillis)

24. the _____ children
    (Gillis)

25. the _____ husbands
    (women)

32

Capitalization

Though professional writers vary somewhat in their use of capital letters, the following rules are standard and will give you acceptable guidance. A small letter is known as a lowercase letter.

Rule 1. *Capitalize the first word and all other words except articles, short prepositions, and coordinating conjunctions in a title heading. When quoting a passage, use the author's capitalization exactly.*

> *title of a book:* The Rise and Fall of the Third Reich
> *title of an essay:* "Sound and Sense in Poetry"
> *chapter heading:* The Status of Women in the Nineteenth Century
> *quotation:* "On that issue Nixon claimed Executive privilege."—*Time Magazine*

Rule 2. *Capitalize all proper names and adjectives formed from proper names.*

Asia	England	Plato	Hollywoodish
Asian	English	Platonic	Oriental

Rule 3. *Capitalize references to the Deity, the names of divine books of all religions, and references to specific religions and religious sects.*

our Lord	Baptist	Bible	the Trinity
His creation	Jewish	Koran	New Testament
Vishnu	Lutherans	the Upanishads	Catholic

Rule 4. *Capitalize the titles of relatives when used with the person's name and when the person is addressed directly, but do not capitalize such titles when used with a possessive pronoun such as* my.

Aunt Margaret	"Oh, Mother, can you come here?"
Grandfather Hughes	Your father is a wizard.

Rule 5. *Capitalize the title of any official when the title immediately precedes the official's name; capitalize the name of a very important official even when his or her name is not mentioned.*

Mayor Karlin   the President (of the United States)
Vice-President Coe   the Senator (of the U.S. Senate)
Captain Castro   the Queen (of England)

Rule 6. *Capitalize the days of the week and the months of the year but not the seasons.*

Tuesday   February   summer   autumn

Rule 7. *Capitalize the names of streets, parks, rivers, specific mountains, cities, states, provinces, nations, continents, oceans, lakes, and specific geographic regions; but do not capitalize the names of directions.*

Todd Avenue	Central Park	the Red River	Mount Whitney
Memphis	Maine	Quebec	Chad
Europe	the Arctic Ocean	Ming Lake	the West Coast
the Midwest	the Near East	the Orient	south (a direction)

Rule 8. *Capitalize the names of buildings.*

the Bijou Theater   the Capitol   the Fine Arts Building

Rule 9. *Capitalize the names of governmental and private organizations.*

the Veterans Administration   the American Legion
The United States Navy   the Lions Club
Congress   the Renegade Knights

Rule 10. *Capitalize the names of historical documents, events, and periods or eras. Do not capitalize the names of centuries.*

the Constitution	the Battle of Midway	the Renaissance
the Bill of Rights	the Diet of Worms	the Second Coming
World War I	the Middle Ages	the eighth century

Rule 11. *Capitalize the names of specific heavenly bodies but not the words* earth, world, sun, moon, galaxy, *and* universe.

Venus   Phobos   Arcturus   the Milky Way   Orion

Rule 12. *Capitalize the names of specific school courses but not of general subject matter areas (unless some other rule calls for capitalization).*

History 3A   history (no course name)
American Literature Since 1865   American literature (in general)

Rule 13. *Capitalize brand names but not the name of the product.*

a Ford car   Camay soap   Atlas tires   Crest toothpaste

Rule 14. *Do not capitalize the names of foods, games, diseases, occupations, animals, plants, or musical instruments. Sometimes, however, a proper name is part of the whole name and should be capitalized.*

tamale	golf	mumps	doctor	an African violet
violets	violin	Hodgkin's disease		cheetah

EXERCISE 32
Capitalization

Directions: In the following sentences encircle incorrectly used capital and lowercase letters. Encircle the letters only, not whole words.

1. After talking to professor wordsmut, i decided to enroll in principles of accounting and some other course in business administration.

2. The culprit was apprehended in the fox theater, which is on second avenue near the sill building.

3. The violin is an instrument that must be played very well or not at all, says major Snuffley; but my Teacher thinks anyone can make some kind of Music.

4. Some Birds fly south for the winter, but when they get to the south in the United States they usually want to go farther south.

5. The state department is part of the executive Branch of the Government, but the secretary of state often ignores the president's orders.

6. While I was talking to the secretary of state, the president interrupted in order to pass on some important News.

7. When i had the Measles, doctor wetsleeve prescribed aloran tablets, which are manufactured by pfelzer & company.

8. An english class can help you in courses such as History 17A and even in subjects like Art and Sociology.

9. My Father was raised as a baptist, but since reading the upanishads he has a strong liking for eastern religions.

10. I think uncle oscar lived with my grandfather until he was sent to an Orphanage operated by the methodist church.

11. In introduction to philosophy we spent most of our time on platonic ideas, which are contained in plato's various Dialogues.

12. Members of the american legion want a literal interpretation of the constitution, just as Fundamentalists want a literal interpretation of the bible.

13. In pre-columbian times the Western hemisphere was the site of several Civilizations, notably that of the incas.

14. In Spring the Robins return to the north, just as tourists do from Miami beach.

15. The sierra Madres are a Mountain Chain in mexico that are somewhat similar to the rocky mountains in alaska.

16. My Doctor is an Atheist, he says; but just the same he winds up in Church on sundays.

17. Most southerners prefer the term *war between the states* to the term *civil war*.

18. The american contract bridge league has several Officers who belong to the famous cavendish club in New York city.

19. If god's will is truly revealed in the bible, then we should study each Book carefully so that we can follow his will.

20. The Third Chapter of *mission to metlakatla* is entitled "a dangerous but successful voyage."

21. The Veterans of foreign wars is an Organization started by Veterans of world war II, but now is open to veterans of the Korean war and the Vietnam war.

22. The antarctic ocean is really an extension of the pacific, for only small islands separate them.

23. My Brother-in-Law, colonel Miller, lives with his Relatives in ohio.

24. If you have studied latin in High School, you will find college courses in french and spanish easy.

25. The chapter I like most in our History book is entitled "plain Men and fancy Women."

33

The Use of the Hyphen

The **hyphen** (-), which is not as long as a dash (—), is a mark used in spelling; it is not a mark of punctuation. Following are rules for its use.

Rule 1. *Use a hyphen to divide a word at the end of a line and hyphenate only between syllables.* Never divide a word of one syllable, such as *ten-th* and *sli-nk*. Do not divide a word so that a one-letter syllable—such as *a-moral* and *slim-y*—is left at the end or beginning of a line. Any good dictionary gives the syllabication of words of more than one syllable.

Rule 2. *Hyphenate spelled-out compound numbers and spelled-out fractions, unless a fraction is used with one of the indefinite articles,* a *and* an.

twenty-two	**two-fifths** of my whiskey (could be any amount)
ninety-eight	**one-half** of the audience
fifty-second	**a tenth** of my earnings

Do *not* hyphenate *one hundred, two thousand,* and so on.

Rule 3. *Hyphenate a compound noun when hyphenation contributes to clarity.*

Job-hunting is difficult.	**Communist-baiting** is dangerous.
Joe's a **left-hander**	**Star-gazing** is fun.

Occasionally, but not often, a dictionary is of help in following this rule.

Rule 4. *Always hyphenate words formed with the prefixes* ex *(meaning "former"),* all, *and* self *and with the suffix* elect.

ex-wife	all-American	self-determination	senator-elect

Rule 5. *Hyphenate words with prefixes when hyphenation contributes to clarity.*

anti-integration	re-entry	de-emphasize	pre-exist

Without the hyphens, the double *i*'s and *e*'s might cause momentary confusion.

Rule 6. *Hyphenate words with prefixes when without the hyphen a different word might be understood.*

re-cover a chair	a **co-op**	**re-act** a scene
recover from an accident	a **coop**	**react** to an insult

Rule 7. *Use a hyphen with a prefix added to a word always capitalized.*

un-Christian   mid-July   anti-Rotary   non-Hindu

Rule 8. *Hyphenate two or more words that serve as a single adjectival in* **front** *of a noun.* This is the most important rule for use of the hyphen.

a **rather-Red-than-dead** attitude	a **civil-rights** case
a **shaggy-dog** story	a **sixteen-year-old** beauty
a **time-certificate** account	**fire-resistant** material
a **high-pressure** salesman	a **rich-food** addict
a **used-up** battery	a **dim-but-visible** UFO
all **seventh-** and **eighth-grade** pupils	all **first-, second-,** and **third-place** winners

Note how the hyphens are used in the last example in each column.

Avoid using quotation marks to enclose a long multiple-word adjectival.

preferred: He took an **I-don't-care-what-in-God's-world-you-do** attitude.
poor style: He took an "I don't care what in God's world you do" attitude.

EXERCISE 33
The Use of the Hyphen and the Apostrophe

Directions: In the blanks provided, rewrite the following sentences, entering hyphens and apostrophes where needed. Also eliminate misused apostrophes. If a name such as *Loises* is misspelled, correct the spelling.

1. Jims thirty third off color joke made even the puritan minded dog tuck it's tail.

   _____

   _____

   _____

2. A dyed in the wool Baptist, my Uncle Morbid's second wife becomes annoyed with his late night forays into our wide open town.

   _____

   _____

   _____

3. Cookie baking turned out to be a full time job for the girls counselor at Camp Owyhee.

   _____

   _____

   _____

4. Jameses half baked ideas blocked his reentry into the All for One Club.

   _____

   _____

   _____

5. Palm reading is a still flourishing art in the arcane wilds of Gypsyland, where Muzeemèes rule is still absolute.

   _____

   _____

   _____

6. Snozzes self appointment as leader of our far from stable little band brought twenty one more defections.

_____

_____

7. The Davises even tempered neighbors were alarmed to discover that the Davises were all ex convicts.

_____

_____

8. The supposedly burglar proof store was entered through a hand dug tunnel under it's north side.

_____

_____

9. The Gonzalezes were worried that payment with twenty two dollar bills might arouse the managers suspicions.

_____

_____

10. The childrens fathers low class third wife tried to learn what the hard working teachers taught the children.

_____

_____

_____

298

34

The Rules of Punctuation

Though Part 2 of this text covers the most common rules of punctuation, all the important rules are codified in this chapter for reference or study. The rules are numbered for each kind of mark of punctuation. The first three marks are presented in one section because they are collectively known as marks of **end punctuation**.

PERIODS, QUESTION MARKS, AND EXCLAMATION POINTS

Rule 1. *Use a period to end a sentence that is not a direct question and is not especially emphatic.*

Maurice asked me to help him with his term paper.
In verbal skills, television is proving to be noneducational.

Courtesy questions are those that begin with *will you* in the sense of "please." They are conventionally ended with periods.

Will you let me know your opinion of this issue.

The "I wonder . . . ." sentence implies a question, but it is ended with a period.

I wonder whether you will help me with my calculus.

Rule 2. *Use three spaced periods to indicate an omission in a direct quotation.*

"The striking and characteristic tone color of jazz orchestra music is the result . . . of brass wind instruments . . . ."

The fourth period in the second omission is the one that closes the sentence.

Rule 3. *Use a question mark to end a direct question.*

Where are the snows of yesteryear?

Do not use a question mark to end an indirect question, such as the fourth example under Rule 1 of this section.

Rule 4. *Use a question mark after parenthetic material within parentheses to show that there is uncertainty as to the accuracy of the information.*

Charles Morton (1627?–1698) operated a school attended by Daniel Defoe.

Rule 5. *Use an exclamation point to close an especially emphatic sentence.*

What a headache you have given me!

Do not overuse exclamation points, for then readers will lose belief in the need for emphasis in any of your statements.

COMMAS

Rule 1. *Use commas to separate three or more constituents in a series.*

The scouts gathered aluminum cans, returnable bottles, scrap metal, and goodwill.

The comma before the *and* is usually considered optional, but really careful writers use it, for sometimes its absence momentarily confuses the reader.

Rule 2. *Use a comma to separate two independent clauses connected by a coordinating conjunction (and, but, yet, or, nor, for, so).*

Our underwater camera seemed to be working perfectly, but the film did not develop into recognizable pictures.
I jumped, for the elevator doors were closing too quickly.

When the two clauses are quite short, the comma may be omitted. But a comma should always be used with *for* as a coordinating conjunction; otherwise the *for* might momentarily be taken for a preposition, causing the reader to stumble.

Rule 3. *Use a comma to set off an introductory constituent (that is, one that comes before the sentence subject).*

Normally, good-humored Joe would not have complained.
In case of an emergency, call my mother at 323–2332.
After all the speeches had been given and the resolutions made, nothing had really changed.

If such an introductory constituent is short and the omission of the comma cannot cause ambiguity, the comma may be omitted. Note how the absence of a comma in the first example would cause momentary ambiguity.

Rule 4. *Use a comma to set off a terminal constituent (that is, one that comes after the main sentence is ended) when there is a distinct voice pause before the terminal constituent.*

Jack is just intelligent, not a genius.
We should all vote, because democracy depends on individual participation in politics.

300

Rule 5. *Use commas to set off parenthetic constituents within a sentence.*

Hard work, my father used to say, never killed anyone.
The spirits of the dead, my mother believes, return at times to observe us.
No experiment, however, has shown any evidence of mental or spiritual survival after bodily death.

Internal parenthetic constituents have the nature of an aside or are connectives such as *however, for example,* and so on.

Rule 6. *Use a comma or commas to set off nonessential adjective clauses, adjective phrases, verb phrases, and appositives.*

Spiro Agnew, who resigned the vice-presidency in disgrace, went on to make a fortune.
Dee Bunker, happy with her inheritance, set out to see the world.
Car no. 26, achieving speeds of over 200 MPH, won the race easily.
The large primates, man's closest relatives, are physiologically almost identical to man.

A nonessential constituent modifies or is in apposition to a noun that is already fully identified; hence the grammatically nonessential constituent is set off by commas, because without it a fully meaningful sentence with a fully identified noun would still remain.

Do NOT set off a grammatically essential constituent, for it is needed to identify the noun it modifies or is in apposition to.

wrong: Thomas Wolfe's novel, *Look Homeward, Angel,* was an instant success.
right: Thomas Wolfe's novel *Look Homeward, Angel* was an instant success.

Since Wolfe wrote more than one novel, the appositive *Look Homeward, Angel* is grammatically essential to identify which novel is under discussion and thus is not set off by commas. Similarly, the sentence

Mrs. Grooby's son Alex is an airline pilot

means that Mrs. Grooby has more than one son, with the essential appositive *Alex* specifying which one is under discussion. If *Alex* is set off by commas, the meaning would be that Mrs. Grooby has only one son, for then the appositive *Alex* would be grammatically nonessential.

Rule 7. *Use a comma to separate coordinate adjectives that come in front of a noun and are not joined by* and.

a sensitive, compassionate woman
an ugly, meanspirited woman

Such adjectives are coordinate when *and* between them will sound natural:

a sensitive and compassionate woman

If *and* between two adjectivals does not sound natural, the adjectivals are not coordinate and should not be separated by a comma. Example:

sounds unnatural: a sad and old man

wrong punctuation: a sad, old man
right: a sad old man

Rule 8. *Set off by a comma an introductory adverb clause unless it is quite short (see Rule 3 of this section); set off an internal adverb clause if there is a distinct voice pause before it; set off a terminal adverb clause if there is a distinct voice pause before it.* This rule is somewhat vague because adverb clauses cannot be simply classified into essential and nonessential categories, as adjective clauses can.

noticeable voice pause: My Uncle Jurgen, **because he would not vote Democratic but hated the Republican candidate,** could only refuse to vote.

no voice pause: The time of day **just before the dew begins to collect** is the best for observation of many species of insects.

noticeable voice pause: The negotiating committee could not accept binding arbitration, **because they knew most of their demands were not justifiable.**

no voice pause: We dissolved our investment club **because we were consistently losing money.**

Rule 9. *In dates, use a comma to separate the name of a day from the month, the date of the month from the year, and the year from the remainder of the sentence. When only a month and year are given, use no commas.*

On Wednesday, July 11, 1922, there occurred one of the momentous events of history.

Look that up in the August 1975 issue of *Scientific American.*

Rule 10. *In addresses, use a comma to separate the name of a person or establishment from the street address, the street address from the city, the city from the state, and the state from the remainder of the sentence.*

Send $10.00 to Herb E. Side, 410 Wilcox Avenue, Colfax, Washington, for an analysis of your handwriting.

Rule 11. *Do NOT use a comma to separate a subject from its verb or a verb from its complement. Do NOT use a comma or commas to set off an essential constituent. Do NOT use a comma to separate noncoordinate adjectivals in front of a noun. Do NOT use a comma to separate two constituents joined by a coordinating conjunction, except in the case of two long predicates with one subject.*

wrong: The book most widely sold, is the Bible.

wrong: The subject of the first lecture was, the nature of neutron stars.

wrong: The famous hoodlum, Al Capone, died of syphilis. (Al Capone was not the only famous hoodlum.)

wrong: I don't like our strict, college rules.

wrong: The professor gave plentiful examples, and clear explanations.

DASHES

Rule 1. *Use a dash or dashes to set off a nonessential constituent that contains commas itself or that is especially emphatic.*

302

The free lunch—coldcuts, variety breads, relishes, melons, and so on—was worth
the high price of the beer.

The prize—a bronze stallion!—was given to the boy whom the girls voted the best
lover.

Rule 2. *Use dashes to set off an internal parenthetic comment that is very
long or that is a complete sentence.*

Roberts' Rules of Order—we had agreed to abide by them—prevented Orris from
dominating the meeting.

✓ **Rule 3.** *Use a dash to set off a terminal constituent that is an explanation or
an afterthought.*

Because I wanted to pass there seemed but one thing to do—study.

You should be guided by your conscience—or behave like everybody else.

Rule 4. *To gain emphasis, use dashes to set off a constituent that would not
normally be set off.*

Professor Fleebitt gave me a valuable—and lasting—lesson in manners.

Rule 5. *Use a dash to set off an initial series of constituents that are then
summarized by a pronoun that serves as the sentence subject.*

Junkies, winos, unemployed scavengers, refugees from the law, and just plain dere-
licts—all were fed a turkey dinner at the Main Street Mission.

SEMICOLONS

Rule 1. *Use a semicolon to separate two independent clauses forming one
sentence but not joined by a connective word.*

The skies were brilliantly clear; everything seemed perfect for a night of astro-
nomical observation.

A comma in place of the semicolon would form an unacceptable comma splice.

Rule 2. *Use a semicolon to separate two independent clauses forming one
sentence with a conjunctive adverb joining them.*

The evidence of the Pluggers' guilt was overwhelming; however, the jury found
them not guilty.

College costs are increasing rapidly; many students, therefore, are opting for low-
tuition state colleges rather than the private colleges they prefer.

Whether or not the conjunctive adverb is shifted to the interior of the second
clause, a semicolon (or period) is still needed to prevent an unacceptable comma
splice.

✓ **Rule 3.** *Use semicolons to separate constituents in a series that have commas
of their own or that are very long.*

I decided to restrict my studies to history, archaeology, and economics in the first
quarter; literature, art history, and musicology in the second; and sociology, anthropology, and psychology in the third.

If the semicolons were commas, the reader would probably be momentarily confused.

PARENTHESES

Rule 1. *Use parentheses to set off a parenthetic constituent—even a sentence or group of sentences—that you want isolated from your main sentence but want the reader to read at that point.*

> The experiment in penology conducted by Jacobs and Franks (they published in 1975 a definitive study of the problem schoolchild) tends to substantiate the conclusion that harsh punishment is not only not a deterrent but increases criminal behavior.

If one or more sentences in parentheses begin after a mark of end punctuation, the period concluding the parenthetic sentence is placed within the final parenthesis. If a constituent or sentence enclosed in parentheses comes last in a sentence but does not begin after a mark of end punctuation, the period is placed outside the final parenthesis.

Rule 2. *Use parentheses to enclose numerals that number items in a series.*

> The most frequently used reading selections in this text are (1) "Logical Fallacies," (2) Bacon's "Idols of the Mind," (3) Robinson's "Four Kinds of Thought," and (4) Russell's "Use of Symbolic Logic."

Note that the *and* precedes the last number.

Rule 3. *Use parentheses to enclose cross-references and bits of incidental information.*

> Epicureanism (see also *hedonism*) is named after the Greek philosopher Epicurus (342?–270 B.C.).

BRACKETS

Rule 1. *Use square brackets to enclose nonquoted material inserted into a direct quotation to make it intelligible.*

> "He [John Kennedy] did not live to become the great statesman that he showed promise of becoming."

Rule 2. *Use square brackets to enclose personal comments inserted into a direct quotation.*

> "Next came to the witness stand Julius Cox [a known perjurer], whose testimony the defense was to rest its case on."

COLONS

Rule 1. *Use a colon after the salutation in a letter to indicate formality.*

Dear Reverend Puffer:

304

A comma in place of the colon would indicate informality.

Rule 2. *Use a colon to introduce a series prepared for with such a phrase as* are the following, were these, *and so on.*

> My findings were as follows: most students are not ready for college at age 18, a college dropout who returns to school after age 26 is likely to make high grades, a young female is more likely to be studious than a young male, and retired people of both sexes who enter or return to college almost all have high motivation.

Do *not* use a colon directly after verbs such as *are, were,* and so on.

Rule 3. *Use a colon after an introductory label.*

nonstandard usage: I ain't got no job.

Rule 4. *Use a colon to introduce a terminal explanatory constituent.*

We found the culprit: a marijuana-eating mouse.

A dash is proper in this position too.

QUOTATION MARKS

Rule 1. *Enclose direct quotations in quotation marks.* If a quotation is interrupted with a connective not in the original, enclose only the original parts with quotation marks.

> Professor Feely said that "the greatest piece of Western music is Mozart's *Don Giovanni*" and that "the plays of John Webster are in some ways the equal of Shakespeare's."

Rule 2. *Use quotation marks to enclose the titles of literary works of all sorts of less than book or three-act-play length.*

> My favorite short story is Faulkner's "Two Soldiers"; my favorite poem is "Terence, This Is Stupid Stuff"; and my favorite chapter in *Moby-Dick* is "The Town-Ho's Story."

Rule 3. *Use single quotation marks to enclose a quoted unit or title within a longer quoted passage.*

> The author of *The History of American Literature* says that "The single most powerful piece of nonfiction of the nineteenth century is Thoreau's 'Civil Disobedience.'"

Rule 4. *Use quotation marks to enclose a word used as a word and not for its meaning.*

> The word "broad" was used as slang as early as the sixteenth century.

However, words used as words are more commonly underlined than enclosed in quotation marks.

Rule 5. *Use quotation marks to enclose a word used in some special or ironical sense.*

The "fairness" of the Fairness Committee overwhelmed me.

The quotation marks indicate irony—that is, that the writer did not think the committee was fair.

Do NOT enclose a slang term in quotation marks just because it is slang.

Rule 6: Quotation marks with other marks of punctuation. *Always put periods and commas within the final quotation marks whether or not they are a part of the quoted segment. With other marks of punctuation, put the mark of punctuation inside the final quotation marks if it is a part of the quoted segment and outside if it is not a part of the quoted segment.*

I have just finished reading Hawthorne's "The Birthmark."
Did Professor Snorff say "No class today"?
Molly asked, "Will you please define *meiosis* one more time?"

Note that an additional period does not end the last example, even though the whole is a statement and not a question.

EXERCISE 34
Punctuation

Directions: The following passage is printed without any marks of punctuation or capital letters to begin sentences, except the first in each paragraph. Punctuate the passage and enter capital letters to begin sentences.

The young marched with the black and now the young are not wanted the blacks do not want us nor are they wrong one of the things that we must face up to just as a parent must face up to it with respect to a child is that when one is struggling for freedom and identity sometimes one must do it alone the rejected sympathetic kindly person the parent or white man does not understand but it is his fault it is part of the process of growing up to grow up on your own.

There are those who don't like the phrase black power it's a very correct phrase anyone who really studies democracy will find out that democracy is pluralistic in character it is those already in power who scorn the presure groups but it is pressure groups whether they be voter leagues formed by women labor unions formed by workers black organizations formed by colored people that in the end count and enter into the total social fabric democracy is a struggle based not only on high ideals it is power against power there is an overarch of principle but the overarch is to hold the ring firm while the contestants battle it out within the limits authorized by the organized society.

The young are not wrong either in their wonder about the scope of violence I tread on very dangerous ground here and I beg indulgence as a quasi-historian and not as a judge I ask you to reflect carefully on the Boston Tea Party on John Brown and the raid on Harpers Ferry on the sit-down strikes in 1937 in the plants of General Motors every one of these was a violent unlawful act plainly unlawful in the light of history was it plainly futile there are occasions on which an honest man when he looks at history must say that through violence regrettable as it is justice of a social kind has worked itself out does that mean that I think that violence is right most certainly I answer ambiguously I cannot know none of us can know until long after this time has gone but I warn those who think that violence is right because history in the three instances that I have cited and many others that one might mention has shown that violence worked I warn them that violence will lead to McCarthy I or McCarthy II to which Senator's philosophy if either will this nation respond [Charles E. Wyzanski, Jr., "A Federal Judge Digs the Young"]

35

Subject-Verb Agreement and Verb Forms

The two chief kinds of errors that occur in the use of verbs are (1) faulty agreement in number between subject and verb and (2) misuse of an irregular past participle for the past-tense form or vice versa.

SUBJECT-VERB AGREEMENT

In grammar, **number** is a term having to do, obviously, with the number of units involved. In English, there are only two numbers: singular (one) and plural (more than one). Nouns and pronouns, which are of course often used as subjects, have number: *book-books, it-they, this-these.* Two singular words joined by *and* are also plural: *a dog and a cat, his coming and going, reading books and watching movies.*

In the third person present tense, verbs also have number:

He talks.	They talk.
It bites.	They bite.
Reading is tiresome.	Reading and talking are tiresome.

The verb *to be* also has number in the past tense:

He was there.	They were there.

In other cases, however, the form of a verb is the same for both singular and plural:

He walked.	They walked.
Reading tired me.	Reading and writing tired me.

This fact of English grammar reduces the chances of making errors in subject-verb agreement.

Uneducated people make many errors in subject-verb agreement, but high-school graduates normally make such errors only in certain trouble spots. Following are brief explanations of these troublesome areas of English grammar.

A prepositional phrase intervening between subject and verb does not affect the verb form. In the following examples the subject and verb are in boldface and the intervening prepositional phrase is underscored.

A **list** of honor students **was** (not were) posted in the library.
The **professor** together with six of the demonstrating students **has** (not have) been
  called to court.
The **mayor** as well as the councilmen **refuses** (not refuse) to endorse the bill.

This trouble area exists because the subject is separated from its verb and thus the wrong word may sound like the subject.

The indefinite pronouns one, each, either, *and* neither *are singular and require singular verbs.* The indefinite pronoun *one* is likely to be involved in error only when a prepositional phrase intervenes between it and the verb. The other three are often misused even without an intervening phrase.

One of the students **was** (not were) given a citation for bravery.
Neither is (not are) acceptable.
Each of the books **is** (not are) a classic of American literature.

The indefinite pronouns *none* and *any* may take either a singular or a plural verb, and thus no error in agreement occurs with them.

A compound subject (*two or more constituents joined by* and) *is plural and requires a plural verb.*

⇒ **One bottle** and **one corkscrew were** (not was) missing.
Watching TV and **playing records are** my sister's chief pastimes.

However, subjects that are compound in appearance but function as singular units may take singular verbs.

Some **gas** and **dust** actually **shows** up in photography. [*Scientific American.*]
Disparate **clatter** and **chatter has** fascinated linguists. [*Time*]

These sentences would not be wrong with plural verbs, however.

In the constructions either (neither) . . . or (nor) *and* not only . . . but also, *the verb agrees with the part of the subject closest to the verb.*

Either the **judge** or the jury **members were** wrong.
Either the jury **members** or the **judge was** wrong.
Not only the **president** but also the various **deans were** at the meeting.
Not only the various **deans** but also the **president was** at the meeting.

The thing to remember is that these constructions do not make compound subjects.

In the there is . . . *and* there are . . . *constructions, the verb agrees in number with the subject, which follows the verb.* In the following examples, the verbs and the subjects are in boldface.

There **was** only a **dollar** between me and starvation.
There **were** three **redheads** in the chorus line.

Note that the *there* has no function except to introduce the sentence. Since either a singular or a plural verb sounds natural following the *there*, careless mistakes are common.

In inverted sentence order, the verb agrees with the subject, which follows the verb. The *there is . . .* construction is one kind of inverted sentence order, but there are other kinds. In the following examples the verbs and subjects are in boldface.

On the front lawn **were** two battered **lawnmowers.**
Behind the billboard **was** a sneaky motorcycle **cop.**

Sentence patterns like these are not especially common, and so they give little trouble.

In a subordinate clause with a relative pronoun—who, which, that—*as the subject, the verb agrees with the antecedent of the relative pronoun.* In the following examples, the antecedent, the relative pronoun, and the verb are in boldface.

The **theory that was** provisionally adopted was Hoyle's.
The **theories that were** at first discarded were later proved correct.

Few writers make errors in this kind of construction, for what sounds natural is usually correct.

The foregoing are the chief trouble spots in subject-verb agreement. The grammar of this particular problem in usage is rather complex, but few mistakes occur in constructions other than the above trouble spots. Concentrate on them, and most of your problems in subject-verb agreement will be solved.

PRINCIPAL PARTS OF VERBS

See Chapter 2 for a definition and illustration of the principal parts of verbs.

Errors occur when the past-tense and the past-participle forms of verbs are confused. For example,

I **swum** a mile

is faulty because the past tense is *swam.* Similarly,

It had **began** to rain

is faulty because the past participle is *begun.* Also a person of some education may occasionally make an error by changing an irregular verb form to the regular *ed* form, as in

The wind **blowed** hard

instead of the correct

The wind **blew** hard.

Actually, few high-school graduates make mistakes in using the principal parts of verbs, but for the record the principal parts of the most common irregular verbs are listed below:

Present	Past	Past Participle
begin	began	begun
blow	blew	blown
break	broke	broken
bring	brought	brought
choose	chose	chosen
come	came	come
deal	dealt	dealt
do	did	done
draw	drew	drawn
drink	drank	drunk
drive	drove	driven
eat	ate	eaten
fall	fell	fallen
flee	fled	fled
fly	flew	flown
freeze	froze	frozen
give	gave	given
go	went	gone
grow	grew	grown
know	knew	known
lead	led	led
ride	rode	ridden
ring	rang	rung
run	ran	run
see	saw	seen
send	sent	sent
shake	shook	shaken
sing	sang	sung
speak	spoke	spoken
swim	swam	swum
take	took	taken
throw	threw	thrown
wear	wore	worn
write	wrote	written

36

Pronoun Case Forms

See Chapter 5 for a definition of *case* and for the case forms of various pronouns. Following are explanations of the chief trouble spots in the use of proper pronoun case forms.

IN COMPOUND STRUCTURES

There is a strong prejudice among educated people against the confusion of *I-me, he-him, we-us,* and so on. About the only likelihood of error here among high-school graduates is the confusion of the cases in compound structures. Few if any native speakers would say

He spoke to **I.**
Me was rewarded.
The letter was for **he.**

But people with little education often say

Tom and **me** were rewarded.
You and **us** should get together.

And even well-educated people are often heard to say

The message was for my father and **I.**
Between you and **I,** I'm glad to be in the stock market again.

Thus confusion of case generally arises only when there is a compound structure.

When you are unsure about the case form of a pronoun in a compound structure, you can test by omitting one of the elements. If you omit the construction in parentheses in the following examples, the correct form should be immediately clear.

The package was for (my sister and) _____.
                                           (I or me?)

Just between (you and) _____, I'm scared.
                                    (I or me?)

(Tom and) _____ may make the Dean's List.
                    (he or him?)

He passed the message on to (Sarah and) _____.
                                                    (she or her?)

An awareness of this simple test should prevent you from making case errors of this sort: But note particularly that the objective form follows *to, for,* and *between:*

> to John and **me**
> for their father and **them**
> for you and **me**
> between you and **me**

AFTER THE VERB *TO BE*

In colloquial usage it is perfectly acceptable to use the objective pronoun form after the verb *to be.*

> It's **me.**
> Was that **her?**
> Could it have been **him?**

In formal or semiformal writing, however, it is still common to use the subjective form in such constructions.

> It's **I.**
> Was that **she?**
> Could it have been **he?**
> The guilty ones were **we.**

WHO AND *WHOM*

The objective form *whom* seems to be disappearing from our language. More and more in colloquial usage, people simply use *who* in all constructions. In formal or semiformal writing, however, the distinction between *who* and *whom* is still maintained. In a question you can test for the correct form by converting the question into an ordinary statement and substituting *he* or *him* for *who* or *whom.* Examples:

_____ were you talking to?
   (who or whom?)

You were talking to whom.
                      ‾‾‾‾‾
                      (him)

_____ did you say is coming?
    (who or whom?)

You did say _____ who _____ is coming.
                                   (he)

Such a test will give you the correct form.

You can also use such a test to select the proper form in regular sentences. If _he_ fits, use _who;_ if _him_ fits, use _whom_. Examples:

Mr. Smith, _____ the council voted to reprimand, decided
                 (who or whom?)

to resign.
(The council voted to reprimand _him_. So use _whom_.)

Profesor Thomas, _____ I believe is the popular choice for
                   (who or whom?)

the award, feels that Professor Verhine should receive the honor.
(_He_ is the popular choice. So use _who_.)

This test is, of course, useful only in writing, for in ordinary talk one does not have time to think the matter through. In any case, when in doubt, it is best to use _who_, for that form is becoming dominant.

IN COMPARATIVE CONSTRUCTIONS

Comparative constructions are those using the words _than, as,_ and _as . . . as._ Both subjective and objective pronoun forms may follow these words, and hence there is often a question as to which form to use. Example:

Professor Jones praised Susan more highly than _____.
                                        (I or me?)

You can test for the correct form by filling out the sentence with a clause that is ordinarily understood:

Professor Jones praised Susan more highly than (he praised) **me.**
Professor Jones praised Susan more highly than **I** (praised Susan).

As you can see, in such a sentence the pronoun form chosen affects the meaning. Here are some other examples of the way to use this test:

Professor Burck is more likely to favor the proposal than _____
                                       (he or him?)

_____ (is likely to favor it).

Dennis defeated John by a bigger score than (he defeated) _____.
                                        (I or me?)

Professor McKeighan gave Ed more individual help than (he gave)

_____.
        (I or me?)

Ed is as good a student as _____ (am a good student).
                                (I or me?)

The test is both simple and reliable.

THE *WE MEN/US MEN* CONSTRUCTION

The pronoun used in phrases like *we girls, us boys,* and so on, should take the form it would take if the noun were omitted. Example:

_____ Americans are a compassionate people.
        (We or Us?)

Use the form that would be used if the noun *Americans* were omitted:

We (Americans) are a compassionate people.

Here are some more examples:

Many foreigners think all of _____ (Americans) are rich.
                                (we or us?)

The administration thinks _____ (students) are too lackadaisical.
                            (we or us?)

Give _____ (students) a book and we'll sell it.
        (we or us?)

If you omit the words in parentheses, you will easily see which pronoun forms should be used.

EXERCISE 36
Pronoun Case Forms

Directions: In the blanks provided, write the proper pronoun forms for the following sentences.

1. ·The coach was feeling sorry for _____ linesmen.
   (we or us?)

2. Between you and _____, Professor Shortfellow's poems are banal.
   (I or me?)

3. If I had known it was _____, I would have left by the back door.
   (they or them?)

4. Pascal is the player _____ I believe will win the Heisman Trophy.
   (who or whom?)

5. _____ do you think will be the Honor Speaker at graduation?
   (Who or Whom?)

6. Professor McCall is more doctrinaire than _____.
   (I or me?)

7. The girl _____ I had been waiting for drove by with another
   (who or whom?)

   fellow.

8. Everyone except Phyllis and _____ was invited to the party.
   (I or me?)

9. Give the signal to _____ appears at the gate first.
   (whoever or whomever?)

10. I didn't know _____ was alluded to in the second stanza.
    (who or whom?)

11. The camp set up by Rosie and _____ was intended for the use
    (I or me?)

    of _____ happened to come by.
    (whoever or whomever?)

12. Nobody but _____ Bluebirds could sing so angelically.
    (we or us?)

13. Was it _____ _____ the police threatened to put in
    (they or them?)   (who or whom?)

    jail?

14. It might have been _____ _____ the police inquired
(he or him?)   (who or whom?)

about.

15. _____ do you think will be the Homecoming Queen?
(Who or Whom?)

16. I must admit that Joan is prettier than _____ .
(I or me?)

17. Father spoke more gently to Susan than _____ .
(I or me?)

18. It was _____ two _____ the article was about.
(we or us?)   (who or whom?)

19. Toby was not as well informed about Spain as _____ .
(I or me?)

20. The ruling did not affect John and _____ as much as _____

(I or me?)

_____ .
(she or her?)

21. The money was divided evenly between my sister and _____ .
(I or me?)

22. If it had been _____ _____ was selected, _____
(she or her?)   (who or whom?)

_____ do you think would have been angriest?
(who or whom?)

23. It was Bill and _____ _____ the director was supposed
(I or me?)   (who or whom?)

to favor.

24. The same letter was sent to both Henry and _____ .
(I or me?)

25. The report prepared by Bill and _____ did not specify _____
(I or me?)   (who or whom?)

was to make the follow-up study.

37
Consistency in Grammatical Forms

The structure of the English language is such that in several ways a statement can be expressed in either of two grammatical forms, with no change whatsoever in meaning. For example, we can make an observation about people in general in the **third person**, as in

One should let **his** conscience be **his** guide.

But we can make the same observation about people in general in the so-called **indefinite second person**, as in

You should let **your** conscience be **your** guide.

Now, of course, such a sentence as the last example can be spoken to one individual, with the *you* referring to, say, Jane Simpson. But we native speakers of English also use with high frequency the indefinite *you* to mean people in general. The fact that in this and other ways English allows us to say the same thing in different grammatical constructions leads to many improper shifts in such constructions, thus producing grammatical inconsistency. The four chief kinds of inconsistency in grammatical forms are explained in the following sections. It is standard conventional usage *not* to make inconsistent shifts in grammatical constructions.

IN NUMBER

In English we can refer to people in general (or to one category of people) with such **singular** words as *one, person, he, student, player,* and so on, as in these sentences:

A **person** should be honest with **himself.**
A football **player** is often highly admired.
A **teacher** should be aware of varying student interests.

The first sentence refers to people in general, the second to football players in general, and the third to teachers in general. But we can also refer to people in general (or to one category of people) with such **plural** words as *people, they, students, players,* and so on, as in these sentences:

> **People** should be honest with **themselves.**
> Football **players** are often highly admired.
> **Teachers** should be aware of varying student interests.

The two sets of sentences have identical meanings.

Since English freely allows for reference to people in general in both the singular and the plural, careless writers often start a sentence or passage in one of the grammatical forms and then improperly shift to the other, producing grammatical inconsistency. Examples:

> *improper shift:* A **person** should be honest with **themselves.**
> *improper shift:* A football **player** is often highly admired, but **they** may lose their popularity overnight.
> *improper shift:* A **teacher** should be aware of varying student interests, but **they** often ignore such differences.

Such an inconsistent shift from the singular to the plural weakens style and violates standard conventional usage.

The singular word *everybody* is often involved in faulty shifts in number, as in

> **Everybody** picked up **their** book.

Some people maintain that *everybody* is in essence plural, since it carries the meaning "all," and that thus *everybody . . . their* and *everybody . . . they* are not inconsistent shifts. But the words *nobody, somebody,* and *anybody* certainly do not imply plurality, and the same people who say *everybody . . . their* also say *nobody . . . their,* and so on. Also very few, if any, native speakers of English would say

> Everybody **are** coming.

Instead, native speakers say

> Everybody **is** coming,

showing that they consider *everybody* grammatically singular, as it is.

Furthermore, look again at the first example sentence in the preceding paragraph. Since *book* is singular, does the sentence mean that everybody owned just one book together and that each participated in picking it up? And if the sentence is changed to

> Everybody picked up their books,

one does not know whether each person had one or more than one book. On the other hand,

> Everybody picked up his book

and

> Everybody picked up his books

deliver perfectly clear meaning.

322

There are probably several reasons for such common but inconsistent shifts as *everybody . . . their, a person . . . they, a musician . . . they,* and so on. But perhaps the chief reason is that *they* and *their* refer to both sexes, whereas most people think that *he, him,* and *his* refer only to the male sex. Thus to avoid what they think is sexism, many people, consciously or unconsciously, speak or write such sentences as this:

> *improper shift:* A free-lance **writer** has a great deal of freedom, but **they** have a hard time earning a living.

Many people seem to think that to use the consistent *he* instead of the inconsistent *they* is a slur on women.

Such a belief, however, is founded on ignorance of the nature of structure words in English. In Part 1 you learned that there is a great overlapping of the structure words in English. For example, the *that's* in the following three sentences, though pronounced and spelled the same, are no more the same word than *dog* and *cat* are:

> **That** book is highly informative.
> The horse **that** won the last race is to be put out to stud.
> I wish **that** every day were Saturday.

Similarly, the *he, him,* and *his* that refer to a particular person, such as Jacques Sierlin, are different words from the *he, him,* and *his* that since 1320 at the latest (see the *Oxford English Dictionary*) have been used in English to refer to indefinite sex or to groups composed of both sexes. For example, in

> Gary left **his** bottle again,

the *his* is a different structure word from the *his* in

> Everybody brought **his** own bottle.

The two words are different just as the *that's* in the sentences above are different, for the first refers to a specific male and the second refers to everybody—male and female—who came to the party bringing his own bottle.

Therefore we recommend that you maintain consistency in number and thus observe standard conventional usage. Examples:

> *inconsistent:* Did **anybody** lose **their** luggage?
> *consistent:* Did **anybody** lose **his** luggage?
>
> *inconsistent:* An **adult** is responsible for **their** personal decisions.
> *consistent:* An **adult** is responsible for **his** personal decisions.
>
> *inconsistent:* If a **winner** is displeased with **their** prize, **they** may exchange it.
> *consistent:* If a **winner** is displeased with **his** prize, **he** may exchange it.

Generally, experienced readers much prefer consistency in number. The inconsistent shift has not yet become fully established as standard conventional usage.

A final note: If, because of your attachment to feminist causes, you just cannot bring yourself to use the consistent *a person . . . he* construction, the construction *he or she,* awkward as it is, is preferable to an improper shift to the plural.

IN PERSON

As we explained in the introduction to this chapter, English allows us to make reference to people in general in the **third person** *one, he, person, student,* and so on or in the so-called **indefinite second person**—*you.* Thus some writers carelessly shift from the third person to the indefinite second, or vice versa, thus producing grammatical inconsistency and nonstandard usage. Examples:

> *inconsistent:* **Students** should not have to take so many required courses. Often **you** just aren't interested in some of the courses required for graduation.
>
> *consistent:* **Students** should not have to take so many required courses. **They** often just aren't interested in some of the courses required for graduation.
>
> *inconsistent:* When **someone** cheats, **he** may get a higher grade, but usually **you** are caught and may lose **your** grade altogether.
>
> *consistent:* When **someone** cheats, **he** may get a higher grade, but usually **he** is caught and may lose **his** grade altogether.
>
> *inconsistent:* A **person** likes to have a good time at a party, but **you** seldom like to pay for it the next day.
>
> *consistent:* A **person** likes to have a good time at a party, but **he** seldom likes to pay for it the next day.

The inconsistent examples here all illustrate an improper shift from the third person to the indefinite second, which is by far the most common source of inconsistency in person. However, we should say that it is *not* wrong to use the indefinite *you.* For example, in a theme on how to play poker successfully, a student might open with such a sentence as this:

> In order to be an expert poker player, **you** must first have a good understanding of the so-called odds.

But then the writer should continue in the indefinite second person and not shift inconsistently to the third person. But we should also say that many composition teachers prefer their students to avoid the indefinite second person.

IN TENSE

Our grammar allows us to summarize events of the past—as in history or the plot of a novel—in either the **past tense** or the so-called **historical present tense** (which is the same as the ordinary present tense). Example:

> In 1678 the so-called Popish Plot **has** caused panic in England, and Titus Oates **is** riding high as the key witness for the prosecution.
>
> In 1678 the so-called Popish Plot **had** caused panic in England, and Titus Oates **was** riding high as the chief witness for the prosecution.

In the first sentence, the *has* and *is* are present-tense forms; and in the second, the *had* and *was* are past tense. But the sentences have identical meaning because our language allows us to use either tense in summarizing past events.

Inconsistency in tense occurs when a writer shifts from the past to the historical present tense, or vice versa, in summarizing events of the past, usually history or the plot of a piece of fiction. Example:

> *inconsistent:* Pete's little brother **has** managed to sneak out of the house and **is** on his way to Memphis to join Pete. He **had** difficulty at the bus station in Jefferson but finally **boarded** a bus for Memphis.
> *consistent:* Pete's little brother **has** managed to sneak out of the house and **is** on his way to Memphis to join Pete. He **has** difficulty at the bus station in Jefferson but finally **boards** a bus for Memphis.

Of course, the consistent passage could be written wholly in the past tense: *had managed, was, had,* and *boarded.* One needs only to be alert and careful to maintain consistency in tense.

IN VOICE

Some statements can be expressed in either the active or the passive voice (see Chapter 4), with no change in meaning. Example:

> *active voice:* The butler stole some whiskey.
> *passive voice:* Some whiskey was stolen by the butler.

Though the active voice usually creates a tighter, more effective style, many times the passive voice is preferable, such as when the doer of the action is not known and the *by* phrase is suppressed.

However, when you have started describing an action in the active voice and continue with the same doer of the action, you should not inconsistently shift to the passive voice. Such an improper shift greatly weakens the style of a passage of writing. Examples:

> *inconsistent:* The professor raised his voice to the class, and they were reprimanded by him for their bad manners.
> *consistent:* The professor raised his voice to the class and reprimanded them for their bad manners.
> *inconsistent:* Our team was 20 points behind at the half, but the game was won by them by two points.
> *consistent:* Our team was 20 points behind at the half but won the game by two points.

In each of the inconsistent examples the first clause is expressed in the active voice, but then an improper shift to the passive voice in the second clause produces inconsistency. The improvement in style in the consistent sentences (both actions in the active voice) should be clear even to an inexperienced reader.

EXERCISE 37
Consistency in Grammatical Forms

Directions: Rewrite each of the following sentences to correct any inconsistency in grammatical forms. Some sentences may be correct.

1. A pro football player works hard, but their income is high.

_____

_____

2. Even when a player is second string, they should stay in shape, for you may suddenly be called upon to play.

_____

_____

3. The cheetah put on a burst of speed and the gazelle was easily caught.

_____

_____

4. In the story Wash is old and ill, but he pretended he hadn't gone to war because he had to take care of the Colonel's plantation.

_____

_____

_____

5. A seal can learn to do many tricks, for they are highly intelligent.

_____

_____

6. The pilot steered the steamer carefully, and the sandbar was missed by a few inches.

_____

_____

7. Many lawyers make high incomes, but if you decide to enter law, be prepared to study hard for several years.

_____

_____

8. If a person is ignorant of the law, they can still be prosecuted for breaking it.

_____

_____

9. When a person is sick they should stay in bed, for rest will help you recover more quickly.

_____

_____

10. A farmer works hard, but their income is usually not large.

_____

_____

11. The Earl of Essex had been Queen Elizabeth's favorite for a long time, but she has to have him executed for treason.

_____

_____

12. If the person elected chairman doesn't want to serve, they can appoint a successor.

_____

_____

13. I worked steadily, and my tasks were finished with time to spare.

_____

_____

14. A dog is good company, and often they protect property too.

_____

_____

38

A Glossary of Usage

accept, except *Accept* is a verb meaning "to receive"; *except* is a preposition indicating that something is excluded; *except* can be used as a verb meaning "to leave out or exclude."

> *right:* I cannot accept your gift.
> *right:* Everyone except me came to the party.
> *right* (though rare): The professor excepted those who had perfect attendance.

accidentally The spelling *accidently* is substandard.

affect, effect *Affect* is a verb meaning "to influence"; *effect* is a noun meaning "the influence exerted on something"; *effect* is also a verb meaning "to bring about."

> *right:* The bad weather affected my morale.
> *right:* The bad weather had an effect on my morale.
> *right:* The prisoner effected an escape.

agree to, agree with We *agree to* a plan but *agree with* a person.

a lot, lots *A lot* is less colloquial than *lots*. Some authorities think *a lot* is colloquial, but most accept it as standard.

all ready, already *All ready* is an adjectival idiom meaning "everyone or everything is prepared"; *already* is an adverb meaning "at this time or before this time."

all right, alright The spelling *alright* is now accepted by dictionaries, but careful writers still use only *all right*.

all together, altogether *All together* is an adverbial idiom meaning that "everyone acts in unison"; *altogether* is an adverb meaning "wholly or completely."

> *right:* Let's sing all together now.
> *right:* That solution is altogether unsatisfactory.

allude, refer *Allude* is a verb meaning "to mention indirectly"; *refer* is a verb meaning "to mention specifically and directly."

right: He alluded to his drinking problem when he spoke of Alcoholics Anonymous.
right: He referred to *Hamlet,* act IV, scene II.

allusion, delusion, illusion   *Allusion* is a noun meaning "an indirect reference"; *delusion* is a noun meaning "a false belief"; *illusion* is a noun meaning "a deceptive appearance." Don't confuse *delusion* and *illusion.*

right: His allusion to *Das Kapital* made him suspect.
right: He is under the delusion that he will be a great baseball player.
right: Her apparent beauty was a mere illusion.
wrong: His illusion that he was another FDR irritated the political pros.

almost, most   *Almost* means "nearly"; *most* means "to the greatest extent." *Most* is colloquially used for *almost.*

colloquial at best: Most all the players were declared ineligible.

among, between   Use *among* when three or more items are designated; use *between* for two items. Occasionally *between* is used colloquially for *among.*

amount, number   *Amount* designates a quantity that cannot be numbered; *number* designates a quantity that is divisible into units.

right: an amount of sugar
right: a number of books
colloquial at best: a large amount of books

and etc.   Do not use the redundant *and* with *etc.*
and, but   It is not wrong to begin a sentence with *and* or *but.*
and/or   Many authorities advise against the usage "All swimmers and/or waders must obey the lifeguard." Other authorities accept the usage, and there seems to be no sound reason for avoiding it.
anecdote, antidote   An *anecdote* is a little story. An *antidote* counteracts a poison.
anxious, eager   *Anxious* means "uneasy or apprehensive"; *eager* means "strongly desirous of."

colloquial at best: I was anxious to go to the party.

anyway, any way   *Anyway* is an adverb meaning "in any case"; *any way* is a noun phrase.

right: I was broke, anyway.
right: I couldn't find any way to solve the problem.

around   Avoid using *around* (or *round*) to mean "about."
as, as if, like   Some authorities think *like* as a conjunction is colloquial.

colloquial to some: It looks like it may rain.
standard: It looks as if it may rain.
colloquial to some: Do like I do.
standard: Do as I do.

average, median   An *average* is the total sum of the scores on a number of tests or other items divided by the number of tests. The *median* is the score exactly in the middle of a number of tests or other such items.

330

awful, awfully Both *awful* and *awfully* should be avoided as intensifiers.

> *low colloquial:* I'm awful (awfully) sorry about your accident.

bad, badly *Bad* is an adjective, *badly* an adverb.

> *right:* I feel bad.
> *right:* My car runs badly.

because clause as subject *Because* normally introduces an adverb, not a noun, clause.

> *colloquial:* Just because you're intelligent is no reason for you to be conceited.
> *standard:* Your being intelligent is no reason for you to be conceited.

because of, due to Many authorities prefer *because of* as an adverb and *due to* as an adjective.

> *preferred:* Because of the rain I was late.
> *preferred:* My failure was due to my poor study habits.

being as, being that Avoid these low-level constructions. Use *because* instead.
beside, besides *Beside* is a preposition meaning "at the side of"; *besides* is a preposition or adverb meaning "in addition to."

> *wrong:* We brought everything beside beer.

between See *among*. Never use "between you and I," "between you and he," and so on. The object form of a pronoun must be used after *between*.

born, borne *Borne* is the past participle of *bear* when it is in the active voice; *born* is the past participle in the passive voice.

> *right:* She has borne six children.
> *right:* She has borne her poverty with elegance.
> *right:* He was born in France.

burst, bust *Burst* is the standard usage; *bust* is at best low colloquial. The principal parts of *burst* are *burst, burst, burst*. There is no such word as *bursted*.
but that, but what

> *colloquial:* I don't know but what I'd avoid that store.
> *standard:* I don't know but that I'd avoid that store.

can't help but

> *colloquial:* I can't help but feel sorry for Tom.
> *more formal:* I can't help feeling sorry for Tom.

censor, censure *Censor* is a verb meaning "to suppress or restrict publication of supposedly objectionable material." It is also a noun meaning "one who censors." *Censure* is a verb meaning "to find fault with or condemn as wrong." It is also a noun meaning "the expression of disapproval or blame."

> *right:* The government should not censor novels.
> *right:* Such behavior is subject to censure.

cite, site, sight *Cite* is a verb meaning "to indicate or mention"; *site* is a noun meaning "a place where something is, was, or is to be"; *sight* is a noun or verb having to do with vision.

right: He cited a chapter from the Bible as proof.
right: The site for the new building was poorly chosen.

colloquialism, localism, regionalism   A *colloquialism* is "a word or phrase suitable for informal usage"; a *localism* or *regionalism* is "a word or phrase used only in one locality."

wrong: I heard many colloquialisms (meaning localisms) in the hills of North Carolina.

complement, compliment   *Complement* means "something that completes or a number or amount that makes a whole"; *compliment* means "to give praise." Each can be used as a verb or a noun.

right: He complimented her on her dress.
right: The Fourth Division had a full complement of troops.

conscience, conscious   *Conscience* is a noun meaning "a knowledge or feeling of right and wrong"; *conscious* is an adjective meaning "aware or alert."

contemptible, contemptuous   *Contemptible* means "deserving contempt"; *contemptuous* means "showing contempt."

right: He is a contemptible person because of his bad habits.
right: I was contemptuous of his pomposity.

continual, continuous   *Continual* means "occurring at close intervals"; *continuous* means "without interruption or cessation."

could of, would of   Illiterate misspellings for *could have* and *would have.*

council, counsel   *Council* is a noun meaning "an official group"; *counsel* is a verb meaning "to give advice" or a noun meaning "advice or adviser." *Counselor* comes from counsel.

right: The city council voted new taxes.
right: I asked my teacher to counsel me.
right: He gave me good counsel.

credible, creditable, credulous   *Credible* means "believable"; *creditable* means "worthy of praise"; *credulous* means "willing to believe readily or easily imposed upon."

right: Your story is credible.
right: His kind actions were creditable.
right: A credulous person is an easy mark for a con man.

data   *Data* is a plural and most writers use a plural verb with it.

right: The data support his conclusion.

delusion   *See allusion.*

different from, different than   *Different from* is the preferred usage; *different than* is colloquial.

preferred: John's book is different from mine.

disinterested, uninterested   *Disinterested* means "impartial"; *uninterested* means "having no interest in."

332

right: The judge was disinterested.
wrong: John was disinterested in his studies.

double negative See *hardly.*
due to See *because of.*
eager See *anxious.*
effect See *affect.*
enthuse Many authorities prefer *be enthusiastic.*
everyday, every day The single word is normally used as a modifier. The two words are a noun with a determiner.

> *right:* That's an everyday affair.
> *right:* I go to the movies every day.

everyone, every one The single word is an indefinite pronoun meaning "everybody." The two words are a noun (cardinal number) with a determiner.

> *right:* Everyone should folow his conscience.
> *right:* Every one of the members contributed.

everyone . . . their Though commonly used, this phrase is not as acceptable as *everyone . . . his.*
except See *accept.*
expect, suspect *Expect* means "to look forward to or anticipate"; *suspect* means "to think probable or likely."

> *right:* I suspect he will fail.
> *colloquial:* I expect he will fail.

farther, further *Farther* relates to physical distance; *further* refers to degree and quantity. More and more, *further* is being used as synonymous with *farther.*

> *right:* I cannot walk any farther.
> *right:* Do you have anything further to say?

fewer, less *Fewer* refers to separate items; *less* refers to a quantity that cannot be divided into separate items. *Less* is used colloquially for *fewer.*

> *right:* I have fewer marbles than you.
> *right:* I have less sugar than you.
> *colloquial:* I have less marbles than you.

fiancé, fiancée The *fiancé* is the male and the *fiancée* the female.
folk, folks *Folk* is mostly used as a modifier, as in "folk music." *Folks* refers to the members of a family or to a group.
fortuitous, fortunate *Fortuitous* means "occurring by chance rather than design." *Fortunate* means "happening by a favorable chance" or "favored with good fortune."
fulsome *Fulsome* means "offensive," as in "fulsome praise." The word is not related to *full.*
get, got, gotten These words are used in many colloquial idioms, such as "Get going with your project." But they need not be avoided in semiformal writing.

good, well   These words are difficult to separate, for both are adjectives and *well* is also an adverb. But most usages are acceptable now. You should, however, avoid using *good* for *well* in such examples as these:

>   *right:* The car runs well.
>   *right:* John did well in algebra.
>   *right:* John carried the joke off well.

hadn't ought to   The phrase is low colloquial. *Should not* or *shouldn't* is the standard expression.

hanged, hung   Use *hanged* in referring to persons being suspended in a noose. Use *hung* for other uses.

>   *right:* The criminal was hanged.

hardly   Never use the double negative *can't hardly, won't hardly,* and so forth.

he, she   When a singular pronoun of indefinite sex is needed, use either *he* or *he or she* (or *his* or *his or her(s), him* or *him or her*).

healthful, healthy   *Healthful* means "giving health." *Healthy* means "having health."

height, heighth   *Height* is the accepted spelling and pronunciation.

himself, hisself   Only *himself* is standard. *Hisself* is vulgate.

human, humane   *Human* as an adjective means "having the attributes of man." *Humane* means "characterized by kindness and sympathy."

if, whether   Use *whether* to introduce a noun clause.

>   *right:* I don't know whether I can come.
>   *colloquial:* I don't know if I can come.

illusion   See *allusion.*

imply, infer   *Imply* means "to suggest or hint"; *infer* means "to draw a conclusion about."

>   *right:* As he talked, he implied I was a fool.
>   *right:* From the conversation I could infer that John was displeased with Joan.
>   *wrong:* As he talked, he inferred I was a fool.

in, into   *In* shows location; *into* shows direction.

>   *right:* He was in the house.
>   *right:* He walked into the house.

incidentally   Avoid the spelling *incidently.*

incredible, incredulous   The negative of *credible* and *credulous.* See *credible.*

indefinite you   Some composition teachers prefer their students to avoid the indefinite *you.*

>   *not acceptable to some teachers:* To succeed in the business world, you must first of all be tenacious.
>   *acceptable to all:* To succeed in the business world, one must first of all be tenacious.

infer   See *imply.*

inside of   Colloquial for *within.*

>   *preferred:* I will see you within a week.

334

invite Do not use as a noun.

> *substandard:* I received an invite.
> *right:* I received an invitation.

irregardless Avoid altogether. Use *regardless.*

its, it's *Its* is possessive; *it's* is a contraction of *it is* or *it has.* Never use the illiterate misspelling *its'*.

> *right:* Its waterbowl is empty.
> *right:* It's raining.

it's me, it's I *It's me* is colloquial. In formal situations use *it's I.*

kind of, sort of Colloquial. Prefer *rather* or *somewhat.*

later, latter *Later* is an adjective or adverb meaning "at a time after a specified time"; *latter* is an adjective or noun meaning "nearer the end or the last mentioned."

> *right:* He came later than you.
> *right:* Of the three methods described, I chose the latter.

lay, lie *Lay* is a transitive verb meaning "to place an object somewhere"; *lie* is an intransitive verb meaning "to be in or take a reclining positon." The principal parts of *lay* are *lay, laid, laid;* the principal parts of *lie* are *lie, lay, lain. Lay* is used colloquially for *lie,* but most teachers oppose such usage.

> *right:* I will lay the book on the table.
> *right:* Yesterday I laid the book on the table.
> *right:* I have laid the book down many times.
> *right:* The book is lying on the table.
> *right:* I will lie down this afternoon.
> *right:* Yesterday I lay down.
> *right:* I have lain down every day this week.

lead, led *Lead* is not the proper spelling of the past tense of the verb. The pronunciation of the metal *lead* confuses some people.

learn, teach The use of *learn* for the meaning of *teach* is vulgate and should be avoided altogether.

leave, let *Leave* in the sense of *let* is vulgate.

> *nonstandard:* I have the habit of leaving nature take its course.

less See *fewer.*

liable, libel *Liable* is an adjective meaning "responsible or legally bound or likely to have"; *libel* is a noun meaning "slanderous references" or a verb meaning "to slander."

> *right:* A man is liable for debts contracted by his wife.
> *right:* The gossip columnist was sued for libel.

lie See *lay.*

lightening, lightning *Lightning* is the noun meaning "a flash of electricity in the sky." *Lightening* is a verb meaning "making lighter."

like See *as.*

localism See *colloquialism.*

loose, lose *Loose* is an adjective meaning "unfastened"; *lose* is a verb meaning "to mislay or to be deprived of."

loud, loudly As an adverb, *loud* is colloquial.

> *colloquial:* Don't talk so loud.
> *standard:* Don't talk so loudly.

majority, plurality In an election, *majority* means "more than half the votes." *Plurality* means "the largest number of votes among three or more candidates, with none having a majority."

maybe, may be *Maybe* is an adverb meaning "perhaps or possibly"; *may be* is a form of the verb *to be*.

moral, morale *Moral* is an adjective meaning "right or ethical"; *morale* is a noun meaning "a mental attitude or condition."

> *right:* All moral acts are recorded in Heaven.
> *right:* The troops' morale was high.

most See *almost*.

nohow A vulgate term. Avoid in all writing except dialogue.

nowhere near Low colloquial. Avoid in semiformal writing.

nowheres A vulgate term. Avoid in all writing except dialogue.

number See *amount*.

old-fashioned, old-fashion *Old-fashion* is sometimes used now colloquially, but *old-fashioned* is the standard adjective.

on account of the fact that Just use *because*.

onto, on to *Onto* is a preposition. *On to* is an adverb plus a preposition.

> *right:* The dog trotted onto the playing field.
> *right:* We went on to our destination.

oral, verbal *Oral* means "spoken"; *verbal* means "pertaining to written or oral language." *Verbal* is now much used for *oral*.

passed, past *Passed* is the past tense and past participle of the verb *pass; past* is an adjective and a noun meaning "of a former time."

> *right:* I passed calculus.
> *right:* The time for reconciliation is past.

plan on, plan to *Plan on doing* is colloquial. *Plan to do* is standard.

prepositions It is not wrong to end a sentence with a preposition.

principal, principle *Principal* is an adjective meaning "chief" and a noun meaning "the head of a school or money used as capital"; *principle* is a noun meaning "rule, law, or doctrine."

> *right:* Stockholm is the principal city of Sweden.
> *right:* Algebraic principles are not difficult to learn.

proved, proven Both are now standard as the past participle of *prove*.

quick, quickly As an adverb, *quick* is colloquial.

> *colloquial:* Come quick.
> *standard:* Come quickly.

quiet, quite *Quiet* is an adjective meaning "not noisy, calm"; *quite* is an adverb meaning "entirely." The words are pronounced differently, *quiet* having two syllables.

> *wrong:* Children, keep quite.

raise, rise *Raise* is a transitive verb (takes an object) meaning "to put something in a higher position"; its principal parts are *raise, raised, raised. Rise* is an intransitive verb meaning "to go to a higher position"; its principal parts are *rise, rose, risen.*

> *right:* Will you raise my salary?
> *right:* Smoke does not always rise.

real, really As an adverb, *real* is low colloquial, but it is standard as an adjective.

> *colloquial:* I had a real good time.
> *standard:* I had a really (very) good time.
> *standard:* The real facts of the case never came out.

reason is because, reason is that Both expressions are now acceptable, but *reason is that* is more suitable for semiformal writing.

reckon *Reckon* is colloquially and regionally used to mean "suppose." It should not be used for this meaning in semiformal writing.

refer See *allude.*

regionalism See *colloquialism.*

rhyme, rime Either spelling is correct.

scarcely Avoid the double negative *can't scarcely.* Use *can scarcely.*

set, sit *Set* is a transitive verb (takes an object) meaning "to place something in a position"; its principal parts are *set, set, set. Sit* is an intransitive verb meaning "to occupy a seat or to be in a sitting position"; its principal parts are *sit, sat, sat.*

> *right:* Yesterday I set the phonograph on the floor.
> *right:* Will you sit in this chair?
> *right:* I have sat here all day.
> *wrong:* He set down
> *wrong:* He has set here all day.

shall, will Formal rules for the use of these modal auxiliaries no longer hold. Whichever sounds natural is acceptable.

site See *cite.*

slow, slowly Both have been adverbs in English for over a thousand years. *Go slow* and *go slowly* are equally correct.

so As a conjunction, *so* is generally considered colloquial, but many professional writers now use it as standard.

> *colloquial to some:* The rain didn't let up, so we abandoned the game.
> *preferred by many:* Because the rain didn't let up, we abandoned the game.

sometime, sometimes, some time *Sometime* is an adverb meaning "at some future time." *Sometimes* is an adverb meaning "at times" or "occasionally." *Some time* is a noun with a determiner.

right: Sometime I'll get my degree
right: It snows here sometimes.
right: We spent some time with Susan.

sort of See *kind of.*

split infinitive Some stylists oppose the placing of a modifier between the *to* and the verb of an infinitive, such as "to better understand." They prefer "better to understand." Nevertheless, split infinitives are not errors. But usually the style will sound better if the modifier is placed before the *to* or after the verb.

> *awkward:* I want to learn to better play the game.
> *smoother:* I want to learn to play the game better.

such as Do not use a mark of punctuation after this connective.

> *right:* Bring comfortable clothes, such as slacks, sport shirts, and loafers.

suppose, supposed To omit the "d" of the past participle is a serious error. When the "d" is needed, the word will normally be preceded by a form of the verb *to be* and will be followed by an infinitive. The same distinction is to be made for *use* and *used.*

> *right:* I was supposed to vote today.
> *wrong:* Was he suppose to come?

suspect See *expect.*

than, then *Than* is a conjunction used in comparisons; *then* is an adverb of time.

> *right:* John has a higher IQ than Shirley.
> *right:* First we ate; then went to the opera.

themselves, theirselves *Theirselves* is strictly vulgate and should always be avoided.

these kinds, these sorts These are the correct forms. *These kind* and *these sort* are nonstandard.

toward, towards There is no essential distinction between these words.

try and, try to *Try to* is preferable.

uninterested See *disinterested.*

used to See *suppose.*

well See *good.*

where . . . at Avoid the *at* if it is unnecessary.

> *right:* Where is he?
> *colloquial at best:* Where is he at?

whether See *if.*

who, whom Colloquially, *who* is now commonly used as an object except directly after a preposition. In semiformal writing, only *whom* should be used as an object.

> *colloquial:* Who did you mention?
> *standard:* Whom did you mention?
> *unacceptable:* To who should I give the receipts?

whose, who's *Whose* is a possessive pronoun; *who's* is a contraction for *who is* or *who has.*

wrong: Who's book do you have?

would have Avoid using for *had.*

right: If he had studied, he would have passed the exam.
colloquial at best: If he would have studied, he would have passed the exam.

would of An illiteracy. Use *would have.*

you See *indefinite you.*

your, you're *Your* is a possessive pronoun; *you're* is a contraction for *you are.*

wrong: Your supposed to come at eight.

Index